WRITING WORDS THAT SELL

To John Yates, who has written more good "words that sell" than anyone we know.

ABOUT THE AUTHORS

Since the early 1970s Canadian-born, Bedfordshire-based **Suzan St Maur** has been working as a professional copywriter and scriptwriter in the United Kingdom, EEC countries, and North America. She has written and produced material for consumer and business-to-business advertising, public relations, sales promotion, business television and business theatre. She now specialises in corporate and educational scriptwriting, and is recognised as one of the top ten such specialists in the UK.

Former actor and director **John Butman** is based near Boston, Massachusetts, and in the last fifteen years has established his reputation as one of the USA's leading writers and concept creators in business communications on the East Coast of America. He has written brochures, scripts and speeches for many of the top 100 corporations in the United States. More recently, he has been involved in similar projects in Europe, and is now in considerable demand as a business communications creative director and scriptwriter in Britain.

St Maur and Butman met in London, England, while both involved in writing projects for one of the UK's leading business communications agencies. The concept of this book grew from their mutual concern at the lack of sales writing ability and understanding on both sides of the Atlantic, and their desire to share their combined experience and knowledge with a wide range of readers.

Writing Words That Sell

SUZAN ST MAUR AND JOHN BUTMAN

LENNARD PUBLISHING 1989

Lennard Publishing
a division of Lennard Books Ltd

Lennard House
92 Hastings Street
Luton, Beds LU1 5BH

British Library Cataloguing in Publication Data is available.

First published 1989
© Suzan St Maur and John Butman 1989

Phototypeset in Linotron Meridien
by Goodfellow & Egan Ltd, Cambridge

Cover design by Pocknell and Co.

Printed and bound in Great Britain by
Mackays of Chatham PLC, Chatham, Kent

ACKNOWLEDGEMENTS

We would like to give grateful thanks to Roderick Brown and Mark Booth ... Nancy and Jeremy Butman ... Laurence Harris ... Jackie and Mac Hercus ... Jean Jackson ... Jane Judd ... London Media Workshops ... Charles Lousada ... George Lynde Jr. ... Renee Marshall ... The Open College ... Debbie Sinfield ... Videotel Productions Ltd ... John Yates ... and everyone else who gave us both practical help and moral support while we wrote this book. And last but not least, our grateful thanks to Spectrum Communications, for bringing these two damned good writers together in the first place ...

SUZAN ST MAUR AND JOHN BUTMAN

CONTENTS

INTRODUCTION

The need for good selling techniques does not stop at encyclopaedia or insurance salespeople. In an increasingly competitive marketplace, there comes a time when *any* business is obliged to sell itself, and the product or service it offers. Of course, the foot-in-the-door approach is not only undesirable in most cases, it is also very old-fashioned. Selling and particularly selling on paper and through audio-visual media has become a very subtle and sophisticated skill.

It is a well-known fact that many verbally-successful sales people often experience a problem when they try to put their conversational success on paper. Selling "off the page" (a term cribbed from direct response advertising), and through the script of an audio-visual presentation, require different skills to those used for even the most carefully handled face-to-face sales talk.

Selling through the written word often plays the crucial role of opening doors, permitting one-to-one verbal selling to follow. Very frequently, written or pre-recorded sales material is the first contact you will have with a potential customer. As the saying goes, first impressions count. Here, the quality and content of such written or pre-recorded sales material undoubtedly represents the difference between success and failure.

Large businesses have been quick to realise that the written selling word, be it for print or screen, needs an expert hand to write it. That's why copywriters and scriptwriters, hired through advertising agencies, consultancies and production companies, are in such demand. Smaller businesses or smaller departments within large businesses, however, do not usually have a large enough budget for high-quality, professionally written material. Such funds as they may have will be spent on design, print, and production; the words will usually be written by a member of their own staff. And in the majority of cases, it is unfair to expect these people to be experts at writing words that sell. They're experts in their own fields, of course; but communicating on paper is a *separate area of expertise in itself*, and not normally within the portfolio of business executives and managers, no matter how good they may be at their own discipline. It is sad to see efficient, worthwhile companies undersell themselves, and create the wrong impression for their customers, through a lack of writing ability. Yet it is an all-too-common problem.

Similarly, there are times when salesmanship is required *within* a company; and written communication skills become every bit as important as they are externally. New ideas, plans, strategies, and directions must be sold on paper and through formal presentations, by one department to another; by management to sales force; by personnel departments to employees; by junior management to board members; and so on. Naturally, in these circumstances there is usually an in-built obligation to look favourably on the selling proposition. But selling on the strength of no-choice obligation is dangerous. If any company's policy is to be carried out successfully, obligation is not enough; enthusiasm and commitment are needed, too. Good salesmanship in written communications converts in-company obligation into the right attitudes to make things happen.

Just as it is in the case of external selling, large companies spend considerable amounts on getting their in-company communications right. Writers like ourselves are frequently paid big fees to script a presentation from management to sales force; to write sales brochures from manufacturer to retailers and dealers; and, in an allied but slightly different context, to sell companies to potential employees with things like recruitment videos and brochures.

So: how much hope is there for the smaller companies and departments whose resources do not stretch to professionally written selling words? The answer is, more than they think.

The writing of words that sell, is a craft; not a gift. Crafts can be learnt. Copywriting and scriptwriting skills can be learnt. And that's what this book is all about.

There is no obscure mystique to writing words that sell. There are recognised approaches and guidelines which, once you know them, bring selling words alive. There are a number of short cuts, pitfalls to be avoided, basic psychological techniques, and styles relevant to writing good selling copy and scripts. And although not everyone can become a successful, full-time, professional writer – that takes a certain ability and instinct for the job – everyone who reads this book will emerge from it knowing how to sell themselves, their companies, and their products and services through written words ... more easily, more successfully, and more profitably.

CHAPTER 1

A WAY WITH WORDS:

Style and jargon

STYLE AND JARGON

Probably the most important thing we can tell you about writing style is to forget what you learned at school. Promotional writing is not about being grammatically correct; it's about writing in the way that people speak. Selling anything, from the harsh reality of the can of baked beans, to the intangible concept of a corporate identity, involves direct communication between seller and buyer. The most direct form of communication, and interestingly the earliest form of communication we know, is spoken speech. Prehistoric society was selling ideas and produce through speech long before anything got carved in tablets of stone.

Many people find the conversion from written to spoken speech quite a difficult task. Ironically enough, it is a lot harder to write simply, in the way that spoken speech is simple, than it is to lean on the support of carefully constructed phrases and sentences that come straight from the grammar books we all used to pore over in the classroom. Like any new concept, learning to write in simple, spoken speech means a shift in your attitude; in the way that you think, as well as in the way that you set out one word after another.

Understanding the logic behind the need to write in simple, spoken speech can be made easier if you look at the ways in which sales people deliver a pitch to a prospective customer. Here, a straight, uncluttered, simply-worded sales pitch is probably the most believable one of all. Simplicity implies honesty, conviction and enthusiasm. On the other hand, a wordy, over-long, cliché-ridden sales spiel will often have the prospect wondering what all that verbiage is trying to hide, or if it's actually a replacement for a good, believable sales story.

Writing words that sell involves exactly the same principle. A strong, simple message that says what it means in unfussy language will come over as a lot more credible than large amounts of flowery prose.

Naturally, there is a dividing line between the spoken speech you write for printed material and the spoken speech you write for an audio track. This second category has further sub-divisions when you consider the spoken style for writing narration, character dialogue and live speeches. All these elements are covered later in this book, under their appropriate headings. But there is one very strong common denominator which runs through most of them, and that is what John Yates – one of the UK's most prolific and experienced sales writers – calls the "you" angle.

The exceptions to this are fairly self-explanatory; written material describing the technical functions of a product, documentary film scripts describing the workings of a manufacturing process, and so on, all need to be led by "it" rather than you. But that doesn't mean that "you" can be forgotten, even when the narrative is describing how many times the ionised widget revolves in the galvanised cylinder per millisecond. In these cases, you should remember who it is you're writing for. And even with your ionised widgets, you're writing about "it" for "you"; not for "we", or for "it".

The cruel truth about selling anything by any means is that "you" is the only important part of the deal. It is "you" who will buy whatever is for sale, provided the words "you" manage to convince him or her that he/she should do so. "You" couldn't care less who "we" are, unless by implication "we" can be made into a selling point. For example:

> *'We recommend that the product be compared with those of our competitors'*

won't impress anyone. "You" doesn't need recommendations from you – after all, you're selling something, aren't you? Can your judgement be trusted?

However, turn it around and put the onus on "you". "You", now firmly back in the driving seat, is far more likely to take the bait this way:

> *'If you compare our product with those of our competitors, you'll find that...'*

When you're writing words that sell, you're going to have to forget "we" in the way that you know and love "we" in your day-to-day business life. After all, you don't produce your products or services for "we" do you? You produce them for "you", and so "you" must be placed firmly on the largest pedestal you can find. Professional writers and other message communicators live with "you" on a permanent basis, and in many ways it's easier for them to identify with "you" because in a lot of instances they are a "you" themselves. They are also trained from a very early age to become "you" minded, and because they don't have such a close involvement with "we" and the products/services "we" make, they can keep their creative eyes firmly focused on "you". From your point of view though, as a full-time member of "we", you may find it more difficult to change pronouns than, say, a copywriter or scriptwriter. Yet if you are to write words that sell successfully, you have to think "you" at all times.

And remember, if "you" doesn't buy, "we" can go out of business. Companies all over the world are currently investing fortunes in customer-care programmes, training staff at all levels to look upon the customer as the most important part of their working lives. Yet many of these same companies leave the customer out in the cold in the written material they produce. The customer is just as important when reading a brochure or watching a corporate video as he or she is when standing in a retail outlet discussing a purchase with the sales assistant.

Situations at this Moment in Time

Many satirical publications in English-speaking countries run columns about clichés. Business-speak grew out of lawyer-speak and, more recently, computer-speak, elevated to world class status by the more pompously-spoken business schools of the Western hemisphere. Business-speak has its own fashions and trends, just like the clothing industry; remember "parameters", for example. That was a great favourite of the 1970s and still hangs around today, with many people talking about parameters when they really mean perimeters. "Situations" is another great all-time favourite; a useful alternative to far more explicit words like "circumstances", "conditions" or "problems". Examples include a "no-win situation" (jam) ... "an on-going situation" (permanent arrangement) ... "a management-led situation" (bosses rule) ... and so on. Business-speak clichés can be strung together to make even more gobbledegook that can be translated into something far simpler and more direct: "at this moment in time" (now) ... "within the parameters of our situation at this moment in time" (here and now) ... "outside the parameters of my corporate responsibility" (not my job). In some business circles, it's considered a good thing never to use a short word or phrase when a long one will do. Business clichés that develop out of that upside-down principle are supposed to lengthen simple thoughts and make them sound more business-like, more assertive, more corporate. Nonsense. Business-speak clichés are just a prop for people or companies to lean on while they figure out what it is they really want to say, and then how to say it.

THE VALUE OF POP CONVERSATION

Whatever you write, you must try to get yourself inside the reader's head before you put pen to paper and almost become that reader. This does not mean you have to become a mental contortionist. It means that you should find out who your reader or viewer is, and learn about how he or she thinks; what his/her needs are; how much importance he/she attaches to the value of your product; and so on. Many companies pay market research organisations huge fees to find out this information, and if it is your company's policy not to let one corporate sneeze out of the building before researching the market for it, then that's fine. But common sense has a great deal to do with it, too. Many organisations find they spend a lot of money on research which tells them what they already knew, which was based on common sense. So although good old-fashioned horse sense is hardly the scientific way to assess your audience's needs, it can be a cheap and effective alternative, especially for the small business.

Getting inside the reader/viewer's head involves a great deal of grammatical rule-breaking. That's because people don't speak to the rules, although reasonably educated conversation is loosely based on them. One of the main points about writing how people speak is to keep statements and thoughts as simple as you can; and that is the basis on which grammatical rule-breaking becomes relevant, too.

A thought which is expressed correctly in grammatical terms, like this ...

> (Well known brand of artificial sweetener):
> *'The taste to which the world is turning ...'*

is lumpy and awkward. The grammatically incorrect, but far more human way of saying it, is ...

> (Well known brand of artificial sweetener):
> *'The taste the world's turning to'*

This line is taken from a real advertising campaign that was running in the UK at the time this book was written.

Another favour that popular conversation has done for words that sell is to invent completely new words, or at least some new uses for old ones. And, in turn, advertising and copywriters have created some new ways of using words. There are a number of everyday words which you won't find in a good dictionary: "read" as a noun, as in "this book is a good read"; "blonding" as the present participle of "blonde" used as a verb; "cheese" as a verb, as in "anyway you please it, cheese it". And these examples aren't made up; they're taken from recent and current advertising campaigns (at the time of writing).

As is the case with many things, before you can break the rules and get away with it, you have to know what the rules are. Whoever thought up the idea of using "cheese" as a verb, had to know how to use a verb in the first place. Whoever picked up on the popular usage of the word "read" as a noun, used it in a way that was strong, simple and effective; it came from an ad for three new novels, and the full baseline ran like this ... *'Three sizzling summer reads from'* (well known publisher.)

Picking up on popular conversation for use in writing words that sell means listening to what people say – and particularly, listening to what typical representatives of your target market say. It may sound obvious, but you don't use popular teenage words and phrases if you're selling holidays to senior citizens. And you don't use trendy street slang if you are selling a new drug to doctors. If you don't already know how your target audience talks and thinks, find out.

Jargon

The dividing line between specialist language and jargon is dangerously thin. Words that one person might think an indispensable part of the vocabulary, another might consider deliberately abstruse. And business language today is growing ever more specialised, to the point where a visitor from a former decade would be totally in the dark when reading an ordinary business document.

It's difficult, if not impossible, to write effectively for many industries without being tempted to use specialised language that sounds like jargon. However, the question of whether it really sounds like jargon or not is a decision for you to take. *Webster's Third New International Dictionary* describes jargon as "technical terminology or characteristic idiom of specialists in a particular activity or area of knowledge". There is nothing wrong with that, except that jargon is also "often: a pretentious or unnecessarily obscure and esoteric terminology". Pretension and obscurity in selling documents are not good.

The technology business, particularly the electronics technology business – and especially computing – has the most complicated specialist vocabulary and the greatest number of newly coined phrases or new meanings for existing words. This makes sense. The computer industry is new, in comparison to banking or insurance or hospitality or retail, and its vocabulary is still developing. If you complain that computing has altered the meaning of the word "architecture" forever, think how banking must have changed the meaning of the word "draft", for example. There is no doubt that computing language will gradually work itself into general usage. Much of it already has – think of such words as "software" and "information" systems and "programmer". Many computing terms (borrowed from other usages originally) have also been returned to the language in non-computing terms. To "crash" for example, is often applied to a general, catastrophic, complicated and serious malfunction of any kind of system. A "bug" is any kind of small, annoying and recurring malfunction in any type of procedure.

The audience decides

When you're writing business and selling documents you should always be searching for words that are the most accurate, least open to misinterpretation and best suited to the tone of the document. People with excellent vocabularies often find themselves wanting to use a word in general conversation that they believe to be the best word for the job – let's say the word is "inchoate" – but hesitating to use it because some people will not understand it, and it will have the effect of confusing (or irritating) the listener.

The most important, and really the only determining factor in your decision about where specialist language leaves off and jargon begins, is the audience. You must decide, with every word, whether or not your audience will understand the word, or can grasp the meaning from the context. If you decide that most of them won't understand it, you have two choices. You can use this word anyway, but explain or define it in the writing. This requires more words and takes up space – and may put a lump in the flow of the argument. Or you can choose another word or phrase. You can also take the risk and use the word without explaining it – and hope that some people will look it up, hear it again, or learn what it means somehow or other. This is a rather high-handed approach and should only be used if the central meaning of the document does not depend on that word.

You might think that when you write for the general public you would use the least specialised language – and the most colourful, non-technical phrasing. However, how often do you really write for the general public? It's pretty rare that selling documents of whatever type – from speeches to television advertisements to brochures – are genuinely aimed at everybody.

Overall, you can assume that external audiences will have less understanding of and tolerance for specialist language than internal audiences. However, when it comes to language – as opposed to messages – you may be able to broaden your definition of "internal" a bit. For example, if you're writing a speech for a conference of plastics engineers from a variety of companies, they might be considered an internal audience – because they will have a common vocabulary.

Let's consider some computing terms, and try to determine where specialism in the name of accuracy ends and where pretension and deliberate obscurity sneak in. Take the terms "end-user", "host", "system", "network", "desktop", "mini", "third party", "application", "protocol", "connection", "remote", "multi-vendor", "integration", "transparency" and "architecture". Today most people in the computer industry, whether technical people or not, would understand these terms. They would certainly not consider them to be pretentious or obscure. Many business people using computer systems, but not in the industry itself, would agree.

When you're writing for either of these groups, using such specialist language without explanation and without apology makes sense. In fact, to try to avoid it would probably lead to awkwardness and an amateurish tone. For example, the word host has come to mean the main computer in a system, the one that essentially runs the show, be it a huge IBM mainframe or simply the largest PC. To use the word "host" is, in computer circles, accurate and clear and far more elegant than a phrase like "the main computer in the system that runs everything".

In hospitality or travel, you have "destination" referring not so much to the country you're visiting as to the place you are ultimately going to, whether it is a resort, city, bungalow, hotel, shack or boathouse. In manufacturing, you have the terms "discrete" and "process"; "discrete" meaning "the manufacture of separate parts which are then assembled into a whole", and "process", meaning "the manufacture of a single end product by working, modifying or adding ingredients". The financial services industry is notorious for its terminology, including terms such as "instrument", meaning a financial phenomenon that helps you do something with money.

Such words have to be considered as acceptable usage because – even if some in the audience would consider them pretentious – they are generally accepted by those who must use them most, and help to simplify your writing. So generally accepted terms within the industry, even if they are not known to the general public, are usually acceptable in sales writing internally.

Unfortunately, in much business communication, jargon is used as a weapon. This might seem to make a great deal of sense. The reason is obvious; if you use language that others don't understand, you can create an advantage for yourself. Your listeners will have to pretend they understand what you mean, which means they won't really understand what you mean, which means you can alter your meaning later if it suits your purpose. Or they can choose to ask what the hell you do mean, which exposes them.

In business meetings, you will often sit silently while someone uses an acronym or phrase that you don't know. The other members of the meeting listen contentedly, with knowing expressions on their faces. However, if you finally choose to query the speaker, you often find that no one else knew what the phrase meant either. So don't be afraid to ask. Don't allow people to bully you with jargon.

It's not surprising that, as specialist language has grown more complex – and as the sheer number of specific, identifiable things there are in the world has multiplied – there has also evolved a new kind of generic language to help define categories of new things, and make life a little simpler. So now, instead of screws and nails, we have "fasteners". Instead of glue or tape we have "adhesives". Rather than parts or bits, we have "components" and "units". Rather than typists or computer operators, we have "end-users". We have "elements" and "platforms" and "systems" and "modules". Although it is easy to use these terms – because they are so broad and inoffensive – they're not terribly exciting. Use of too many generic terms leads to a kind of generic writing indistinguishable from any other.

ACRONYMS

The great banes of the business writer's existence are the acronym and the abbreviation. The number of these used in every type of discipline has grown beyond control. Why it is that people have the urge to create one for any and every phenomenon is a mystery. For example, in FMCG, or "Fast Moving Consumer Goods", you have SKU's or "Shelf Keeping Units". This means, essentially, anything you put on a shelf in a package whether the package is a bag, a tin, a carton, a bottle or anything else. SKU is therefore a more inclusive term than "item", or "product", or "thing". But, to any but "internal" or trade audience its use would be out of the question.

From MRP (manufacturing resource planning) to RDB (relational database) to AGV (automated guide vehicle) – treat acronyms and abbreviations as severe forms of jargon. Avoid them, or spell them out at least once, at the beginning of the document. Fewer people understand the meaning of generally used acronyms than you might think. If you ask someone who has a habit of reeling off these phrases just what a QRX is, he may not actually know. If he doesn't know, there's a good chance that he may not really know what the thing does, either.

Choosing the correct style and use (or not) of jargon and clichés depends very much on your ability to take yourself out of your own shoes, and put yourself in those of your target audience. Achieving this takes practice, but it's not difficult; all it needs is a bit of common sense, role-playing, and honest appraisal of your company and its products or services. If you can manage to use those elements consistently, you'll be well on your way to writing words that sell – successfully.

CHAPTER 2

FOUR STEPS TO GOOD WRITING:

The method

THE METHOD: ART VERSUS CRAFT

This is a book about a particular type of writing; writing words that sell or, more broadly, writing words with a particular and definable purpose. This type of writing is in contrast with what is often termed "creative" writing, or writing that is primarily intended for self-expression.

People tend to have strange and complicated notions of what writing is all about, and how it is accomplished. This may be because they consider writing, in general, to fall into the category of art. Art, by its very nature, is mysterious and indefinable. The tales of seemingly undisciplined writers and artists are legion. The image of the tortured artist, habitually intoxicated, who lives beyond rules, endures.

But the type of writing we're concerned with is essentially a craft. It can be defined. It has learnable rules and guidelines. It has steps and processes that can be followed each time you set out to write.

Unfortunately, this does not mean that this type of "writing with a purpose" is particularly easy. It isn't. Good writing of any type requires discipline, concentration, organisation and a certain amount of will-power.

But if you approach writing as a job, it can be made easier than if you approach it as a divine mission. If you are reasonably diligent in following a series of steps, you will be more or less guaranteed to produce a document that is clear and readable, and that is written with a minimum amount of personal pain.

Thinking and writing

The relationship between thinking and writing is extremely complex. Thinking is essential to the act of writing, and the act of writing seems to stimulate and facilitate thinking. A major mistake people make when setting out to produce a business document is to try to think and write at the same time. It can't be done.

It may appear that the two happen at the same time, but actually they are happening sequentially. A bit of thinking is followed by a bit of mechanical writing, which is followed by a good stare out of the window (a clue that thinking is taking place), which is then followed by a prolonged pound at the keyboard.

It's quite acceptable to think and write in this way – in alternating bursts – particularly for shorter documents. However it's not the most efficient way to write, and because writing with a purpose is usually created under some amount of pressure, efficiency and speed are virtues.

To try to think and write at the same time, is to do the last thing first. That is, you're trying to create a final draft before an initial one. As with other crafts, this is difficult – like trying to make a chair without having first drawn a plan, selected the wood and shaped the individual pieces.

In writing, as in thinking, people need to get to know a subject, organise it in their minds, try out a few thoughts in (sometimes) incoherent fashion, and ultimately reach a final, polished thought which can then be spoken or written – and easily understood.

When you try to produce a finished document by sitting down (or standing up, as some writers prefer) and forcing it to come, you may find youself facing the well-known "terror of the blank page". You get a headache, you procrastinate. You suffer.

Thinking seems to be a wonderfully meandering process that involves a lot of data collection, reacting, sudden crystallisation of ideas (often called inspiration) and constant reworking and refining. Writing should follow this thinking process. It should not be a stark, abrupt or isolated task.

Of course, in the world of purposeful and businesslike writing, you're probably writing to a fixed deadline. The document is required on Thursday at 14:00 and no later. There must be something on paper by that time, or else. This is why a process is so helpful. If you know what the process is and if you've tailored it to your own thinking process, you avoid much of the terror of the blank page.

So when the moment comes for you to position yourself before whichever recording apparatus you prefer – word processor, type-writer, cards – it is entirely possible for that moment to be a pleasurable release, rather than a torture.

The key point is: if you don't know what you think, you won't be able to write it down.

THE BASIC STEPS IN THE PROCESS

No matter what you are writing – a speech, a memo, a brochure, an advertisement, a script, a treatment or proposal – the following steps apply. Depending upon the task, you may be able to de-emphasise one step or may need to spend more time on another. But, generally speaking, all the steps always apply.

Input

You can't expect to write anything without having some raw information as grist for the mill. Information doesn't necessarily consist of facts. It may be visual information, or emotional impressions or anecdotes. You may not even need to venture outside your own memory to find the necessary information, although you probably will.

Wherever the information is stored, you must begin with a period of research or gathering-in. This sounds absurdly obvious. However, many people try to start writing without enough basic information. They then find themselves trying to gather – or, worse, create – information and think and write all at the same time. They are, in short, trying to do three things at once – when doing two is impossible and just one is reasonably difficult.

In the worlds of advertising, public relations and marketing today, to create an advertisement, image statement or product positioning without doing any research is considered amateurish and unprofessional. Whether this trend has gone a bit over the top – to the point where research has become an expensive replacement for common sense – is another issue.

The kind of information you need depends on what you're writing. You should look everywhere, ignore nothing and never believe anybody when they tell you that the information you want is unavailable. Your sources are the same as those that journalists, scholars and authors use: documents, books, interviews, objects, photographs, events.

It's useful to make notes, take photographs or sketches, record audio tape and gather objects during the research phase. In this way, the writing process has already begun.

(N.B. See Chapter 5 for more on research.)

Distillation

Of course, the gathering-in never really stops. At some point, however

– a point that comes when either you run out of time or reach your saturation point – the research period begins to taper off.

As it does, a period of distillation sets in. This is the time to allow your mind to work its marvellous and mysterious methods. Quite unbidden, the brain will sift and catalogue, compare and analyse the data and words and pictures and conversations as soon as they start pouring in. Gradually, some bits begin to rise to the top. Others sink. Things you thought were important disappear. New things you hadn't really considered force their way forward. Don't ignore any of these clues and subconscious orderings. They are absolutely critical to any piece of writing.

Careful, though; this process is not entirely within your conscious control. You can't force it. You can only allow it to happen, and not muck it up. It works best in odd moments; in the car, in the shower, during your sleep, when talking about other things.

It is during this distillation phase that an irreducible thought nugget should appear. What is an irreducible thought nugget? It is, like a sub-atomic particle, a quantity – such as an image or word or phrase – that will not go away, which cannot be broken into smaller quantities and which seems, somehow, to be essential to the document you are planning to write.

Let's say you're working on a video script about a country hotel. The irreducible thought nugget might be an image; delphiniums in the lounge ... or, if you're writing a speech about the development of a new car model, it could be a comment somebody made: "This is the most amazingly complex process in the world."

If you're lucky, your irreducible thought nugget will not be an obvious repetition of something heard or seen – it will be a synthesis, it will have a touch of freshness, or inspiration, about it. For example, if you're writing a script for a multi-image show to open a sales meeting, your nugget might be ... "Selling this product is like convincing the Queen to finance a voyage to the New World."

All of your research is a quest for this thought nugget. It rarely fails to offer one up. The trick is to recognise it when it appears and to trust it. This is simply a question of experience and listening to what your own mind is telling you.

A common, and destructive, mistake is to ignore this distillation phase and move directly from the gathering-in phase to the spewing-forth phase. When you try to force the creation of an irreducible thought nugget, you often end up creating a false one. A false thought nugget is extremely difficult to dislodge. You may never find your way back to a "clean slate".

Make a list of points

Now, place yourself before the typewriter, word processor, blank tablet, marker board or flip chart and write down everthing you can remember about the subject at hand. Don't try to order your thoughts. Don't write complete sentences if you don't want to. Don't worry about spelling, grammar, factuality, layout, phrasing or originality, don't worry about what is right or wrong. Don't worry if someone else in the room laughs at you. Do not refer to notes or tapes. Just spill it out.

This listing process is best done in one great rush of mental regurgitation. It can be done with a group of people, or alone. It should be done when you feel relatively keen and alert – not at the end of the day or after a bibulous lunch. Some of the points may be facts (but they needn't be accurate – you can check them later); others may be impressions or thoughts. For example, here are some of the points from a real list made for a corporate image video.

> *Strategy*:
> Solutions vendor
> Hardware/software/support
> Long range systems integration
> Discrete manufacturing
> Auto/aero/plastics/appliances
> *Solution suite*:
> Product design
> Third party vendors
> Total systems supplier
> *Today*: seen as design solutions company
> *Target markets*: not the big biggies. £25–£100 million sales or divisions
> Objective: the leader in product design
> Influence that segment
> Be seen as a major player
> Target audience: Directors, VPs
> Mfg. guys concerned with; reliability/quality/delivery

This particular list ran to about six pages. But you can see the idea. It is a spewing out, with no imposed order or emphasis. It can be a fantastic mess.

The list of points is something you can keep returning to. It is the one place where the distilled data still exist; a list of everything that's probably important or relevant to the project.

Outline

This is arguably the most important step in the process and, therefore, the most difficult. Outlining consists of two tasks.

Editing. An outline is composed of points from your list, but does not contain them all. In making the outline, you're deciding which points must be included in the document, and which points can be dumped. You always want to include the smallest number of points you need to do the job. Deciding how many points you need and which ones they are is a matter of judgement. How you develop a good sense of judgement is a topic outside the scope of this book. But bear in mind that if you are someone who knows a great deal about the product or service you're about to write on you should already know which points you need, provided you can see the wood for the trees. Remember, though, whatever you're writing needs to be put together for the benefit of the reader/viewer/audience, not you or your chairman. The right choice from your point of view won't necessarily be the right choice for your sales force, your customers, or your dealers, so always make your choice while standing in the recipient's shoes.

Ordering. In addition to editing, the outline is an ordering of the selected points. Ordering tends to be more complicated than editing, because you're now trying to connect a series of random points into a clearly reasoned argument. You're trying to find the logic behind them. You are, in fact, trying to create order out of chaos. For those who understand physics, you'll realise that this is an audacious act. You are attempting to defy entropy which is the basic trend of the universe towards disorder.

However, it can be done. It simply requires a good stint of undistracted ratiocination. There's no trick to it, nor is there an easy way around it. You just have to sit down and think. However, once you've accomplished this task, the rest of the job becomes a lot easier.

The outline is the blueprint for everything that follows. Writing without an outline is like trying to put up the steel framework and the cladding for a building at the same time. It's very heavy work.

Prose

If you've followed all of the above steps, the writing of actual prose can be fun. The most important caveat here is that, you still can't write the final draft first. Usually, a document needs three drafts.

The first draft is a pouring out. It is the putting of flesh on to the bones of the outline. You use it to test the validity of the outline, and to give yourself a feel for emphasis. It helps you develop a style and tone.

The second draft adjusts the emphasis and order, removes or adds points, and further develops the style and tone. But it's not until the third draft that you should worry about polish and ornamentation. This is not to say that finely honed "wordsmithing" is not important; it's just that you have a better chance of choosing the perfect word or creating the luminous phrase if your mind is free from structural issues.

It's much easier and safer to dance on a solid platform than on one you think may collapse. Your pirouettes will be a bit crisper, your leaps a bit higher. And you're less likely to break your neck.

Don't combine steps

As you go about the process, it is important that you avoid the temptation to do two things at once. This may seem embarrassingly obvious. However, people regularly get confused as to just what they are about at any given moment. You are much better off if your mind is fully focused on one task at a time. This doesn't mean that you must clear hours or days to devote to the creation of an outline, for example. Given the nature of a typical business day, where it has been estimated that a manager spends an average of seven minutes per issue at any given time – this will not happen.

It does mean that for whatever time you have you're completely clear on which task you want to work on. This is where the step method is so helpful. Rather than clearing time simply to "write", now you can schedule time to make a list of points or write a second draft. The more often you go through the process, the easier it will become to estimate how much time you need for each step.

DON'T SKIP STEPS

If you skip any of the above steps, you're asking for trouble. You may find that everything takes longer than it should. You get headaches, you may find yourself in a daze, your eyes glazing over. If time is short, as it usually is, the trick is not to skip steps but to compress them. All of the above may have to be accomplished in a morning. or an hour, or in ten minutes if necessary.

If you have ten minutes to write a page, spend your time accordingly; take a minute to gather information. List the points in 30 seconds. Distil it for another minute. Write an outline in two minutes. Write a first draft in two minutes, second draft and third draft in one each. That's a total of eight-and-a-half minutes. This then gives you an entire minute-and-a-half to use as separation between tasks.

Separation is important. If you can take a minute or an hour or a day between each step you give your mind time to settle, store and reset itself.

When facing particularly tight deadlines, some writers will use pleasantly artificial time demarcations to separate steps ... smoking a cigar, for example, walking around the block, a trip to the shop, a brief chat about golf, the obsessive stacking of papers or straightening of paper clips. The point is to get your mind on to something else, for however brief a time.

There is a tendency to want to skip steps when you have too much time as well as too little. You figure that there is no pressure, and you don't need to constrict or limit the process. Wrong. Even if you've got three months, don't skip steps.

Extremely experienced writers may appear to skip steps. It's most unlikely, however, that they do. They may create a list of points or an outline in their mind, rather than on paper. They may be able to sit down and write a single draft that seems polished but is, in fact, rough – given what they could accomplish with two additional drafts.

Essential considerations

All the above fits into the category of process or method. As you go about the process, there is a short list of essential considerations to keep in mind. These may or may not actually appear in the document. They should always be in the back of your mind as you write.

It being a complicated world, and business being a rapidly changing phenomenon, it is wise to consider and often include a bit of background information in your writing. This has a number of advantages and positive benefits.

It locates your audience in space and time. You know what your concerns are and what you intend to talk about. Your reader, or your audience, does not. They're thinking about holidays and profits and tennis and redundancies and all sorts of other issues. You need to remind them, fast, of what you are talking about, why, and deliver any historical information that is critical to the understanding of the new stuff you're about to deliver.

This gives you a chance to interpret history in a positive light for your purposes. Let's say you're writing a speech for a press conference to introduce the new ZX90 Component Module Unit. By spending a few minutes describing the market scene that led up to the development of this amazing new product you can make it appear that the world was living with a great, unnoticed lack before the ZX90 burst on the scene.

It gives you a chance to gain agreement, before raising any controversial or difficult issues. You can select the bits of history that are positive or appealing to your audience. By reinforcing or invoking these you help to get the audience with you and on your side.

You may not need to include background in your actual document, but the more you know the better the writing will be, and the more pitfalls you'll avoid. Suppose, for example, that the ZX90 CMU bears a striking resemblance to a tortoise. So, you decide to draw several parallels between the fine qualities of the ZX90 and tortoises. Long life. Steady gait. Thick skin. Then, a month into the work, you learn from an old timer that a competitive CMU was actually called Tortoise and had a tendency to catch fire, which resulted in the competitor being taken to court and finally going bust. The tortoise approach goes out of the window, and you get egg on your face. A little early foraging into product history, and that of their competitors, would have saved you a lot of time, trouble and tortoises.

OBJECTIVES

This is really at the heart of any type of business or sales writing. You must determine, very early on and with great clarity, what your objectives are. What do you want the audience/readers to do, feel or think once they have encountered this bit of writing?

You can create awareness. This is a rather clear objective. Small companies operating in a marketplace where there are massive competitors, start-up companies, or companies that are moving into new markets, need to let people know what they are doing. They simply need to get their names on the mental shortlist of those people who are in a position to choose their products or services.

You can change or influence attitudes. Many business communication endeavours are designed to change attitudes. From brochures to videotapes to company meetings to press background sessions to print and television advertising, much of what you write is not selling anything tangible; it doesn't ask you to part with money. It *does* ask you to think about some issue or company in a particular way; *our* way. Attitude-changing can certainly be considered as selling, because it attempts to use persuasion for a long term gain. But it is low-key, high-level selling.

If change of attitude is the objective, you need to determine what the current attitudes might be and how, specifically, you would like them to change. For example, many computer companies were founded by engineers and are engineering-driven. In recent years, however, they have been challenged by marketing-driven technology companies.

This has created intense competition and has also created a need for some large companies to change the attitudes of their employees towards the importance of the customer.

Or let's suppose that a retail shop has long made its profits on low-priced clothing with little or no service support. It finds that the bottom is dropping out of this market (or the chairman now wants to become respectable). So it embarks on an advertising campaign to change attitudes towards the shop, by showing designer fashions and helpful sales people and talking about quality and the importance of the customer, but never mentioning price.

Or, the most difficult type of attitude-changing. This is when a company undergoes some terrible débâcle. A huge loss, a scandal or gross negligence. A remarkable case of attitude "control" took place in the United States after several containers of the headache remedy Tylenol were poisoned (through no fault of the company) and several people who took it died. A well-orchestrated campaign that included press coverage, public relations efforts and television advertising fought the fears and shaken confidence head on, by reinforcing all the positive feelings people had for the drug. It worked. There is undoubtedly a well-written document somewhere at corporate headquarters that clearly states the objectives of that campaign.

If you write without clear objectives, you'll wander and waffle and confuse everyone. A clearly stated objective is perhaps the chief characteristic that distinguishes this from other forms of writing ... particularly from the "creative" forms. Poetry and fiction may have the effect of changing your attitudes, or making you take action, but it is unlikely that this was the primary intent of the writer. One fiction writer said he wrote a famous novel "to get rid of it". It is quite possible that the writer of selling documents has precisely the same intent but that is the hidden agenda, not the stated purpose. And that's something we look at later in this book.

THE AUDIENCE

Determining who your audience is (and what you want them to do – see above) is absolutely vital to selling and business writing. Advertising agencies spend vast quantities of money and hours of research analysing who is buying, was buying, should be buying and would never buy their client's product or service. We cover this subject in more detail later in the book, particularly where it relates to advertising. But for now, let's look at its overall relevance.

Understanding who you're talking to focuses your thinking and sharpens your writing. Clear proof of this is the writing you find in corporate brochures that really are aimed at everybody. They tend to take a vague, bland, inoffensive and extremely generalised tone. This is because the writer doesn't know the audience and can't know what attitudes, opinions, religions, national or regional concerns are at stake.

The more you can focus on your audience the more precisely you can tailor your message. If you're writing a speech to be delivered to an internal sales force of thirty-five people, you may know each of them individually. You can really work with their particular concerns, even their personalities. Perhaps the need to understand your audience is most compelling when you're writing a presentation or document for the boss. The managing director or chairman tends to be a highly visible character in most companies, whose likes and dislikes, personal history, strengths and weaknesses are not only well-known, but may also have passed into corporate mythology. This is perhaps the one case, apart from writing to one's family or lovers, when knowing the audience too well can be a disadvantage.

Knowing who your audience is, is one thing. Understanding them is quite another. If you are writing for a conference of new car dealers, for example, but you're not actually in the car business, you may have a clear impression of the breed taken strictly from your experience as a car buyer. This is certainly useful, but it probably isn't enough, because the car dealer has problems too ... pressure from the corporation, short supplies, increased competition, impending legislation, and so on. You have to know what the concerns are. You have to identify and understand your audience and try to see the issues from their point of view.

KEY MESSAGES

Once you've looked into the background, determined your objectives and identified the audience, now you can start to identify your key messages. You must do the other things first because the key messages will differ according to what your objectives are and who you are talking to.

You don't want to be dealing with too many key messages at once. One is best. Two is OK. Three is getting a bit tricky. If you've got more than four, you're not thinking or editing hard enough. *The point is to determine the key messages; not every message you can think of.*

Identifying the messages, selecting the key ones, may be a fight between the writer and everybody else involved. The non-writers will have a natural tendency to want to say everything good about the subject. If you are writing a corporate image video, for example, there will be a desire to say too many things; that we are the leader in high technology, but that we are also tops in service, and that we feel a great responsibility to the community, and, oh yes, we have a corporate culture that is also first-rate, and on top of that we have an excellent record on the environment, and overseas development, but research and development comes first. You've got to decide.

Whenever possible, and that is almost always, the messages should present at least one USP – unique selling proposition. (Even our business has its acronyms.) The USP is simply a best, or a first, or better, or only, something that your company, product or service has that no one else has, or has as much of, or had as early as you, or does as well as you.

If you're working with high technology companies, banks, delivery services and volume car companies – you'll have a hard time developing memorable, unique key messages with real USPs. This is because they are basically all alike. If you can't find something obvious, look for something more subtle. Was yours the first delivery service to use large trucks running deliveries overnight? Is your computer software company the smallest, but fastest-responding, servicing organisation? Does your bank have its roots in an industry/activity that has made history (we loaned Scott the money to explore the Antarctic)? Research ... painstaking, detailed research ... will tell you a lot more than how the ZX90 CMUs brass widgets were made. It might also lead you to a USP that no one else would have dreamed of.

One final note: Just the good news, please

Always remember that selling documents and business communications in general are vehicles for the delivery of good news. No one wants to hear the bad news cold; no one wants to review miserable past history. So, no matter what has to be said, you'll have to find a way to make it sound and look like good news – no matter how bad it is. We hope this book will help you do so.

CHAPTER 3

SELLING TO YOUR COLLEAGUES, ON PAPER:

Business documents

THE ROLE OF INTERNAL WRITING

It seems that there's more writing being churned out in governmental and business organisations today than ever before. Researchers in the United States estimate that about 1.3m pages are stored in filing cabinets and desk drawers across the nation. In London, the local government records have grown so fat that if all the pages were laid end to end you'd have a trail of paper 2,400 miles long. Paper documents are piling up by 20% per year, and by the year 2001 it is estimated that recorded knowledge will be accumulating four times faster than the human population. If you venture inside any business organisation these days, large or small, you'll find volumes of paper everywhere. To be in business today is to be living under a volcano of reports and memos, proposals and other documents smouldering on the corner of your desk. And for more and more people, there is another source of yet more written information – the desktop computer or workstation.

Where does all this writing come from? Is it necessary? In large organisations, a great deal of the documents that are produced are redundant or overlapping. The description of a new product, for example, is written by product engineers. Some of the information is then used to write a marketing document. Then both are combined into a presentation to industry analysts. Then all three are amalgamated into a report to the chairman. All of these are then used to brief the advertising agency. The agency dissects it to create a document that simplifies it all. Soon, the file on something as nondescript as the ZX90 CMU is bulging with reports, memos, presentation scripts, speeches and briefs. Human nature being what it is, errors are introduced along the way. More paper is generated to try to correct things. The simplest subject comes to require a filing cabinet full of paper.

Decentralisation of companies exacerbates the tendency. With employees in different offices, departments, cities and countries a lot of paper is generated because messages can't be delivered face to face, or over the telephone. And the advent of electronic data and word processing equipment – rather than creating a paperless office, as some predicted – has made it so easy to create and revise documents, to print and reprint them, that people can blithely generate weighty, beautifully printed documents in hours that would have needed days to produce just a few years ago.

The writer of internal documents should keep all this in mind when nestling before the trusty word processor. It's highly unlikely that your readers are eagerly awaiting that report or proposal from you, so that they can spend a leisurely hour or two savouring every well-chosen word. So, don't write a document unless it's necessary. And when you do, make it as brief and to the point as possible.

Sounds a bit negative, doesn't it? But there are many good reasons for writing internal documents. First, remember the relationship between writing and thinking. The very fact that thinking is involved at all in writing (or should be) distinguishes it from many activities undertaken during the normal business day – such as going to meetings or trying to reach someone on the telephone. Writing a document demands that you take the time to think your subject through clearly and completely. If you can do this, your colleagues will be forever grateful. They may not agree with what you write, but at least the initial pain of structuring and ordering has been undertaken for them. Now their job is to find the flaws in the form and the weaknesses in the argument – not build the structure itself.

The written document, therefore, is a catalyst. Once "you've got something down on paper" you're dealing with a tangible quantity. With internal documents, it often doesn't matter how good that something is – as long as it's not complete rubbish – because the real role of the document is to give people something to react to and to edit. The number of times you will hear people say, "I'm not a good writer, but I'm a good editor", or "I can't generate ideas, but I know good ones when I see them", will convince you, eventually, that the role of the writer is important. Words on paper are concrete. They bring order and meaning to people's swirling thoughts and spoken ideas.

Once written, the internal document brings consistency; it is a form of getting your story straight. Write your objectives down and pass them around and it is amazing how people will actually take them in, repeat them, stick to them and refer to them in a consistent fashion. Even in huge corporations with offices all over the world, you'll find some clearly defined corporate thinking usually articulated in a short, simple document.

This is not to overstate the role of writing. Writers do not, you may have noticed, ascend to the chairmanship as often as financial or sales people do. However, it's a rare chairperson who is a rotten writer.

Internal writing and politics

If writing words that sell is a different discipline from writing words of self-expression, writing documents for internal consumption is even further removed from "creativity" as it's usually understood. In a video script or advertisement, you are trying to reach out to others and make them understand – you may even be able to inject a good bit of your own humour or style into the writing. Much of internal writing, however, is about protecting yourself. About concealing your personal interest under the mantle of corporate objectives. About finding ways to compromise – making your ideas blend with those of your colleagues. Once you accept these rules, then you can see the discipline as a game – one that everyone plays and knows that everyone else is playing, and keeps on playing no matter what.

All the steps of the writing process (research, distillation, outlining, prose) apply to the internal document. One of the basic considerations, however, takes on extra significance: your audience. When writing for external audiences, you are an anonymous writer. No one knows your name. No one cares to know it. If something in the writing does not please, it will have little effect on you as a person or as a writer.

However, when writing internal documents, everything you write may be held against you. Your readers may know exactly who you are and, if they don't, they can find out. So you need to consider your audience extremely carefully. The natural assumption you might make when writing an internal document is that, because we all work for the same glorious company, we are on the same side – I can write the bad news, therefore, I can be completely honest about the hidden agendas. This sounds good in the abstract. In reality, however, every company is a chaos of conflicting personal motives, deep-seated jealousies and ambitions, hatreds and loves. There is constant jockeying for position, constant searching for credit, constant building of internal kingdoms and sieges against others. Although everyone is on the same side – in the broadest sense – there are plenty of times when common purpose seems to be absent.

For the most part, your readers will assume that – whatever you write, and no matter how much for the good of the company it appears there is also a personal motive involved. You are seeking a better position, more money, recognition, a different location, more furniture, a free lunch. They are probably right. This is acceptable, as long as the personal objective is not at odds with the corporate objectives and as long as you don't go over the top. So, you need to be clear about your own personal objectives, messages and audiences when writing a document. Hidden agendas within hidden agendas! Probably the most successful business people are those whose personal objectives are most consistent with corporate ones. It will certainly show in their writing.

Of course, there are great advantages to writing for internal consumption that you may not enjoy when writing for external audiences. If you're writing for a large organisation, you won't know all the individuals, but you will have a certain amount of shared history and culture. If you know specific people in your audience, you can write with an extremely sharp focus. You may know your subject matter already, as well. If so, your research should take less time and may consist only of a thorough racking of the brain.

These advantages may also be pitfalls. There is a good chance that the audience will understand the subject matter as well, or better, than you do – and is less likely to be tolerant of errors, incorrect assumptions, wild predictions, rumours or self-serving reinterpretations of history. And, if you know the audience, it's likely that they also know you. They'll recognise your style, they'll be aware of your own personal agendas. They may know your strong and weak points. You are out in the open and the open is a place that many people in business organisations would prefer to avoid – thus the rather woolly, non-committal tone of many internal business documents.

Always keep your audience in mind – not just who they are, but also in which *direction* you are writing ...

UP. That is, writing to people who have more power, a more senior position, more knowledge, more resources, or more capability than you have. They will tend to assume that you want something from them, and they will probably be right.

DOWN. People in the opposite positions to those above will tend to assume that you want them to do something for you, and they will probably be right.

LATERALLY. To colleagues who have an equal status in most respects. They will not know why you are cluttering up their desks with more bits of paper, but will hope that you make it clear as quickly as possible.

UNDER THE TABLE. If you believe a piece of information or

strategy should be strictly personal or confidential, don't write it down. There is very little within a company that is not unofficially known by at least one or two people who aren't supposed to know it.

Structure

There is little obligation on the part of internal readers to receive your latest missive in polite fashion. You need, therefore, to approach your reader in such a way as to get – at the very least – a fair reading. It is always wise to assume the worst, and approach your reader as if he/she is ...

- in a foul mood
- reading and talking on the telephone at the same time
- late leaving for lunch or the airport
- basically opposed to your idea
- in no mood for negatives
- incapable of handling more work
- uncertain which day it is
- working on two projects at once
- feeling ill.

Establish your subject. The first thing you must do – briskly and clearly – is to establish your subject matter. Let the poor recipient know what's on your mind. This is best done with a title or headline. It's important that this be chosen keeping the "good news" axiom in mind.

Let's suppose that you're writing a proposal document to the managing director for some new office furniture, including a leather sofa. A clear and direct title would be ...

"Re: New furniture acquisition".

Clear and direct, but no good. Why? Because acquisition suggests the outflow of capital, which triggers the automatic internal reaction in MDs which goes: ACQUISITION = EXPENDITURE = REDUCED PROFITS = NEGATIVE IMPACT ON ME. This gets you off on the wrong foot.

Instead, title the proposal ...

"Improvement of working environment".

This is slightly better, in that the word "improvement" is positive, and also because no acquisition is mentioned. However, although willing to appreciate the positive tone, any managing director worth the title will instantly recognise that furniture acquisition is what's probably required to improve *your* working environment. It also comes across as a personal request; we want to improve our lives without thought as to what impact it will have on the business.

Now it so happens that just last week the MD was in your work area when an important client arrived. The client was, in fact, coming round to inspect your premises before confirming the details of a major new contract. Alas, there being no suitable sofa handy, the client was forced to lean against a desk. Unfortunately, a bit of indelible ink had been spilled there by a careless graphic artist and there were terrible results.

With this in mind, your proposal is now entitled ...

"Proposal for the creation of a client conference area".
Naturally, the MD will still recognise this as a thinly veiled bid for additional creature comforts. At the same time, he or she will also recognise the strong and undeniable benefit for *the company*. Creation is positive action, and to an enlightened manager anything that improves client satisfaction is a good thing. But the "hook" of this title is the deep-seated psychological one – you are proposing a solution that will help the MD avoid future pain and embarrassment.

The example is a bit frivolous. But the rules apply no matter how serious the subject. The title should be positive, should be seen to benefit the *company*, not just one or a few employees, and, if possible, have a strong personal attraction to the reader. The clear and positive title slices through the thicket of the reader's other concerns. In the midst of chaos and personal trauma, at least here are six or eight words of clarity and hope. I think I'll read on.

Locate the reader. Now it is time to locate your audience, quickly, in time and space. You need to let them know what you're writing about and why, and deliver any relevant background information they might need. This is often done in the "as you know" or "as you remember" mode, so as not to insult the reader on the off-chance he or she actually does know or remember something of the subject matter. For example ...

When the company-wide "putting people first" programme was announced about two months ago, you asked all of us to find new or better ways to serve our clients.

At that time you had a brief meeting with all of us in graphic arts, and we talked about various ways that we might improve our presentation methods and the quality of our presentation visuals.

Many of the actions we identified have been taken. You remember, of course, the great success of the specially mounted illustrations presented to ZX Ltd. In fact, the chairman liked them so much that one of them is now hanging on his wall.

Note that, in establishing a bit of history, you can also put your own case in the best light. Lots of positive stuff here.

Establish some areas of agreement. Now, you need to set up your argument. The best way to do this is to establish some broad areas of agreement, and very gradually move towards specific proposals. Peace negotiators and policemen talking to people on window ledges use this technique regularly. Diplomats don't start negotiations by saying: "Good morning. We want you to destroy 178 medium-range missiles. In return, we will build 16 fewer submarines."

No, you begin by establishing agreement that you want peace and harmony between your two nations and then that one way to ensure the peace is through a lessening of tension about nuclear weapons, and then that tension could be reduced through a reduction of medium-range weapons, and then that perhaps a deal could be made involving medium-range missiles and submarines and, finally, that perhaps 178 and 16 are the respective right numbers to consider.

In this way, the exact moment when the reader stops nodding the head is clearly defined. If the nods stop at "peace and harmony" you've got big trouble. If it stops at "178 and 16", your job is a lot easier.

In the case of furniture, you might continue ...

> Although these efforts have been successful, they all have been directed at serving the client better when we are on their location. We haven't done much, however, to improve our service for clients who visit us here at the studio.
>
> We think it is just as important – perhaps more important – that we present a proper image here at home as when we go to them. And, in light of the fact that client visits are rapidly increasing, the need is even greater. Just in the last week, for example, we received seven different clients on 12 different occasions. Over the past month, we've seen some 23 clients in about 40 meetings.

Facts always help.

State the problem in terms of opportunity. Next, you need to define the opportunity (which is probably a problem in disguise) that your proposal is best suited to take advantage of.

> Although our client contacts at the studio have been successful, we're not able to give them really first-class service. Although our drafting equipment and photographic gear is first-rate, we have no comfortable seats, decent tables or adequate presentation easels. This is not surprising, considering the fact that we were set up as a work space and had intended to meet clients in the boardroom.

However, times have changed and – in light of the "putting people first" objectives – we'd like to take advantage of this opportunity to give our clients a good impression of what we do.

Even if you are facing a horrendous situation, there is no point in trying to establish blame for it – thus the "this is not surprising" line. It's especially unwise to place blame if there is any chance it may land on the reader to whom you are supplicant.

State your proposal. Now, it's time to state your case and state it plainly. The reader knows you're leading up to something, so don't try to disguise the fact.

We suggest the establishment of a client conference area, within the graphic arts department. It would consist of a seating arrangement – probably a sofa and several comfortable chairs – a large table to accomodate illustrations and blueprints, a multi-purpose presentation system (possibly the ZX90-P CMU from ZX Ltd.) and a new lighting system.

State the benefits. Your proposal is nothing until you have stated the great benefits it will bestow upon the company, and no doubt, upon the reader.

We believe that such a conference area will improve the receptiveness of our clients to our presentations. As you know, much of what we do calls for subjective and non-rational judgements – the appraisal of colours and designs, for example. By presenting the company's work under the most flattering lighting conditions, supported by a high-tech and substantial support system (the ZX-90 CMU) and with our clients comfortably seated in attractive chairs – we can only expect to improve our image and give ourselves the greatest opportunity to have our work accepted.

Of course, client acceptance means fewer revisions and reworking. We have found that client-ordered changes – not errors, but merely stylistic adjusments – account for about 18% of our workload. If we could reduce that by even 5%, we would more than pay for the new arrangement in the first year.

Ask for the sale. Sounds awfully good. Hard to turn down. The final step is to tie it all up, and make it clear what you want the managing director to do.

The company is going through a period of change. We're all looking for new ways to improve our image and serve our clients better. We think that the creation of a new, reasonably priced client conference area is in line with these objectives.

We want to proceed to create detailed plans and costing proposals for your approval. The estimated costs and schedule for doing so is attached.

Keep it brief. Above all else, keep internal documents brief and to the point. The reason most selling documents, reports and memos are too long is because it's *much harder to write short documents than it is to write long ones*. Writing long documents is an exercise in brain spillage – it has nothing to do with editing and selecting and ordering and clarifying.

Abraham Lincoln (American president from 1861 to 1865) was once invited to deliver an address, and was asked how long he would need to prepare it. "It depends", he said, "on how long you want me to speak. If you want me to speak for five minutes it will take two weeks to prepare. If you want me to speak for an hour, it'll take a week. If you want me to talk all day, I'm ready now".

One large multi-national conglomerate is reputed to have had a rule for internal memos; they would not be read by senior management if they were longer than a page. The theory was that any idea – no matter how large it was – could be expressed in one page or less. Behind this rule was a hidden agenda; if you couldn't state your idea in clear enough terms you were probably incapable of implementing it or seeing it through.

Know your objectives. Perhaps the worst thing that you can do is to create a piece of writing that does not have a clear objective – that is, does not clearly state what you want from the reader. Suppose for example, you have a general feeling that your particular department is not performing as well as it should and that you are losing business as a result. You decide that you want to do something about it. You may have the urge at this point to write a memo to someone, with copies to everyone, that spell out your concerns.

It may express a concern about product quality, a feeling that there are not the proper staff people in position, that the competition has a vastly superior product or service. You may include the warning that something had better be done, and soon, or else, and no buts about it.

This is not a selling document. It is ranting; it will be perceived as self-indulgent and worthless. Why? Because it is negative. It may attempt to place blame. It places the writer in a position of superiority to that of the reader. And, the action is: be better. How? This document should not exist.

The basic reason for writing, of course, may be perfectly sound. Your product or service may be miserable. It may be necessary for everyone to shape up quickly – and you may even be vastly superior to your colleagues in this area. However, if the objective of your document is to convince your colleagues of your correctness, it won't be effective. You need to find some general areas of agreement on broad goals and then lead the reader inexorably to a specific conclusion.

Good writing cannot improve a bad idea. Of course, if your idea or proposal is without merit, there is very little that the writing can do about it. Good writing is designed to clarify and simplify – and if the concept or idea you are attempting to write about is clearly unworkable or simply foolish, the well reasoned document will expose it. There is, of course, a bit of camouflage and protective editing that the clever writer can accomplish – but that is the stuff of propaganda and ruthless advertising, and not what we are all about.

Use of the "we". Like it or not, when you're a member of an organisation you're expected to adhere, to a reasonable degree, to the goals and principles of that organisation. No matter what your personal objectives may be, it's unlikely that you can accomplish much without the support and collaboration of your colleagues. Use of the "we" rather than the "I" acknowledges them – and makes it all the more likely that, if you deserve credit, they will find a way to give it to you. You may even resort to the indirect as in: "It was felt that ..." The important thing is to share the process with those who actually participated in it.

There are two opposing forces at work in business organisations that make writing a bit tricky. The first is the "not-invented-here" syndrome; if we didn't think it up, it can't be any good. There is an equally strong feeling that "if an outside expert says it, it must be true". You have to be careful, therefore, when quoting anybody as an expert – internally or externally – and careful in attributing any ideas to anybody in particular.

Dissociate your tone from the tone of the message. The generic "businesslike" tone is neutral and unexcitable. There is no whining, no crowing. No emotion is necessary. It is optimistic and positive. It seldom entangles personal emotions with business issues. If, for example, you're the plant manager and have just discovered that 86% of the CMUs the plant is churning out are defective, you do not begin your report to the board by cringing ...

> I didn't know this was going to happen! I'm terribly sorry and ashamed! I hate myself! If only I could go back in time to the moment I bought those 47 milling machines from that bankrupt toolmaker! Oh why, oh why, do these things happen! Please don't hurt me!

No, despite your deep mental and emotional anguish the tone of your writing should be chirpy ...

> It seems that, despite a reputation for excellence, our new milling machines are not doing the job. Now, at least we understand why that toolmaker went out of business! My team and I are working day and night on a solution to the quality problem – and see it as a great

opportunity to streamline the production line, something we've been wanting to do for some six months now.

Passion and deeply felt conviction are rare commodities in business writing. They are wonderful to behold, wonderful to possess. Business writing, however is all about rationality and clarity – not self-expression.

Writing on the computer

Many business people today are writing documents and messages on computers. This has changed the way people communicate, and the way they write. If you are on an electronic mail system in a large company, there are some style issues to consider.

Headlines. Electronic messages are usually sent from one mailbox to another, each identified with a short headline. The recipient checks the mailbox and sees a whole list of headlines. If the headline is intriguing, that message gets looked at first. And if the memo requires some urgent or protracted action, your memo (the one entitled *"Re: furniture acquisition"*) may never be viewed at all.

Size of the sheet. There is a natural tendency when writing with a typewriter to think in terms of paper pages. This is also true with word processors, because the end product is still the printed page. However, with electronic mail, the page is governed by the size of the screen. In many word processors it's 24 lines. It is, therefore, a clever electronic mailer who confines messages to a single screen – so that the message can be read without having to scroll up or down.

Ease of use. E-mail systems are relatively effortless to use, after you've learned the system, and they eliminate the need for link between computer and printer – where all kinds of problems can occur. Unfortunately, although this makes life easier, it does tend to increase the number of messages created. The responsible writer, therefore, communicates only when really necessary and doesn't gum up the system with exchange of motoring and sporting news.

Finally …

Much internal business writing is less about wordsmithing, and more about how to get people's attention, how to avoid corporate traps and how to ask for what you want. If you are a good corporate political animal, the chances are you will be a good corporate writer. In short, although external audiences don't like to hear or read rubbish very much, internal readers like it even less – and they can take revenge.

CHAPTER 4

FREE PUBLICITY – THE BEST KIND?

Public relations

WHAT IS PUBLIC RELATIONS?

There were a lot of very bad jokes about PR people in the 1960s. One of the worst was that the way to tell a PR man was by the way he drank his gin and tonic while simultaneously talking a load of hot air. PR men were supposed to have kipper ties (trendy then), cheap suits, and eyes that could swivel around 360 degrees of a crowded room. No one quite knew what they did, other than churn out the occasional press release and load their expense accounts by lunching journalists at fancy restaurants. PR ladies wore pearl necklaces and Gucci shoes, spoke in donkey-braying accents, and knew a lot about art.

One of the reasons why PR people got sent up was because PR is not an easy discipline to define. OK, PR – and advertising, for that matter – of the 1960s did attract a good many chinless bores who went into those industries largely to fill in the time between social occasions. And as the business world of that era carried a great many more passengers than it can afford to now, they managed to last quite a while before somebody got around to firing them. But there were a lot of serious-minded professionals around then, too. And although it was rather more journalism-orientated in the 1960s than it is today, with the now-famous press release assuming a very prominent role, PR is, and always has been, a multi-faceted operation.

London-based PR consultant Laurence Harris agrees:

> Going back a decade or two, a lot of ex-journalists used to go into PR. It was a natural progression for them. In those days, PR demanded a very high skill in the writing area, because PR tended to be very much press relations-led so you'd spend your whole day churning out press releases, articles and so on.
>
> Nowadays, PR is usually the promotion of an individual company

or product to a specific market, creating an image for that company using the various tools associated with PR, like press, TV, radio and so on. The main difference between PR and most other forms of marketing is that PR, by its nature, is an attempt to promote a product to its selected markets without paying for the media space or time that you would normally associate with advertising.

But, although PR has now expanded to take in all sorts of other disciplines like conference organisation and media interview training, the age of the good old press release is not dead. The unpaid promotion of any product or service still involves communicating with the media, and even when you're dealing with a radio or television station you are still likely to be asked for written material of some kind to explain what your promotional effort is all about. So, onwards and upwards ... to the writing skills you need.

RESEARCHING YOUR MEDIA

Before you start writing for any medium, it is necessary to understand all the influences and nuances that are likely to affect the success of your efforts. In the case of writing press releases, you need to understand the publications and/or broadcast organisations you select pretty well before you can write effectively for them.

Assuming that you have made your target media selection – and there are a number of other books on the whole of the PR function which will give you good advice on this – you need to find out who reads the publications, and/or who listens to or watches the broadcast station. Most publications and broadcast stations will tell you about the people they appeal to, but in most cases a little common sense is all you'll need. And the nature of the readership/viewership/listeners will provide you with a major clue as to the right way of approaching your press release.

Local newspaper readers will be interested in stories which have a local connection; national publication readers will be interested in the hard news value of a story; technical publication readers will be interested not only in hard news but in, for example, the research and development which went into a new product, and its technical superiority over its competitors.

Editors: A rare breed

Editors of all publications receive PR press releases by the truckload every year. They throw the vast majority of these into the wastepaper basket. Before we look at how to create press releases that editors read and use, it helps to understand what these people's responsibilities are.

It is the editor's job – with his board-level colleagues – to structure the editorial policy of the publication concerned, and then see that it is put into practice. Editorial policies vary very widely, according to the type of readership. But they all have one thing in common, and that is to attract and hold readers' loyalty. This way, the publication stays in business and the editor eats; simple. Now, there's nothing that destroys readership loyalty faster than poor quality, boring editorial, or articles that stink of advertising copy. With the possible exception of "advertorial" – favourable feature articles produced by the publication in exchange for the purchase of rather a lot of advertising space – anything that goes into the editorial columns of a publication must be of genuine hard news or feature news interest to the readership. That's a simple, basic fact that the majority of press release writers forget, and that's why their pieces of paper go straight into the garbage or, in these conservation-conscious days, into the recycling plant.

Editors are also busy people. When they look at a press release, it has got to catch their imagination within the first line or two; they haven't got time to read through three paragraphs of turgid prose to look for something interesting. So, writing a press release involves using your imagination.

As Laurence Harris says:

> If you have a product in front of you which is probably not much different from a dozen or so others that are available, you have to look for some different angle; some story element that is either there already, or that you can genuinely introduce into it. This will make it of use to the editor or journalist who is to receive it ... so your first task is to produce a press release with an angle, so that the editor can feel he has got a justifiable reason for putting it in his newspaper, magazine, or whatever.

WRITING PRESS RELEASES: THE ANGLE OF THE DANGLE

Finding the best angle to use for a press release can involve a little lateral thinking. Very often, you'll find your angle by using your imagination and moving one step on from the actual facts of the story concerned. Another quote from Laurence Harris:

> Let's suppose you are producing a press release about a new booklet your company has published on, say, school industry links, which is a pretty boring subject, from a general readership's point of view. You have to find an angle that will make it more interesting. One angle might be research data; newspapers love facts and figures. So if you found out that the school-leaver population was going to drop

enormously in the near future, and that industry is going to have a harder task to recruit people in the next few years, then that's an angle which would make it of much greater human interest. You could then find some research data from your government's education body, and use that concept to build your press release on. Your headline might then read, *'40% Shortfall Predicted in School Leavers Population: Industry Left Without a Workforce by 1995?'* ... something like that. It instantly grabs the readers' attention and makes them think 'there's a story here, something interesting'. You can then back up the headline with some statistics and then go into why, as a result of this, the booklet has been produced bringing industry and schools together.

Human interest is the key with all forms of general media. Specialised media are a bit different (see below). But in general publications you can't go far wrong if you can find an angle – or a hook – that emphasises the beneficial effect your announcement will have on people. This then automatically puts your company and product or service in a favourable light. And do remember that something which is of great interest and importance to you and your colleagues is not necessarily of interest to readers of a publication.

Let's say your company, Doggo Petfoods, has bought some land adjacent to the existing factory and intends to build a new puppy food factory on it. The fact that you're investing a couple of million pounds or more, and that projected sales of puppy food are looking good, is of no interest whatsoever to the local community. Here's the wrong way to do it, starting with the headline:

'Doggo Petfoods Announce Plan to Build New Factory'.

... then followed by a lot of talk about Doggo Petfoods and its five-year growth plan. Boring, boring, boring, even though the entire board and management committee might have been up six nights in a row working out the finance and strategy.

Readers of publications are just like advertising consumers; they want to know what's in it for them. Puppies, as we know, are usually cute and cuddly, so they can grab attention. There's one angle for you: a story based on the projected growth of the puppy population as families buy more dogs, and the need for special food to allow them to grow up healthy and strong. You could have a photograph taken of a group of puppies from different breeds of dog, with a can or two of Doggo puppy food clearly visible in the foreground, and your headline might run something like this:

'The Puppy Population Explosion: Pups Are on the Up and Up'.

You'd then go on to say how this fact has been noticed by Doggo, and that they are expanding to be ready for the predicted future.

Another angle for the same story would be the increased number of jobs available at Doggo once the new premises are functioning. This is also of considerable interest to readers, especially young people who will be looking for jobs there when they leave school a couple of years hence. So, you could lead in with a headline like this:

'100 New Jobs for Local Dog Lovers by 199X'

As many people are dog lovers, and many of those who aren't will cheerfully pretend they are if they need a job, that's an attention-grabbing headline. You would then go on to point out that the jobs the new premises will create will not require any training or previous experience, as full training will be given. You can also work in a few other facts about Doggo Petfoods, provided they're consistent with the story line.

Finding your angle isn't difficult; it just requires some thought and an ability to stand back and look at your corporate selves objectively. Outside advice is very helpful. But if you can't afford the services of a PR consultant, you can bounce your ideas around with your family, friends or colleagues who may view your particular project with less close involvement, and therefore provide you with some fresh food for thought.

WRITING PRESS RELEASES: STYLE AND STRUCTURE

The writing style you use in a press release depends very much on the publication or publications it is intended for. The obvious thing to do is to buy copies of those publications, study their editorial content, and try to copy their editorial style as far as possible. Sometimes, though, you may want to send out releases to a number of different publications within a category like the national newspapers, which have varying styles. In this case, here's Laurence Harris's advice:

> You cannot go too far wrong if you emulate the style that is used by a good national newspaper ... you can do no better than study the language and style of writing that is used in this type of publication. It's punchy, it's interesting.

Writing styles are many and varied, but for PR purposes you're only likely to need to know about three: hard news, feature news, and technical articles.

Hard news is almost self-explanatory. This is the tough, no-nonsense, no-frills style of writing you see on the front pages of most good publications. They answer the classic journalistic questions of what, when, where, who and how, tightly and punchily. If your story is that newsworthy, you don't even need to work too hard at finding a cuddly angle. The facts should be interesting enough in themselves. Let's take an example:

Jobs Scare Resolved at Doggo Petfoods
Gordon Setter, Chairman of local company Doggo Petfoods, announced today that the threat of 200 job losses at their XXXXX-town plant was now past. The company's financing has been strengthened by its recent merger with Catto Petfoods, and its future now looks secure well into the next century. "The jobs scare was only temporary," said Mr Setter, "but now that our financing has been secured for the next ten years we can guarantee not only existing jobs but plans for expansion into a new brand of puppy food, which will mean additional jobs for local people in the future."

Enough said. The story has answered all five questions thoroughly, but with no wasted words or extra padding. And with an issue as important to local people as this one, it would have been in bad taste to put in too many plugs for Doggo products. However, a few basic, promotional facts have been put over, in an appropriate style.

Feature news style is softer, and can go into more detail, fleshing out the bones of the hard news story. Let's return to Doggo's puppy food press release, assuming we've chosen the puppy population explosion angle:

The Puppy Population Explosion: Pups Are on the Up and Up
Recent research commissioned by local company Doggo Petfoods shows that the dog population in this country is increasing at the rate of 30%. By 199X, there will be more than 500,000 dogs living as pets with their families, the research predicts. That means there will be more puppies for families to look after; as many as 5,000 new puppies in XXXtown alone.

So how can local people do the best for their puppies without spending a lot of money? Doggo Petfoods chairman, Gordon Setter, has this advice: "Obviously, exercise, grooming, proper veterinary care, correct sleeping accommodation and gentle but firm discipline are all important," says Mr. Setter. "Our recently published leaflet, 'Caring for your Puppy', goes into that in some detail. But probably the most important thing is correct feeding. Puppies need a careful selection of vitamins and minerals in their diet, as well as the right balance of protein, fat and carbohydrate. Yet to make up this correct diet out of ordinary meat and biscuits can be expensive."

Doggo Petfoods has plans to build a new factory in the town to produce a new type of puppy food that combines just the quantities and proportions of all the nutrients puppies need, at a price their owners can afford. The factory, planned to open in June 199X, will produce three different varieties of the as yet unnamed puppy food, for small, medium-sized and large dogs. And the resulting expansion of the company will mean over 50 welcome new jobs for the area.

Gordon Setter pointed out that they'll be looking for local people who love dogs to work in the new factory. Recruiting for staff will start in January, 199X, and full training will be given.

The style goes into more detail; it contains longer quotes than would be suitable for hard news; and it contains a little more in the way of opinion than would be the case with hard news. However, if the editor of the publication liked the story but wanted to cut it down for lack of space, it would be very easy to sub-edit down ... a point worth remembering when you're writing a feature-style press release. Always make sure that the main issues of the story are structured in a way that can bear editing, without the editor or sub-editor having to rewrite it. After all, they're busy people; a release that can be prepared quickly for inputting or typesetting is far more likely to get used than one which has to be reworked. Let's see how the editor might approach the pruning job; bold type is what should stay, faint type is what should be removed:

The Puppy Population Explosion: Pups Are on the Up and Up
Recent research commissioned by local company Doggo Pet-foods shows that the dog population in this country is increasing at the rate of 30%. By 199X, there will be more than 500,000 dogs living as pets with their families, the research predicts. That means there will be more puppies for families to look after; as many as 5,000 new puppies in XXXtown alone.

So how can local people do the best for their puppies without spending a lot of money? *Doggo Petfoods chairman, Gordon Setter, has this advice: "Obviously, exercise, grooming, proper veterinary care, correct sleeping accommodation and gentle but firm discipline are all important," says Mr. Setter. "Our recently published leaflet, 'Caring for your Puppy,' goes into that in some detail. But probably the most important thing is correct feeding. Puppies need a careful selection of vitamins and minerals in their diet, as well as the right balance of protein, fat and carbohydrate. Yet to make up this correct diet out of ordinary meat and biscuits can be expensive."*

Doggo Petfoods has plans to build a new factory in the town to produce a new type of puppy food that combines just the quantities and proportions of all the nutrients puppies need, at a price their owners can afford. The factory, planned to open in June 199X, will produce three different varieties of the as yet unnamed puppy food, for small, medium-sized and large dogs. And the resulting expansion of the company will mean over 50 welcome new jobs for the area.

> *Gordon Setter pointed out that they'll be looking for local people who love dogs to work in the new factory. Recruiting for staff will start in January, 199X, and full training will be given.*

The bones of the story are still there, but without the quotes which act as padding – albeit useful, informative padding. Let's see it now, after the edit:

> *The Puppy Population Explosion: Pups Are on the Up and Up*
>
> **Recent research commissioned by local company Doggo Pet- foods shows that the dog population in this country is increas- ing at the rate of 30%. By 199X, there will be more than 500,000 dogs living as pets with their families, the research predicts. That means there will be more puppies for families to look after; as many as 5,000 new puppies in XXXtown alone.**
>
> **So how can local people do the best for their puppies without spending a lot of money?**
>
> **Doggo Petfoods has plans to build a new factory in the town to produce a new type of puppy food that combines just the quantities and proportions of all the nutrients puppies need, at a price their owners can afford. The factory, planned to open in June 199X, will produce three different varieties of the as yet unnamed puppy food, for small, medium-sized and large dogs. And the resulting expansion of the company will mean over 50 welcome new jobs for the area.**

Finally, we come to the style you need to adopt for a technical publication. Here, you should still stick to answering the five ques- tions, but you can afford to go into more detail. Also, the "what's in it for me?" aspect of the readership changes. Readers of a technical or other specialist publication are not necessarily interested in the good of human kind, or at least if they are they will read about it in general publications. Targeting your story should be a lot easier here, because this is a field you or some of your colleagues will know intimately. It should not be too hard to find an angle when your readers are likely to have the same interests as you.

Technical editors and their readers are interested in facts and figures and, provided you don't bore them with profuse or irrelevant detail, you're free to use as many as you like. The writing doesn't need to be as chatty as it does for general publications, though good, clear style is still important. It is a wise precaution – just as it is with every other type of PR writing – to study the style of the technical publication you're aiming at, and try to emulate it.

Structuring a press release really means getting things in the right order. The place to start is with the headline. This needs to catch readers' (and editors') attention, and make them want to know more. Then, the first paragraph should expand on that headline, with one or two interesting further facts to explain it (see above examples). The main body of the release should expand further and, if it is a feature style story, should contain a quote or two from a senior person in your company, or someone who is connected with it. Quotes are often made up in the writing of press releases ... and this is not a crime, provided you show your draft to the person who is supposed to have spoken the words, and get his or her agreement. It's just that putting over some of the information in quote form gives a lively feel to the article; but unfortunately not all spokespersons are that articulate, have the time, and can express the sentiment you want them to express in exactly three lines.

Writing style should always be concise, and the language should be straightforward and uncluttered. It's difficult to teach people to write simply, and the truth is that it *is* harder to write simply than it is to write at length. The following two ways of writing the same short piece, taken from the course notes of one of Suzan St. Maur's video and AV writing workshops (London Media Workshops), illustrate the point and, although originally intended to show how to write bad and good spoken speech, are just as relevant to writing press releases.

> *Version One:*
> The object in question is made of light wood, containing
> a cylindrical core of carbon. At the end of this
> instrument it is necessary to sharpen the surrounding
> wood in order to achieve a conical point. In this
> respect it is possible to hold the object in the hand,
> and through the application of the correct degree
> of pressure the carbon point will convey an image upon
> a piece of paper placed directly beneath it. At this
> moment in time it is not possible to demonstrate the
> action of this object as it would appear to have been
> temporarily mislaid.

> *Version Two:*
> I'm talking about my pencil. It's made of wood, with
> some carbon in it. If you sharpen one end, you can
> write with it. I can't show you how it works, because
> I've lost it.

WRITING PRESS RELEASES: FLAGGING THE READER DOWN

Press release headlines are crucially important, and deserve a few paragraphs to themselves in this book. This is what gets the reader's attention, and this is also what gets the editor's attention as he or she flicks through the daily batch of ten or more press releases. Of course, many publications will rewrite or change your headline, and this is their privilege; they may feel that their version is more in keeping with the style of the publication, or that yours is too long or too short to fill the available space correctly, or they might just be zealous perfectionists who won't use a press release headline on principle. However, you have still got to flag the editor's attention if you want anything published at all, so your headlines have got to be good.

Which of these two headlines would attract your attention quicker?

'Doggo Petfoods Launches New Bark Dogfood'
'New Bark From Doggo Gets Better With Every Bite'

Much of the theory behind writing good headlines is similar to that of finding the right angle for your story, and so it would be duplicating things to say too much about how to arrive at the line you need. However, writing good headlines involves punchy, lively thinking and punchy, lively writing.

In truth, the headline that's right for your press release is a brief, gutsy summary of your angle. But sometimes, creating a headline that summarises your angle might be too long; and long headlines are not a good way to catch the editor's eye. One of the great favourites in Britain is the pun – an effective way to catch eyes in almost any language.

Laurence Harris again:

> We recently launched a new road sign. This was an electronically controlled road sign which flashes up information to motorists. It is the first time that words on signs have been used to inform motorists; the product provides intelligent, advance information to drivers about traffic jams and other traffic problems ahead, so that they can avoid them. The headline we used was *'No Jam Tomorrow'* ... and then we went on to say how this could alleviate traffic jams, and that from now on there would no longer be such a thing. It was a little bit of a pun, but it caught the eye and was very successful.

Puns are fine and dandy provided they are relevant. They can even be corny, provided they are relevant at the same time. The adaptation of a well-known phrase or saying is a useful device, too, because readers (or editors) tend to identify with a short phrase they know well. Hence:

'New Bark From Doggo Gets Better With Every Bite'

... as above. This works, because although it is a playaround with the old line about a dog's bark being worse than its bite, it actually contains a promise of what's to come; in this case, the story would go on to say that new BARK is so tasty dogs will be clamouring for more ... the new product's flavour is such that the dog's appetite is whetted at the merest sniff of new BARK, and so on. What wouldn't have worked would be:

> 'Doggo Teaches Old Dog New Tricks'
> 'New Bark Isn't Up the Wrong Tree'
> 'New Flavour For Man's Best Friend'

This is because although the lines are cute, they aren't relevant. Perhaps it's true to say that the way to write good headlines is a lesson that could be learned from the advertising world; make them punchy, make them as short as you can get away with, make them funny, make them corny; but whatever else you do, make them *work*, and make them use whatever vehicle you choose to sell the reader the idea of reading on for further information.

WRITING PRESS RELEASES: A FINAL WORD

Lastly, ensure that the press release is sent out on company stationery. If you send out releases on a regular basis, it's worth getting special paper printed; otherwise make sure that the following information is typed in.

- The company's name and logo, if relevant.
- Your address and phone number, plus the name of the person at your company who can answer any further questions and be available for the publication to interview, should it want a more detailed story about your release.
- A sentence across the top of the paper that says something along the lines of *"Latest news from Doggo Petfood"*; this will signal the fact that your piece of paper is not a bill or a mailshot selling office stationery, but an interesting piece of editorial material that deserves priority attention from the editor.
- An embargo notice, if relevant; useful if you want a story to break at roughly the same time in publications with slightly different copy deadlines. Embargo notices i.e. something which says *"not for publication before September 5th., 199X"*, may ensure that your story comes out everywhere at around the same time.

TALKING TO THE BROADCAST MEDIA

Whereas this topic is not about writing words down on pieces of paper, as such, apart from your coffee and sandwich order, it certainly is about *speaking* words that sell, in the PR context. And it involves choosing the words very carefully.

Broadcast media interviews ... that is, going on radio or television to talk about your business or other activity ... have become an art in themselves. Radio and television interviewers are trained and very experienced at asking questions, often awkward ones, and practised interviewees are just as good at responding in a way that makes them or their companies look good no matter how much pressure the interviewer puts on them to do otherwise. For the inexperienced interviewee, a good interviewer with a plastic smile and sharp verbal teeth can be terrifying. With a little knowledge on how to handle interviews, though, you can come through even the harshest experience unscathed.

In nearly every major city in the Western hemisphere, you can take a course on media interviews. This training facility has become big business, often run by ex or current media interviewers who put you through a "mock" interview, record it on videotape, and then take your performance apart and show you how to put it back together properly. For most executives whose companies play a significant part in a community, one of these courses is a good idea. Even local radio and television will sometimes want to interview a representative of Bloggs Bearings Ltd. if the factory is facing potential closure, they plan to build a new plant, their chimneys are puffing out what the district conservation society thinks is toxic smoke or the local frog population is threatened with reduced breeding grounds in the factory's car park, or any other activity which is likely to affect the neighbourhood. Company representatives will be called upon for an interview to put their side of the story. To refuse, can be seen as an admission of culpability. To do the interview, and get it wrong, can make the company look bad even if it doesn't deserve to. Knowing how to put your case becomes essential.

Another, rather more positive, reason why two or three people in a company should know how to be interviewed, is for promotional purposes. Suitably worded press releases sent to a broadcast station stating some piece of genuine news about a company can interest its editorial people and result in a request for someone to go on air and elaborate.

Finally, going on air in a non-specific capacity ... the managing director of Bloggs Bearings Ltd. answering questions about how to grow orchids on a radio phone-in show, and casually mentioning the company's name ... can help to gain recognition for Bloggs Bearings. That's all part of the PR process. But if the MD knows his orchids, all he or she needs to understand about the PR relevance of the exercise is that more than one or two discreet plugs for Bloggs would be a no-no. Wall-to-wall plugs would have two consequences; one, the MD would never be asked to discuss orchids again, and, two, he or she would put Bloggs Bearings in a bad light. Discretion is vital; but the spin-off PR, with press releases about the MD's radio stardom going to local newspapers, and internal PR with an article about the radio show in the company newsletter, could be useful.

Where words that sell really count are in the first two categories; defending your position, and promoting a new product or service. Let's take a look at a few tips on how to get your words right; however, bear in mind that a full training course for the likely interview candidates in a company, will teach them much more than is possible in this book.

The first thing to consider is that radio and television stations are uncharted waters for the average business person, and the sheer unfamiliarity of the place can make you nervous to start with. It's important to remember that these stations are ordinary places of business just like yours. The fact that there are people in headphones lurking behind double thicknesses of glass and strange machines whirring around you is purely a matter of course in the running of the station's business. If you took one of the station's technicians down to your place of work, he or she would probably feel just as out of place and uncomfortable watching your production line or computer activity as you do in the sound-proofed recording studio. The red glow of the "on air" or "recording" light in the radio or television studio does not signal Armageddon; it merely tells everyone that it's time to go to work. Keep the whole thing in perspective, and keep reminding yourself that broadcasting, just like your own industry, is not entirely staffed by man-eating tigers.

It helps a lot to do a little preparatory research before you are interviewed. Sometimes, of course, this isn't possible – especially when there has been a sudden piece of news and you need to comment on it pronto. However, in normal circumstances you will have a little time to learn something of the broadcast station, and the programme on which you will appear. Listen to, watch, or tape the programme concerned beforehand, so you know its style and approach.

Make sure you and the broadcast station know what to expect of each other. If you have a PR consultant, he or she will normally do this for you; if you don't, do it yourself. Before the programme, and preferably some time before, find out just what aspect of the topic the interviewer wants to highlight. This will give you a bit of time to prepare your material. You should also make sure that the broadcast station knows who you are and what you and your company do; a short, tightly written briefing document should be sent to them as early on as possible.

Get to the broadcast station as promptly as you can. Don't arrive three hours in advance, as you'll build up excessive nerves and probably wire yourself up on their coffee which will make things even worse. Just allow enough time to park your car, go to the bathroom, smoke a cigarette (unhealthy, but soothing for some), settle in comfortably, and relax. Then, try to have a chat with the interviewer before you go on. This isn't always feasible, especially if you're to make an appearance on a three-hour drive-in time radio show, where you're likely to be ushered into the studio during a commercial break or weather report and start a few seconds later. But, with television, you're likely to have time to talk to the person who will interview you, or at least a researcher who will then brief the interviewer. The purpose of this conversation is to run through the questions the interviewer may ask, and generally get to know the person a little. Not all interviewers will tell you the actual questions you should expect, and this isn't necessarily to catch you off your guard. From the interviewer's point of view, he or she will want your replies to sound spontaneous, and so will want to keep one or two small surprises up the professional sleeve. That makes good radio or television and, provided you know your subject matter, you'll handle any surprises easily. But most interviewers will give you a good general idea of what will be asked so you can call those issues up on your brain's computer and have them handy.

On the air part one: How to approach the interview

One very basic tip is to listen carefully to the questions. This sounds ridiculous, but when you're a bit nervous in your unfamiliar surroundings, staring at a dangling microphone in a radio studio or at a cold, hard camera lens on television, you can be sufficiently distracted to let questions go in one ear and out of the other. Remember that any kind of studio microphone, radio or television, is very sensitive and can pick up a fly buzzing ten feet away. Don't shuffle your feet or tap the furniture with your fingers, as the sound may well come through. Sit still, breathe deeply, and concentrate on the interviewer.

Even with radio, you should always look at the interviewer when you're replying to questions. That will help you to concentrate, as a human face responding to what you say is reassuring. Don't be put off by the fact that the interviewer doesn't *say* anything while you're talking; he or she may well smile or nod to encourage you, but grunts, yesses, noes, oh reallys, and so on that are common in normal conversation are out of the question because more than one voice at a time will confuse the soundtrack.

With radio, remember that the audience does not have the benefit of seeing you. All you've got to put across your message is your voice. So try to speak in a lively tone, avoid clichés and jargon, and avoid plugging your product or service *unless it's relevant* to the subject matter. Be natural; to quote John Yates (one of Britain's leading direct mail writers) entirely out of context, address the listeners "as if you were standing next to them in a pub or cocktail bar". Don't be pompous or opinionated, and remember that all but a few of the listeners will know nothing whatsoever about your business – so speak in simple, comprehensible language.

With television, you do have the benefit of being seen, but that's a double-edged sword. Remember, one of the biggest shocks many people get is seeing themselves on television or video; you never look as you expect to. One of the great advantages of doing a media interview training course is that you're likely to get the chance to watch yourself on videotape. And you'll be surprised how what your mother always called an endearingly crooked smile looks like an evil, twitching leer! The camera doesn't lie, really; it just magnifies all your acne scars, open pores, nervous twitches, and uncomfortable posture. A gesture with your hand or eyebrow that would hardly be noticed in real life makes you look like a demented windmill through the cruel eye of the camera. Many stage actors have had to learn to reduce their exaggerated theatre "body language" when they've turned to acting on television or film, for exactly the same reason. Seat yourself as comfortably as possible, look at the interviewer and, no matter how hostile you feel towards him or her, be pleasant. Keep your hands still, as far as possible without looking as if the interviewer has tied them behind your back, and keep your head still no matter how animated your discourse. Even slight movements of the head can look as though you're bobbing for apples. If all the above guidelines make you feel nervous just to think about them, do a training course; or, failing that, practise with a good friend who can play the interviewer's part and observe your behaviour.

Your clothes should be carefully chosen, too. Don't forget, your clothes speak volumes, or wardrobes, about you and the organisation you represent. Loud, jazzy numbers reflect precisely that. Dress according to how you want viewers to perceive you and your company. And there are a few technical points to observe, too.

Television stations can be hot, especially under the powerful studio lights, so use an anti-perspirant and avoid thin clothes through which any perspiration could show. Also avoid vivid patterns and stripes, plus the colours red and white, as these can create fuzzy reactions with the camera. If the studio uses chromakey (colour separation overlay, a technique whereby you project background pictures apparently behind the subject) you should also avoid the colour blue, but this is something you can check out before you go to the television station for your interview. In either radio or television interviews, it's a good idea to avoid wearing heavy metal watches or bracelets because if you should put your wrist down on a table or desk top the resulting clunking noise might be picked up by the microphones. Even the rustle of crisp, freshly ironed cotton or linen can be picked up by a sensitive lapel microphone, but don't worry too much about that one – usually, the technicians at the broadcast station can sort it out.

One final word on the approach to the interview; watch the booze. Those of us in the business who advise speakers on anything, be they conference presenters or potential broadcast media interviewees, sympathise with the speaker's view that one drink will help to relax the nerves and smooth the conversation – but don't support it. The Police say that even one small alcoholic drink can impair your judgement in the driving seat of a car; the same is true of your ability in the hot seat of the interview studio. If you must, just have one; if you can, though, stick to soft drinks, tea or coffee.

On the air part two: how to say your piece

Once again, a good training course will put you through detailed studies of how to go about answering questions and handling the interviewer. However, there are a few basic tips which will help you if you get caught on the hop, before you've had a chance to enrol on a course.

Let's look first at the straightforward type of interview which has been set up for PR purposes by you or your PR consultancy in order to gain recognition for your company and its products and services. You may be required to participate in an interview as a "generic" industry spokesperson, or your company may have announced a new product, service or activity which is of local or national interest. However, you can bet your bottom dollar that the interviewer is not going to sit there and cue you to perform as a walking, talking, breathing advertising commercial. The interviewer will be looking for an angle – a hook (see section on press releases) – which is likely to be of interest to the listeners/viewers, and what most interests them is not necessarily what most interests you or your sales director. If you even attempt to do a sales pitch, the interviewer is likely to become hostile and stop you, and to an extent this is understandable because a sales pitch is likely to make the listeners/viewers feel hostile towards the broadcast station. And that's bad for the interviewer's business.

What is likely to interest the interviewer and his/her listeners/ viewers are issues relevant to as large as possible a sector of the audience. These are likely to centre around human matters, or commercial matters that are pertinent to the good of the community or a significant group within it.

It is important that you accept this, and answer the questions accordingly. When answering, try to put yourself in the listeners'/ viewers' shoes, and structure your statements with them in mind. However, do remember that, provided you have something important to say, it is not a crime against humanity to use radio or television as "free advertising". And, to be fair, if the broadcast station has done its homework it will have ascertained beforehand just what it is you do have to say, and will naturally assume that you will work in a mention of your company, products or services. So unless you overdo the plugs, no professional interviewer should get hostile with you for a fair and reasonable mention of what you have to sell.

Probably the best and most acceptable way for you to work in your own messages, benefits and achievements is through giving examples to illustrate your direct answer to the interviewer's questions. Examples are wonderful things in PR terms, because they can be set up as a genuine part of the overall non-commercial response you're giving, and subtly bring in a number of facts about you and your company at the same time.

Let's say that Bloggs Bearings has just won a huge, long-term contract from a customer, and the extra work involved is going to generate fifty new jobs in the area. You, as the spokesperson for Bloggs, are being interviewed on local radio about it. The interviewer is keen to find out if this is just a temporary boost to local economy, so asks you ...

> INTERVIEWER:
> "Fifty new jobs – that's good news. But we
> hear a lot these days about growing competition from
> foreign manufacturers in engineering, making goods of
> high quality and selling them here for lower prices.
> How do you see British manufacturers competing against
> that sort of threat? What have you got that the
> foreign competitors haven't?"

YOU:
"Well first of all there's British companies' loyalty to
and moral preference for British made goods. That
counts for something. OK, our prices are higher in
some cases, but then we pay higher wages to our
workforce to keep up with the higher standards of living
we have here. Most of our British customers appreciate
that. More important in a competitive field, though, is
that our service is reliable, with the sort of long-term
experience we have, and because of the fact that we are
on the spot rather than hundreds or even thousands of
miles away. That's worth paying a little more for, in
itself. Then, there's quality; we pride ourselves on
quality in the British engineering industries, and it's
something we work very hard to keep at the forefront of.
So with first-class service and top quality, we're
genuinely giving our customers added value.
   Let me give you an example. Last month one of our biggest
customers telephoned me at Bloggs Bearings, and said they
needed 5,000 titanium bearings for a very special new
machine, by Monday morning. This was Friday afternoon.
So, our workforce dropped all their plans for the
weekend and designed the bearing using our new computer-
aided design technology, got tooled up and manufactured
the whole order of 5,000. They carried on working
through the nights as well, and we got that order
delivered to the customer's door at 9 o'clock Monday
morning. We didn't charge any more for the bearings
than the usual market price; the rush order and special
design are all part of our service. I'm sure many of
our colleagues in British engineering would have done
the same. But how many of our foreign competitors could
have managed that?"

Congratulations. You've answered the broad question – why customers should pay more for British-made goods – and you've also
managed to bring in the facts that your workforce is good, you've got
the latest technology for design, your dedication to quality is absolute,
and your service is excellent. You then managed to bring the conversation back to general terms, by generously suggesting that some of your
British competitors might be almost as good. And you haven't got the
interviewer's back up, because you've worked your own message into
an overall statement that genuinely answered the question. The sell
came into the example, not the reply itself, and didn't sound out of
place.
   Some interviewers like to ask awkward questions in the belief that

putting interviewees on the spot makes for more entertaining radio or television. If you should get one of these, don't be intimidated, and whatever you do don't try to fluff your way through it. That will make you seem shifty and uncertain of your ground. If you believe the question is awkward and/or difficult, say so; honesty is very important in any type of interview. Say that this is a difficult question to answer, and then say why it is. Finally, outline the main points that you can in response to it.

The last, and most important, point to consider about even the most straightforward of broadcast interviews (or interviews for publications, for that matter) is to know your subject. Remember, even the unsighted world of radio can expose your innermost weaknesses to the public ear, and television doubles the risk. Trying to bluff your way out of a question to which you don't know the answer will drop your credibility rating right down. If the worst comes to the worst, say you don't know, but will find out and let the viewers know the answer. But that is a measure which should be reserved only for emergencies. No matter how busy you are, a broadcast media interview is very important to your company in PR terms, so make sure you find the time to prepare for it properly. Not only will you save your company from the embarrassment of looking bad through its representative – you – but you will also save yourself from being any more apprehensive than is strictly necessary. There's nothing like ignorance and lack of preparation to make any interviewee climb the walls with stage-fright.

On the air part three: The defensive interview

This is the type of interview that no PR consultant in his or her right mind would ever seek for you. There has been a problem with your company – real or manufactured – and the press are after you to comment, and/or to defend yourselves. To a large extent, the following few paragraphs apply to press interviews as well, but at least with reporters from newspapers how you sound physically and/or how you look are not so important.

With the broadcast variety, it is vital that you stay calm and don't panic. If you handle the problem properly, not only will you be seen to defend your company well, but you can even turn the whole issue around to do your company some good. So, in reality, a well-handled defensive interview can involve speaking words that sell ... albeit subtly.

Radio and television reporters love to "doorstep" unsuspecting victims when there has been a sudden newsworthy occurence. In fairness to them, as news reporters it is their job to find out what's going on, get the various parties involved to comment, and report it all back to their audience as soon as possible. It's essential not to over-react to doorstepping, because there's nothing more image-zapping than a company representative humming and haa-ing, trying to make something up. If you don't yet know what's going on, say so; and then quickly point out that an immediate enquiry has been launched into the accident/incident/whatever, and that you'll have more information for them in so many hours' time. Once you have the information, give it to the reporters; you must be seen to keep your word.

Whatever you do, don't dehumanise any problem. All reporters, unless they write for the specialised business press, are interested in the "people" issues of any crisis or incident involving companies. Don't preface a rebuff by saying "it's not our company policy to ...", no matter how tempted you may be to use it. Even if it isn't company policy to talk to the press, the alternative if you're doorstepped is to make your company look hard and uncaring, which is bad news from every imaginable point of view. So it's better to say that you don't know the answer to that question yet, and rather than speculate, you're going to find out the facts and let the public know just as soon as the investigation is complete.

Another common instance of doorstepping is when there is a dispute between the management of your company and the trade unions, or between the company generally and an external group. Reporters, in the correct belief that a public argument is entertaining for viewers or listeners, will attempt to get both sides airing their views. Don't be drawn into this one, even if you're told that the other side has given an interview saying you're about as amenable as Attila the Hun.

Let's suppose that there has been a lightning strike at Bloggs Bearings, and you're told that the union negotiator has just given an interview saying that, although you'd been ensconced in a meeting for eight hours, no progress has been made. The interviewer asks for your comments:

> *YOU*: "It's still early days yet, although
> it was a long meeting today. With an issue as
> important as this, we can't expect any quick, easy
> answers. As it happens, I thought we *did* make
> some progress [if this is true], and we'll be back in
> there first thing tomorrow to continue. We've all got
> much more work to do and, if you'll forgive me, I must
> get on with mine now."

This way, even though you may privately think the union negotiator would do better dressed up in a Mickey Mouse suit, you kill the public argument stone dead and deflect any further controversy. If the union person is watching, he or she can't argue with the fact that there's more work to be done, or with the fact that you're intending to do your share.

If you're lucky, you may have a little more time to prepare yourself for a defensive interview. In this case, you might well turn a negative into a definite positive. Let's take an example. Bloggs Bearings is selling some land to a property developer, who intends to build executive homes on the site. Local people are worried that this might mean Bloggs is in financial trouble and is cutting back, with the possible loss of jobs. The interviewer leads up with all this, then asks you why the land was sold instead of it being used to expand your business and create more jobs ...

> *YOU*: "Well, like a lot of companies these days,
> we are under a certain amount of financial pressure,
> yes. Competition is growing, especially from overseas
> manufacturers who have much lower overheads and can
> undercut our prices. And as you know, expansion costs
> money. To do that, we have to borrow money, which
> gets expensive in interest rates. But by selling this
> land, we have released quite a lot of money which we
> can now invest in the company. That means all the
> existing jobs are secure. It also means there's some
> money to invest in new machinery, which we badly need
> to stay competitive. The way things were looking before
> we sold the land, we might have had to stop manufacturing
> some of our components here and imported them from
> Japan. This way, with our new machines, we keep all
> our products 100% British, and may even
> need to increase our workforce once the new machines
> are installed."

> *INTERVIEWER*: "But surely you need that
> land to expand into?"

> *YOU*: "No. The new ways of manufacturing our
> products, with new machines, take up less space. And in
> any case, we still own fourteen acres of land around the
> factory, which we can use in the future, should we need
> it. But expansion these days means smaller, more
> efficient machinery, with more room for the people
> who work with it to move around and do their jobs
> better. Take our XYZ bearing, for example; the

machine we're currently using to make that takes up
eighty-five square metres. The new one we can now
afford to buy takes up just forty square metres,
although the number of people working it remains the
same. In fact, we're planning to buy a second one
to make XYZs next year, which will double our output,
create ten new jobs, and all in virtually the same
factory space."

INTERVIEWER: "So do you foresee any job
redundancies at Bloggs Bearings?

YOU: "No. As I just said, we plan to double
the output of the XYZ bearing next year, with ten new
jobs. And that's just one of our range of 200
products."

You not only have deflected the bad news aspect of the interviewer's questions, you have also caught him or her on the hop. Often an interviewer will keep trying to cast a negative or aggressive light on the interview even after he or she should have stopped; if you're quick to spot this, you can turn it to your advantage. In the last few lines, you have hinted that the XYZ expansion will result in ten new jobs, and that your other products may experience similar growth. You have also managed to cover a number of sales points, and reassured the viewers/listeners on the fact that Bloggs Bearings is on the up and up. You have also given a very fair and honest answer to the interviewer's question before you got into the sales points, which satisfies the media's need for truth, and your need to make your company look deservedly good.

CHAPTER 5

THE WONDERFUL WORLD OF MEDIA ADVERTISING:

Advertising copy introduction

INTRODUCTION

The subject of advertising is as broad as it is tall. There are dozens of good books on the subject, and most people in business will know how important it is and how it works already. Writing for advertising is a different story; advertising copywriters make very healthy livings and for good reason. Writing ads isn't easy, but it's not a mystical art either; you can learn to do it competently, provided you understand the basics of what it's all about. In the chapters that follow, you'll find the basics explained in words of one syllable; but this in itself isn't enough. Once you understand the basics, practice is what makes perfect, as in most things. Budding, would-be writers often ask us how they can improve their skills and the best answer we can give is that they should write a lot. The more you do, the better you get. Even top professional copywriters will look at a perfectly acceptable advertisement they wrote five years earlier and wince, because they believe they could do the same job better now and they're probably right.

Of course, in this book we're only giving you a snapshot of the basics of how to write ads. If you look through any good newspaper or magazine, watch commercial television or listen to commercial radio, you'll see and hear dozens of ads which totally contradict what we say in terms of structure and approach. That's because the experts who have written them have learned the basics a long time ago, and are now experienced enough to twist them around effectively. This is not something we would recommend that you do, until such time as you are similarly experienced. However, as you'll see when you read on, one of the main issues we hammer home is that advertising copy should sell benefits rather than features. And even in professionally written ads that appear to break this rule totally, you'll find implied benefits somewhere, however subtle the approach. For example, some ads will run a headline or main theme which is the mirror-image of a benefit ... pointing out to you the disadvantages you're likely to suffer if you don't buy the product/service in question. Other ads – especially those for slighty contentious products like cigarettes and alcoholic drinks – just use a clever way to get you to think about and remember the product's name, and that's all. But however vague the inference might be, there's always a connection to a benefit somewhere.

If you're not a full-time professional writer, and most readers of this book will not be, our recommendation is that you start out simply ... don't try to be a sophisticated, slick copywriter, because you're likely to get it horribly wrong at first. And an attempt at slick advertising that doesn't work is going to do your product/service a lot of harm. Strong, simple, gimmick-free ad copy may not win you awards at advertising industry festivals, but it will sell your product or service well. By showing you how to approach that exercise, we will be making a much better contribution to the success of your business than if we were to show you how to play around with cute words that don't really achieve anything.

Writing words that sell, like any other type of selling, is not something you can pick up in a couple of evenings' study; it's an acquired skill. So read on, then try out what you've learned, and keep practising. It's not only a case of the more you do the better you get; it's also true to say that the more you do, the more you'll enjoy it. Creating ads is good fun, as well as essential in the running of most businesses; and it gets easier, once you know how. Here's how to start!

RESEARCH: THE KEY TO GOOD SELLING COPY

If you're going to write effective advertising, you need to know as much as possible not only about your own product or service, but also your competitors' products, and about the consumers to whom you are advertising. This is not as simple as it sounds. And talking to your marketing people (if you have them) will not always reveal the whole picture in the way you need to see it.

Let's look first at your product or service. If you talk to many experienced copywriters, they will tell you that to merely sit the product on your desk, or read through a number of documents about a service, is not enough. Obviously, if whatever it is you're advertising is a brand new product or service, untried and untested, you're going to be a bit lighter on background than would otherwise be the case. But there's still a lot to learn.

One of the best places to start your research is right at the source. Talk to the person or people who dreamed up the idea of the product or service. Ask them what their thinking behind it was. Find out if (1) the item was developed to fill a specific gap in the market, (2) if it was produced as an offshoot of an earlier idea, or (3) if it was produced on the basis of the producer's particular abilities. Let's use a country hotel, offering conference facilities, as an example. (1) Was the hotel built especially, because there were no similar hotels offering conference facilities in the region? (2) Was the conference suite added on to an existing country hotel? Or (3), did the hotel have an old ballroom, which the owners thought could be usefully turned into a conference suite? The answers to these questions will have different effects on your approach to the creation of your advertising. Finding the best approach then allows you to pull out the most relevant benefit or benefits of your product/service, from the target audience's point of view. But more of that later; meanwhile, let's get to know the facts first of all. So how would your approaches differ for examples (1), (2), and (3) ?

In the case of (1), your approach would be to launch the hotel itself, along with the conference facility. You would be heralding an important addition to the local business community ... *"at last, the hotel and conference facilities you need, on your company's doorstep"*. In the case of (2), the hotel has been there for centuries, but the conference facility has just been added. So you're selling a new addition to something that's already established ... *"now, your company can enjoy the old-world charm of Dinosaur Manor ... with the new-world conference facilities you need"*. And in the case of (3), you're selling a new concept of an existing facility; *"now, the old-world charm of the ballroom at Dinosaur Manor can be put to new-world conference and meeting work for your company"*. These aren't exactly cracking headlines, but then what the research stage is for is to get the approach right before you go on to look for a good "idea" which will convey your product/service "promise". And although the "product" in all three examples is roughly the same, the approach you need for each is different; and background research is what reveals the differences.

Another aspect of your research should be to go out and touch and feel. This applies as much to advertising as it does to the research behind any piece of promotional or documentary writing you'll ever do. Go and watch a product being made, if you haven't already. Talk to the people who make it. Sticking with the example of Dinosaur Manor, go and spend some time at the hotel; talk to the staff about (1) the excitement and challenge of working in a brand new hotel or (2) the traditions, anecdotes, ghosts and famous guests which have emerged from the history of Dinosaur Manor. Try to put yourself in the consumer's shoes, and perceive the services and facilities at the hotel as he or she would. Don't fall for all the old clichés like "steeped in history", "luxurious surroundings", "delicious international cuisine", and so on. They all say that. Try to find the personality of the place, the USP (unique selling proposition) that makes it different from all its competitors. Once you've found that personality ... and it's a rare product or service that doesn't have one ... it's up to you to bring it alive in the advertising you write by exposing it as a benefit to your target audience. That's what's going to sell it most effectively.

Of course if the product you're to write about is a brass screw, you're going to have a problem finding personality within the product itself. One brass screw is much the same as the next. But personality in this context doesn't need to be restricted to the product. In a sense, personality and USP can be taken to mean the same thing; they can both be turned into benefits. And if there's no USP in the product, start looking elsewhere. Does the product offer a price advantage over its competitors? Is the after-sales service second to none? Are there special discounts and promotions attached to the product, so that there is a special incentive for dealers/retailers to stock it and sell it hard? Does the manufacturer's name traditionally stand for better quality, greater efficiency? Does the product come recommended by a famous expert or celebrity? All of these can become strong, benefit-led advertising approaches.

A good place to go next is to see the people who will be selling the product or service at the sharp end. This could be sales people, demonstrators, retailers, front-of-house staff at Dinosaur Manor. Assuming that the product or service (if new) has already been announced to them, or at least that they've heard informally about it, get them round a table ... buy them a drink or a coffee and get them chatting freely. You'll learn a lot more about the ways in which the product or service has been received (in the case of an existing item) or how it is likely to be received (in the case of a new one) from these people, than you will from their bosses who don't actually deal face to face with customers any more. (Sorry, friends, but it's true.) Another area these people will tell you about is the next area you need to research; the competition.

The obvious facts, like who else is in the market, how much their product or service costs, what their service involves compared to yours, and so on, should be readily available in your initial briefing material. But by talking to the people at the sharp end, you'll pick up a lot of little nuances and snippets of information which the briefing documents leave out. Like if your product is cheaper and better than Brand X, why is it that Brand X outsells yours in shops? Is it because the Brand X merchandising people get out into the shops and put up bigger and more prominent displays? Is it because your product's distribution is poor, whereas Brand X keeps the product flowing into the retail outlets? Are the sales promotion/dealer promotion/discounting schemes of Brand X better than yours? Etcetera. Now of course, unless you're the managing director, there's not much you can do to put right any problems you dig up during your research – although, depending on your status, you can always make recommendations for improvements.

What you, as the writer of advertising, can do is to make allowances for any problems you uncover in the advertising you write. If Brand X has bigger and better displays in the shops, look at the packaging of your product. Does it have any distinguishing marks about it? Or if it hasn't, can the packaging be changed to make it more distinctive? In your advertising, you can emphasise the look of the product ... a) by showing it in the ad, and b) by referring to it, if relevant, with a pay off like this ... *"Munchkins: the chocolate bar with the bright red label ... at your grocer's now"*. If distribution of your product is sketchy, or if for some reason retailers are a bit sluggish stocking it, you can use your advertising to get consumers to ask for it ... *"Ask your grocer for Munchkins: the chewy, chunky chocolate bar your kids will love!"*

In an ideal world, of course, all the little problems suggested above will be solved long before you're called upon to write ads. No manufacturer in his or her right mind is going to invest in an advertising campaign for Munchkins or anything else without ensuring that the back-up for the product is in place all the way along the line. But smaller problems, particularly if your product hasn't exactly got the weight and expertise of a mega-million manufacturing organisation behind it, can often be overcome in the way the advertising material is written.

Once you've conducted your research this far, and learned not only the background to your own product or service but also the ins and outs of how your product and the competition works on the ground, this is a good time to take a long hard look at the competition's advertising and other promotional material. Your product or service's sales people will no doubt have learnt of their customers' feelings about the competition, and will have passed this on to you. You should now compare that information with the competition's ads and literature, and see how it stacks up. Does the material describe the product or service fairly? If it is a service which requires a lot of detailed information, is it the right sort? Do customers feel they're getting all the facts they need? Or do they feel that the competition's advertising is too flashy, without being informative? And so on.

Then, look at the material yourself. Is it inviting to read? Do you find it clear and informative? If you were interested in buying that product or service, would the ads and leaflets inspire you to reach for your cheque book? Is the writing style in any way patronising or sexist? You can learn a lot, or at least learn to avoid a lot of pitfalls in your own writing, by observing and absorbing the shortcomings of others aiming at the same market as you.

THE RIGHT WRITING FOR THE AUDIENCE YOU WANT

The last area of research you need to cover very, very carefully is the consumer ... the person you are attempting to reach in the advertising you write. This person is the only one who really matters in your life; so you've got to get to know him or her very well. If you're in a large organisation that spends considerable amounts of money on advertising, an independent research organisation is usually commissioned to provide you with this information. In other circumstances, though, you may be called upon to do it yourself.

So let's look at the two examples we've already set up; Munchkins, and Dinosaur Manor's conference facilities. They are very different in nature, with very different potential purchasers.

Munchkins purchasers are a tricky one, because pretty well anyone likes to nibble on the occasional chocolate bar. A major international soft drinks manufacturer who shall remain nameless defines its market as anyone with a mouth between six years old and death, and Munchkins appeals to a similar group, though children younger than six like chocolate bars, too. So, here, we're not looking so much at *who*, as we are at *why*, *when*, and *where*. You need to find out who the major groups of purchasers are, yes; chances are in the case of Munchkins they will be individual purchasers buying for themselves, most likely school-age children, teenagers and young people up to 25 ... and parents buying one or a number of products to take home and stuff into children's mouths as a treat when they come home hungry. But that's guesswork; the marketing staff or consultants working on Munchkins should be able to tell you this based on market research results.

If, however, Munchkins is being produced by a cottage industry with no formal marketing facility, it's time for you to take a trip to your local supermarket. Watch the chocolate counter; see who buys the existing products. Notice if a lot of children and young people are picking the product up ... or is it a parent who reaches out first? Which products do the children like, and which products do the parents prefer? Are they the same products, or are they different? Go and talk to shop-keepers who sell chocolate bars. Ask them who buys which. Ask them at what time of day they sell the most ... morning or evening (likely to be parents) or mid to late-afternoon (children on their way home from school)?

Now, too, is a good time to start piecing together the other information you've gathered, combining it with your growing knowledge of the consumer you're aiming for. Let's say Munchkins are made by a small cottage industry, to an old traditional recipe that contains no artificial colours, flavours, or sweeteners. It costs a few pennies more than the nearest competitor, as it's not mass produced by robots. Meanwhile, during your trips to your local shops and supermarkets, you've noticed that parents tend to go for the more traditionally packaged confectionery ... not the ones with the astronauts and space ships on the wrappers. They also buy quite a few "healthy" candy bars made with dried fruits and so on.

So, what does this tell you? It's reasonable to assume that children don't give two hoots about traditional recipes, and unless they're the offspring of millionaires will not choose a chocolate bar that costs more of their hard-scrounged pocket money than absolutely necessary. Parents, though, probably feeling guilty about keeping their kids quiet with sugar-filled bribes, are likely to be attracted to the traditional, healthy recipe (reflected in the traditional, healthy packaging) of Munchkins. They won't be as worried about spending a few pennies more if they know that although sugar may rot the children's teeth, at least the product doesn't contain a lot of chemical junk that will make them turn hyper-active, collapse with an asthma attack, or break out in a rash. So, there's your target market, and your copy approach ... *"your kids will love the traditionally tasty quality of pure chocolate Munchkins"*. (But check with the lawyers and food technologists first).

Moving swiftly on, let's look at the market that lies out there for Dinosaur Manor, supposing it's not a new construction but an elegant old place with a bright new conference suite that's grown on one side like a boil. Assuming that Dinosaur Manor has been socially feeding and entertaining the good burghers of Lower Dinosaur by the Water for the last 500 years, and that this social market is still nicely sewn up, your task is to attract the local business market which has previously been holding meetings internally or, sensibly, in exotic palm-fringed locations thousands of miles away. Getting to know this consumer is much easier, but it is still not just a matter of *who*; the *why*, *when* and *where* aspects are also important.

First of all, you need to know if Dinosaur Manor should attract only local business, or whether there is a case for bringing companies out from cities up to 100 miles away or more, as well. Ideally, there should be two different advertising campaigns for Dinosaur Manor, if this is the case. Businesses further than 100 miles away are going to need accommodation and recreation as well as the conference facilities and incidental catering, because no business person wants to drive 100 miles home on six hours' work, a large dinner and two bottles of Château Dinosaur burgundy. So, this group will require advertising material that offers the total package. Local businesses, however, may just want to hire the conference suite, or parts of it, to hold meetings away from the office/factory/plant/works. In this case we're talking space only, with perhaps coffee and biscuits, or a light buffet lunch and a bar facility.

It is very important that you find out about both local and semi-local businesses' attitudes towards going out to a conference venue, and also assess their needs on a long-term basis. For the more widespread group, it is reasonable to assume that there's likely to be a fairly average mix of types of business, ranging from large to small, industrial to service. But within the local community, especially if there are some large organisations within easy reach of Dinosaur Manor, it will help you to know exactly who they are and what sort of meetings they're likely to hold. Are there businesses nearby which will have weekly or monthly meetings? In this case, your advertisements and leaflets should talk about regular arrangements, discounts for frequent bookings and so on. Price, and discount deals, will be very important in the decision-making process here. One-off conferences will be more influenced by the package offered than necessarily by the price alone.

The big city businesses will be attracted to the beautiful country surroundings and the chance of some suitably rural pursuits when delegates have time off. They will also appreciate the quiet and calm of the surroundings, especially if their offices are slap in the middle of a city centre with wall-to-wall traffic jams and a popular shopping arcade right outside their boardroom window. Local businesses whose employees know Dinosaur Manor well will not be as impressed by the magnificent formal gardens and adjacent golf course, because they've heard it all before. They'll be more interested in the fact that they can inexpensively hire a quiet, modern room equipped with an overhead projector, notepads and bottles of mineral water for a couple of hours, without any phones ringing, and fit all their executives around one table, which they can't necessarily do at their own headquarters.

Alright, the market for Dinosaur Manor is easier to identify than that of Munchkins but, here, once you've identified the market, you've got to get to know the animals within it pretty well. There are a good many reasons for that, largely based on the difference between the two products. Munchkins is a product that costs a fraction of someone's weekly salary, is probably an impulse purchase, and disappears into the oblivion of the consumer's alimentary tract within a few seconds.

Dinosaur Manor's conference facility involves buying a meeting that's planned days, weeks or even months in advance, costs hundreds or thousands of pounds, and is likely to influence delegates for some time afterwards.

If all of the above section on researching your consumer sounds dishearteningly confusing, don't worry. You are not writing to some super-schizoid mega-headed Hydra who can devour the entire conference suite at Dinosaur Manor while simultaneously eating a Munchkins chocolate bar. You are writing to another human being; an intelligent, breathing, walking, talking person just like you. David Ogilvy, one of the best copywriters of the twentieth century and certainly the most famous, once said words along these lines; the consumer is not an idiot, she is your wife. Now for those of us of the female persuasion this could also mean that the consumer is pretty strange, but then you must remember that David Ogilvy flourished in the days when both advertising and sexism were at their most energetic. When you're writing to *your* consumer or customer, it is usually possible to conjure up the image of that person – the typical consumer who is likely to want to buy your product or service. Try to think of him or her as you write; imagine you are in conversation. That makes for good copy ... but more of this below. What all your research, all your background foraging, all your talking, touching and feeling add up to is an overall understanding of what you must write. Certainly, many copywriters recommend that you should allow all this vast input of information to settle for a while before you pick up your pen or lay your fingers on the word processor keyboard. Most of us in promotional writing of whatever variety experience the pangs of cerebral indigestion during the research phase of a project. But like the other kind, this indigestion passes with time, and your brain should automatically extract the salient points you need to help you into the "distillation" phase we describe in Chapter 2 – ready for you to write some valid, hard-hitting words that sell.

STYLE AND APPROACH

Although the general rules for the style of writing words that sell are described in an earlier chapter, there are a number of further thoughts which will help you write advertising copy, and here they are.

The best thing anyone can teach you is to go straight to the point. That sounds easy and obvious; it isn't. As with all promotional writing, you should, in the main, forget about third parties and stick to you and us. Keep your writing like a personal communication between you and your target audience members, one at a time. But whether you're talking about press or broadcast media ads, you have very little time in which to communicate your message and do your persuading. Even the mega-giant corporations seldom take television air slots longer than two minutes. And research shows that the vast majority of people, when looking at a press ad, will see the illustration, read the headline, perhaps glance at the cross-heads, look at the pay-off, and *that's all*. At best you've only got a few lines to get your points over.

Bearing that in mind, you can begin to see that brevity is beautiful. Even headlines should be short, although a long headline – provided it's very strong – will usually be read. In the sections above, we've given you an overview of how to get to the point where you're ready to start writing the actual advertising words. Many of the lines quoted will form the skeleton of the final words you write but, as we mentioned, you should only regard those as the basis for your approach – the gist of the message you want to put over.

The sizzle in the sausage

Deciding on a good, strong approach ... the basis on which to write press ads and commercials ... is something many advertising creative people agonise over for days at a time, and for good reason. However simple your selling proposition is, it's not normally enough in itself to set the world on fire. To say that Blatts Hair Conditioner makes people's hair more shiny than any other product is a strong marketing statement, but it won't exactly get young Cathy reaching for her wallet and running out to the nearest drugstore to buy some.

Although it may sound cynical, Cathy actually doesn't care too much about your product, or what it does. She certainly doesn't care what your product does for anybody else. And shiny hair for her, although it may be quite nice to have, doesn't in itself excite her that much either. What will turn Cathy on, however, is one or more of the following benefits as she perceives them.

- Using the product will make her look more attractive.
- Using the product will help her get ahead in life.
- Using the product will make her feel more sophisticated.
- Using the product will give her the edge on the competition (socially, romantically, at work).

In other words, we come back to the old line that lurks on every consumer's mind as far as you're concerned, and that's *"what's in it for me?"* And while we're on the subject of old lines, here's another one. Don't sell the sausage; sell the *sizzle* in the sausage. It's something that has been taught to budding copywriters for centuries – or at least since

Suzan St Maur was a student copywriter, and that's almost as long ago – but it's still very, very valid.

What works better in any form of advertising copy is selling benefits not features. Features, on the whole, are what the product is; benefits are what it does for someone. And that's the key to all good promotional writing.

Let's take another product which ostensibly does not have any subliminal emotional appeal; a life insurance policy. Now the features of your policy may be extensive … low monthly repayments, investment supervised by the finest financial wizards in the world, good capital growth, no-quibbles cancellation. But these are features. If you want someone to buy your policy, their primary interest is not in any of these features, although of course they are of secondary interest. What your consumer wants to hear is what the policy is going to do for him or her: its benefits. These are different.

- Buying the policy means you will have more money to spend on leisure when the policy matures.
- Buying the policy means you will save money on income tax and be able to spend more now.
- Buying the policy means you will be able to afford a new boat, a world cruise, a holiday home when you retire.
- Buying the policy means that, if you die, your spouse and children will be well taken care of.

One of the main problems you will find if you're writing ads about your own product or service is that you are likely to be very feature orientated. This is understandable; you're involved with its creation, its development, its manufacture, its marketing, and you get paid to spend your time thinking about what it *is*. If you had to focus the majority of your attention on how its buyers perceive what it's going to do for them, as well as all your own responsibilities, you'd be on the way to the funny farm. Agency copywriters, although they're on your side, are sufficiently distanced from the day-to-day activities of your company to see the wood for the trees, and look for benefits from the consumer's point of view. But if you are to write your own words that sell, you will have to learn to see things from their side of the fence as well as your own. It's not that difficult. Really. It's just a case of being objective, putting yourself in the consumer's shoes, and being honest with yourself about your product's benefits to the buyer.

GETTING THE IDEA

So, having examined your research and identified the main benefits of your product or service, you can develop your idea – the overall concept of the words you write. Lateral thinking enters the picture here, and very often there is a snappy, clever way of developing a benefit in creative terms so that it is not merely a plain statement. Take the UK's advertising campaign for a brand of beer, for example. The main benefit it uses is that drinking it makes you feel more refreshed than any other beer does; a manufactured benefit, of course, as technically any beverage with the same ingredients could do the same. However, whether the benefit is manufactured or genuine doesn't really matter; the chances are that Blatt's hair conditioner is chemically identical to 35 other products which could make your hair equally shiny. This is another great advantage of benefits; you can use artistic licence with them, and no consumer in his or her right mind is going to be antagonised by a suggested benefit that's obviously a poetic exaggeration. By laughing at the suggestion that a certain men's after shave is going to make twenty beautiful girls trip over his surf-board, the consumer is also laughing at himself; he knows it's fantasy, but then he enjoys a bit of harmless fantasy as much as everyone else. And, with tongue-in-cheek or not, he quite likes the idea of twenty beautiful girls. Implied fantasy benefits that you'll see in hundreds of advertising campaigns are not cheating; they're an approach that everyone accepts. However, if you lie about features, you can get sued.

What the brand's advertising agency did in the case of this beer was to develop that benefit into a quirky but effective campaign. The idea was to say that it refreshed parts (of you, by implication) that other beers couldn't reach. For readers in other countries who don't know the campaign, the visual treatment was to show two illustrations; one of the subject before it was refreshed, and one of the subject after refreshment. An example of these double illustrations was a notoriously boot-faced soap opera character going from boot-face to smile after having consumed the product. The campaign worked equally well on television and in the press and on posters, and it could incorporate topical issues with quick reponse from the advertising agency. It was a good *idea*, which was developed through both illustrations and headline, and will probably go down in history as one of the more noteworthy UK advertising campaigns of the late twentieth century. It was widely quoted in the media, used by stand-up comics, and alluded to at all levels of society – good ideas get spin-off publicity.

Highly creative advertising ideas are effective if you have a lot of money to spend and wide coverage. At a more modest level, though, such ideas don't always work. If you only have limited funds and therefore fewer opportunities to reach your audience with the message, a kookie idea will have a detrimental effect, because the readers/viewers will not necessarily understand what you're talking about until they've seen or heard your campaign over a period of time. So it is better for lower-budget advertising to be simpler. But that doesn't mean you can't use a simple, strong idea to point out the main benefit or benefits of your product or service.

There is another danger for the inexperienced writer of words that sell, and that is bad ideas. Bad ideas can be heavy, unworkable, sexist, offensive, corny, and a host of other lead balloons. An advertising approach that your mother or lunch companion thinks is really creative might be enough to kill your campaign altogether. Typical examples include heavy-duty, overworked puns ... clichés ... visuals of scantily-dressed girls with a headline that reads something like "Come and get it at Smith's Groceries" ... hackneyed lines like "The finest store in town" ... and word blindness that leads to any advertising such as this gem; "Book your next holiday on an R. Soul luxury bus tour." This headline is actually based on a real-life bus tour operator in the UK, whose name on his vehicles – eventually written out in full for obvious reasons – was Robert Soul. If, after honest, critical appraisal, you feel there's any danger your idea might be a bad one, drop it and use a simple, strong, plain, benefit-led statement. That way you can't go far wrong, and you don't risk becoming the laughing stock of your local business community.

ADVERTISING CAMPAIGNS: SPREADING YOUR MESSAGE

An advertising campaign is a collection of advertising activities as part of one project. Of course, this can mean a series of ads for one medium alone, or even one ad repeated a number of times. But more usually, and especially where you're spending a considerable sum of money on an advertising campaign, it will involve the conveying of your message across more than one medium.

As you'll see from other chapters in this book, each medium is different and copy normally has to be tailored for each one. But there are some important common denominators that must be upheld if the total campaign is to be successful.

The first common denominator is the "corporate image", which can and must be the same over all the visual media. This means that the design style of your company name and logo, plus any slogan or baseline (for example *"AVIS: We try harder"*), should be conveyed in the same visual way throughout. In radio commercials, the slogan or baseline can be spoken by a voice over. This conformity of corporate image means that no one is in doubt as to who the advertiser is, and seeing the corporate image in one medium will be reinforced in the reader/viewer's mind when he or she sees it again, in a different medium, so maximising your total advertising effort.

The same principle applies to the sales message. Naturally you can't really reproduce it verbatim in different media, as all call for their own types of approach. But you can reproduce the concept, or the "idea", translating it for each medium.

Another great advantage is cross-fertilisation between media. For example, lists of stockists or full details of a competition can be given in press ads – and a radio commercial can refer listeners to this ...

> **VOICE OVER:** *"KEEP-DRY umbrellas are on sale in most good stores ... you'll find your nearest stockist in the KEEP-DRY ad in your local paper."*

or this ...

> **VOICE OVER:** *"So get on the road to your holiday of a lifetime, with the SLOW BOAT TO CHINA competition! See your evening paper for details and your entry form."*

Translating your selling "idea" across media needn't cause you sleepless nights. It's just as case of using your common sense. And another thing to remember is that you don't have to change the message very much – in fact to change it too much can be detrimental, because you risk diluting the effect of the campaign. Let's say you're advertising a local restaurant. The radio script might go like this ...

> **VOICE OVER:** (Spanish background music throughout)
> *Now there's even more reason for you to take that special someone to El Salmonella ... this week, we're giving away a bottle of wine to every couple ... turning your evening out into a romantic occasion, absolutely free! And with our table d'hôte menu, your dinner for two at El Salmonella can cost as little as £14. So book your table now at El Salmonella. Look for our ad in your local paper."*

The press ad needs to pick up on the main offer, that is, that this week couples get a free bottle of wine. So ...

> ***"THIS WEEK, YOU CAN TURN AN EVENING OUT INTO A ROMANTIC OCCASION ... ABSOLUTELY FREE!***
>
> *Now, there's even more reason for you to take that special someone to El Salmonella, XXXtown's most romantic Spanish retaurant. For this week only, we're giving every couple a bottle of delicious Spanish wine to go with their meal ... absolutely free. And your romantic evening out is always good value, at El Salmonella. A table d'hôte*

dinner can cost as little as £14 for two. But hurry ... this offer ends on Saturday, June 4th. So phone us now to book your table for your romantic occasion – at El Salmonella!"

You would then display the telephone number, name and address prominently in the ad. You could also reproduce the table d'hôte menu in a box somewhere, if your space is big enough. This should be clearly labelled as a sample menu, unless you do the identical table d'hôte every night.

On the promotional side (although a special offer like this is sales promotion, anyway; more of that in another chapter), you might decide to do a leaflet drop in the more affluent neighbourhoods of your town. The leaflet would be based on the press ad copy, with similar wording. The name, telephone number and address should be more prominent than in the ad. You can also reproduce the menu again, and even write a few descriptive lines about each dish to really whet the appetite.

A television commercial could use the radio script as a voice over, and use some well-shot still photographs of the restaurant's interior, and/or some close-ups of Spanish specialities, for the visuals. Alternatively you could shoot some live action film or videotape of the restaurant, featuring a romantic couple dining by candlelight – although for a local promotion like this a film or videotape shoot might be a bit of an extravagance – particularly when the most attractive part of the selling message (free wine) can be conveyed in two words.

Another medium that might be useful is a small card which you could distribute in local shops and businesses. This should be an abbreviated form of the press ad ...

"THIS WEEK, YOU CAN TURN AN EVENING OUT INTO A ROMANTIC OCCASION ... ABSOLUTELY FREE!

El Salmonella – your most romantic local Spanish restaurant – is giving away a bottle of delicious Spanish wine to every couple dining this week (May 30th to June 4th inclusive) absolutely free! Table d'hote dinners start at just £14 for two. So hurry – phone us and book your table now!

El Salmonella, (address), phone XXXtown 1234."

That message could also be conveyed on posters, and on showcards in the restaurant itself, like this ...

"THIS WEEK, YOU CAN TURN AN EVENING OUT INTO A ROMANTIC OCCASION ... ABSOLUTELY FREE!

El Salmonella – your most romantic local Spanish restaurant – is giving away a bottle of delicious Spanish wine to every couple dining this week (May 30th to June 4th inclusive) absolutely free! Just ask your waiter for details."

Translating an advertising message into a campaign across different media isn't difficult, provided you understand each medium and what it's capable of doing. If you focus on that, you can then adapt the message as necessary without diluting it.

CHAPTER 6

PRESS AND PRINT ADVERTISING:

Including Sales Promotion

WRITING FOR THE PRESS

There are dozens of different types of press ad. These range from the specialist technical ad selling hyper-activated widgets, to mass-market ads selling cooking oil, to one-off ads selling your home. However, they have two things in common; a headline and body copy. And many share another common element; an illustration.

Let's look at how these elements work together first of all. The idea behind an illustration, a headline and body copy is that they tell a cohesive story. In harmony, they work together using all three elements – or two, in the case of a copy only ad – to put your message over in as strong a way as possible. So, it's quite important that there is no duplication, although deliberate repetition may be useful on occasion. The headline should always be tied in with the visual, and it can be used in a repetitive sense if you want the reader to look again and see something which is not necessarily obvious ... either literally or metaphorically. Let's take an ad for Blatt's hair conditioner ...

We assume that the main benefit we're using to appeal to Cathy, our prime target, is that using the product will make her feel more attractive, with the added hint that it will also make her appear more sophisticated and help her to get on in the world. The visual we see is of the back of a girl's head, showing shiny, well-groomed hair. Beyond that we see some people looking at her. The headline reads ...

"Does Your Hair Make Heads Turn?"

The body copy will then go on to say that hair groomed with Blatts conditioner is bound to turn heads in the street and get you noticed in life, because your hair will look shinier than anyone else's. Tongue in cheek, but hinting at a real benefit. The pay off (and remember,

most readers will only look at the visual, the headline and the pay-off)
should go something like this ...

> *"Blatts. Conditioning Your Hair for Success"*

So, in those three elements (if you count the pay-off as part of the
body copy which, in truth, it is) you have got your main messages
across. You will also ensure that there is a "pack shot" somewhere in
the ad, preferably close to the pay-off, so Cathy knows what to look for
when she's next in her neighbourhood chemist or at a beauty counter.

VISUALS

Although these are not strictly speaking a writer's responsibility, no
writer can afford to ignore the importance of visual thinking. This is
especially true when you begin to work with any of the audio-visual
media, but it applies to print as well. For the reasons suggested above,
there is no way that one element of an ad can be developed in isolation
from the others. Of course, you don't have to be able to draw, take
photographs or do elaborate graphics in order to think visually. All you
have to do is broaden your scope out from the "words only" approach,
and attune your mind to seeing the whole ad with all its elements as
one overall concept.

Also remember that a bad visual is worse than no visual at all. Corny
or obviously contrived pictures that show unbelievable scenes, such as
semi-naked girls sprawled over a car, don't fool anybody. (Would even
the most chauvinist male really want to have his wicked way with
several damsels while lying on a cold, hard, uncomfortable expanse of
metal? How would he be able to see out of the windows if they stayed
there while he drove along?) If you must connect sex with the
automotive industry, get a fully clothed but equally attractive female
model to drive the car, or sit in the passenger seat. This is far nearer to
what might happen in real life, and the suggestion of sex is still there,
although in a more subtle way. (Is she driving/sitting in her boyfriend's
car? If you buy that car, might you become eligible to become her
boyfriend? Could she be driving off to, or waiting for you to drive her
off to, a naughty weekend somewhere?) In all fairness, such blatant
sexism regarding motor cars has been largely relegated to the oily
workshop calendars for some years now. But advertisers of cars at
more local level, say a used car dealership, still like to associate their
products with scantily clothed women. What they forget is that an
increasing proportion of their customers are women, who are not
amused to see their gender exploited in this way. Even if your target
audience is, for some reason, 100 per cent male, don't fall for the sexist

gimmicks; there are also a lot of men around these days who find sexism offensive.

Offensive visuals of any kind should be avoided. This includes blood and gore, vulgarity, veiled references to ordure matter, and so on, although there are one or two exceptions. Some charities – particularly those raising money to support famine victims or mistreated animals – will show a pretty horrific picture in order to focus the reader's mind on what can happen without the charity's support. Provided the charity is worthwhile, no one is going to complain about a photograph of a starved child or a slaughtered seal. But offensive visuals do not work when all you're trying to do is to sell a product or service. They may attract attention, but of the wrong kind.

Another point about visuals is that you should not put one in purely for the sake of it, or to fill up the space. Some advertising pundits say that plain, white space in a press ad sells harder than extra words and pictures can. What plain white space does is to draw attention to your ad, which is probably sitting in an otherwise cluttered page. So don't feel pressured to fill every available column centimetre. Putting in a photograph of your factory when you're advertising for staff is a waste of time unless your factory is of such stunning beauty and interest that it will, in itself, beckon people to work in it. But recruitment ads are a subject we cover later in this book, so let's take another example; an advertisement for brass screws.

To put in a photograph or illustration of a brass screw is about as interesting as a shredded newspaper. Everyone, unless they've been living on a remote desert island all their life, knows what a screw looks like. Getting back to what we said earlier on, you need to focus on the benefits, not the features. So don't show a screw, and don't even show someone installing a screw with a smile on his or her face. That's a bit corny. Instead, show someone using the finished article that has been constructed using your screws, without a single screw in sight. Let's say the finished article is a desk, and the person is sitting at it reading the paper. There are cardboard boxes or packing cases around to show that it is a new desk, just assembled. Then top that with a headline that reads:

"Screwed Down Tight ... and There's Still Time for You to Take a Breather."

The features of the screw are that it permits users to install it faster than other screws, because it is made of brass and therefore is easier to work. It also has a special coating which makes the process even easier. All these points you bring out in the body of the copy, always relating them to a benefit. But you have appealed to the "what's in it for me" angle, by telling the consumer what he or she really wants to know — it's going to save time. Essentially the consumer couldn't care less if it's made of brass or ready-mixed concrete, as long as it offers something worthwhile on a personal or professional level. Obviously the consumer wants to know that the product's quality is high, and you bring that out in the main body copy, too — after all, screws that are easy to insert but drop out after three months are not of much use to the consumer, either. Your pay-off can emphasise this, if you like; this isn't very snappy, but gets the point over...

> *"Widgets Brass Screws...Quality That Saves Your Time. "*

HEADLINES

If you have to make a choice as to which of an ad's elements is the most important, most advertising people would go for the headline.

A headline needs to be attention-grabbing, lively, to the point and, above all, it must work with the visual and the body copy to encapsulate your total message in one overall concept. That sounds a bit daunting, but headline writing is not as hard as the highly paid agency copywriters crack it up to be. Certainly, headlines need to be punchy, on the short side, and to the point. That's a little more difficult than it looks, because getting to the point can take time; more often than not, the most obvious and simple line is not the first thing you write down. When Suzan St Maur was searching for the title to her first book — a beginner's guide to jewellery, co-authored with gemologist Norbert Streep — she wrote down over 30 different title ideas before she came up with the final choice. Yet that final choice was the simplest, most obvious-sounding one of all: *The Jewellery Book*.

One of the best ways to arrive at a simple, workable headline is to start by writing down your thoughts as they come to you, based on your orginal idea. Then see if you can develop them, or rather distil them down to a final choice. Taking St Maur's jewellery book title as an example (not a headline, we know, but worked out on the same basis) let's have a look at some of the preliminary thoughts that she went through before arriving at the "obvious".

> *Jewellery on a Budget*
> *Jewellery for Beginners*
> *The Down-to Earth Jewellery Book*
> *A Pauper's Guide to Jewellery*
> *Jewellery for the Inflation-Poor*
> *Jewellery for the Not-so-Rich*
> *The Impoverished Guide to Jewellery*

The Simple Guide to Jewellery
Jewellery: The Facts and the Fiction
A Beginner's Guide to Jewellery

They were all reasonable, but they focused too strongly on one aspect of what the book was all about. It was intended to appeal to people who could not afford very expensive jewellery and just wanted to know how to tell a real stone from a fake one, what sort of wristwatch would offer them the best value, how to read hallmarks, and so on. But longer titles suggesting those points lacked zest and brevity. The final title was simple and, in being so, it automatically suggested simplicity ... the fact that the book was down-to-earth, for down-to-earth readers, about a down-to-earth view of jewellery in general.

Rather more than is the case with book titles, headlines have to get the reader to do something. All this might be is getting them to read on, or look more closely at the visual, or think about their pensions plans, but there is always something they should do. So, headlines should always suggest action of some kind; that doesn't mean they must have a verb in them, only that action is in there somewhere. The action should be straight to the point, and get there via the shortest possible route, too ... to say

"Prices Are Coming Down at Blank's Groceries"
is not as powerful as ...
"Prices Down at Blank's Groceries".
And while we're on the subject, how about a more active word than *"Down"*? Try ...
"Prices Halved at Blank's Groceries" (if it's true)
or *"Prices Slashed at Blank's Groceries"*.

Headlines involving references to people are best written in terms of the first and second persons singular and plural, leaving third parties out. Putting it bluntly, your reader is only interested in the second person, himself or herself, in his or her family/friends/colleagues, and possibly in you provided you are offering to do something for him or her that's of special interest. A lot of headlines offer a promise: our product or service will do something for you that you could not possibly have otherwise. It is often a good approach to take, for the reason mentioned above. Just remember to address it to the reader, not the whole world. To say ...

"Now: A Faster Pizza Ordering Service For All Our Customers"

is weak for two reasons; one, the headline is not sufficiently active, and two, it doesn't point directly at you. It also doesn't make the most of the promise. How about ...

"Now, You Can Enjoy Your Pizzas Even Faster" ...

and while we're at it, let's not fall into the old trap of selling all your competitors' pizzas at the same time. Advertising should be strongly branded, so every reader knows it's not just anybody's pizzas, but Plonk's Pizzas. So ...

"Now, You Can Enjoy Your Plonk's Pizzas Even Faster. ".

Questions are also strong in headlines. Questions can't necessarily get the promise over, but they're very useful if you want to set up the circumstances in which to announce your promise. Let's say you're selling a new bicycle seat that's nicely padded for extra comfort. A strong headline might be ...

"Is Your Old Bicycle Seat Giving You a Rough Ride?"

The body copy would explain how the product benefits you, and the pay-off – which should be very visible if the promise isn't in the headline – should say something like ...

"BYX Bicycle Seats: Miles of Armchair Comfort".

Pressure headlines put added urgency into your promise or offer by setting some sort of time limit or other deadline on it.

"20% Off Your Groceries This Week";
"Install Your New Dishwasher This Week: Pay Nothing Till January 1st";
"Huge Discounts on Carpets While Stocks Last"

... are all examples.

"How to" headlines also work well, provided the "how" to is immediately backed up by the promise.

"How to Win Friends And Influence People"

... is a very old example, but it was very successful. In fact, it was a book title, but served as its own advertisement as well. "How to" ads should contain a fair amount of body copy to justify the somewhat educational tone of the approach; let's say you're selling a videotape that teaches people how to improve their golf. If your headline says ...

"How to Lower Your Golf Handicap in Three Hours"

... you should go on to explain quite a bit about the video and how it teaches you the necessary skills to reduce your handicap, and that the running time of the tape is three hours. Incredible-sounding "how to" headlines are fine provided that you can justify them in the body copy in a reasonable way. Not to justify it reasonably is dishonest and, in many countries, can get you into trouble. So be careful.

Trying to teach people to write headlines is not easy, because a lot depends on whether the person concerned has an instinct for headlines or not. One of the best ways to develop your instinct is to browse through various publications now that some of the basic theory has been explained to you, and examine the ads you see. Try to work backwards, taking the three main elements of the ad and deciding what the original message may have been, and what benefits they are focusing on. See how the "idea" has been developed. This technique was taught for many years at the Watford School of Art in its advertising writing course which has produced many of the UK's top copywriters. Once you understand how ads should be put together, it is easier to understand how the professionals do it, and it is a valuable way to learn how to do it better yourself.

BODY COPY

Most of the important points about body copy have been made already, but there are one or two worth stressing here. The points that apply to the other main elements of an ad – particularly the one about not telling readers what they can already see, and avoiding duplication – are equally relevant to the body copy. The first sentence should always be a development of the headline – not the same again in a different way – and should be powerfully enticing, to lead the reader on into the rest of the copy. Each sentence should flow on from the previous one, so that the whole piece reads as one continuous sequence of thoughts. All the rules of headline writing apply to body copy as well; stick to you and we, be direct, and use short, punchy sentences with no waffle or padding. Keep every thought angled to the reader and the benefits you're offering; by all means, mention the features of your product or service, but always in the context of the benefit that feature offers to the reader. Say a feature of your new pocket calculator is that it stores up to 200 calculations. Say so; but say that it stores up to 200 calculations **"for your easier reference"**. If your product has a large number of features that would take three pages to cover if you were to link them all into benefits, list them as bullet points and section them off in a box somewhere in the layout of the ad. That way, people can refer to them if they want to, and you're free to pull out a few really important features to turn into benefits in the main body copy of the ad. In fact, by showing that your product has a lot of features as listed in the box, you're turning that in itself into a benefit ... especially if you put this cross head over the boxed-off section ...

"More Features to Help You Than Any Other Calculator".

Crossheads are useful to break up longer body copy. As is the case with brochure and leaflet copy, crossheads are used to crystallise the main points of the story so a reader can get the gist of it by reading the crossheads alone. In ad copy, you have less time to get your points across, so keep the crossheads really short and snappy.

Body copy style should, of course, be conversational and have precious little to do with the grammar and phrasing you learned at school. Although this topic is covered in the chapter on style and jargon, it certainly is worth re-emphasising here. Body copy sentences don't have to have verbs in them. They don't have to have nouns in them. They can consist of one word. Why? Because this is how people talk. Don't go berserk and be too creative with punctuation, however. The basic rules you learned at school still do apply to an extent although, if anything, ad copy should be over-punctuated by school English standards. The odd comma or row of leader dots can change emphasis in a very useful way...

"When He Said He Was Going",

"When, He Said, He Was Going".

"Get The Best From Your Calculator Faster Than Ever Before",

"Get The Best From Your Calculator ... Faster Than Ever Before".

The end of the body copy is where the pay-off comes in. We've already touched on pay-offs in a number of places, but here are a few more thoughts.

You should always make it abundantly clear to your reader what you want him or her to do next. However effective your headline, visual and body copy, an inconclusive or vague pay-off can ruin the ad. For many purposes, the name of your product or service, the name of the company if that's not part of the product/service name, and the address and telephone number are enough. In other circumstances you need to say where your product/service can be found, its recommended price, and so on. Sometimes a coupon is included in an ad. If you want readers to actually clip the coupon, write a cheque and send the whole lot off to you, you're talking about mail order; a highly specialised form of advertising which is dealt with in the chapter on direct marketing. Many ads, though, will offer a coupon for readers to clip and send if they want further information of any kind. This can be anything from a brochure or a list of retailers or dealers who stock your product/service, to a request for a representative to call at the reader's home.

The best way to approach the pay-off is to write down on a piece of paper exactly what you want the reader to do, and what alternatives you can offer him/her should the first choice not be feasible. Take the example of the videotape programme on how to improve your golf. You're not selling it by mail order but through pro shops at golf clubs and at local video rental agencies. However, if someone genuinely can't find it, you would be prepared to sell it direct. Here's how you tackle the pay-off of the ad...

> *"IMPROVING YOUR GOLF."* (The title of the video, shown by a pack shot of the video's outer casing).

> *"Available from your club's pro shop and all good video rental agencies."* (The price of the video is rather high, so you don't want to quote it in the ad. If it were cheap, that would be different. However, in this case you prefer to let potential purchasers find out the price at point of sale.)

The coupon copy should read ...

> *"Yes! I Want to improve my golf with the help of your video. Please send me (tick as appropriate) ... a list of stockists ... a full colour leaflet and order form."* (The coupon or the base of the ad should have the company name, logo, address and phone number.) Always leave a reasonable amount of space on coupons for the reader to write in the name and address; insufficient space can discourage them from sending the coupon at all, or if they do fill it in your staff won't be able to decipher the words and you'll have lost a potential customer.

SPECIAL TYPES OF ADVERTISING

There are a number of specialised types of advertising which involve slightly differing techniques. The most important of these – direct marketing – has a chapter of its own. But there are a few others which deserve a special mention, as they occur commonly.

Celebrity endorsements

Advertising based on the endorsement of a celebrity tends to be wide-scale, and needs to be, because celebrities usually charge a lot of money to have their names openly linked with a product. To get the best value for your money, you need to look at a fairly large advertising campaign. The most commonly chosen celebrities for this kind of work are television personalities and sports people, although television personalities in many countries have to be careful about commercial activities as they can affect their credibility in their own field. Commercial activities can also lose them their jobs, particularly if they work for a non-commercial television station. Sports personalities, however, don't have quite the same credibility risk and often badly need the money – especially in countries where official backing and funding of international athletes is less than generous.

The trouble with celebrity endorsement advertising is that the public are not fools; remember, as David Ogilvy said, in his inimitably sexist way, "the consumer is not an idiot, she is your wife". There are not very many people who will truly believe that a famous person is waxing lyrical about your product/service purely because he/she thinks it's great. Most people know that celebrities get paid a lot of money to say these things, and that if they didn't they wouldn't open their mouths. Yet, major international advertisers, advised by top advertising agencies, still persist in using celebrities in extremely large and expensive campaigns, so it must have something going for it.

Without going into lengthy research statistics and psychological profiles, the reasons for this are complex. But if you recall the celebrities you see in the press and on television, you'll see that they tend to be used to endorse products that are clamouring for attention in particularly competitive market places. Such products in the UK are beer, some food products, and double window glazing; all markets where there are a large number of virtually identical products to choose from. So the reasoning here may be that hanging your product on a celebrity might not fool anyone into thinking the celebrity prefers it to the others, but merely that consumers will subliminally associate your product with a celebrity whom he/she would secretly like to emulate. Deep psychological stuff, but when you're struggling for a decent share of a mega-million market in competition with dozens of others, it's worth it.

If you are thinking of getting a personality to endorse your product or service, you need to be very careful in selecting someone who is going to provide you with good mileage. Having a celebrity in your ads is fine, provided there is a very strong link between what that personality is known for, and what you're selling. Putting a celebrity in just for the sake of it (and running the risk of picking the wrong one) can be counter-productive, because it can lose the public's respect for you.

Much as we believe you can write words that sell, though, this type of advertising is a job for the specialists – not only in the selection of the person, but in the way the ads and commercials are put together. It requires the subtlety of approach and skilled writing that only comes with years of experience, otherwise large amounts of your company's money can be wasted.

At a local level, celebrities can be useful for one-off activities; and here, they don't necessarily need to have an an obvious association with the product or service. Say you're opening a new hotel, and you want to attract as much attention from the media as you can. Hiring a celebrity to come and open the hotel officially can be a good PR ploy, as your local radio, television and newspapers are more likely to turn up if there is going to be someone there of good news value. This can be combined with ads in the local press and commercials on local radio which announce the grand opening, to be performed by the celebrity.

Still at local level, celebrities can boost attendance at tourist attractions on special days; getting a famous person to come along to a themed event on a public holiday, and advertising the fact beforehand, can pull in the crowds. There is one very important point to remember when writing celebrity endorsement ads, though; don't let your product or service get lost in the excitement. Always make sure that your message, and your promise (the benefits you offer your target audience) are strongly represented in all advertising material.

In the case of an ad for a special event at a tourist attraction, for example, make sure you allow enough space to promote all your important benefits in the ad, as well as the fact that Mae West will be there to sign autographs for the children. Theme the ad, by all means ...

"It's Going to be a Wild West Day at Blinkers Park This Saturday!"

The body copy of the ad should sell all the wonderful things you and your family can do on the day; the fact that Mae West will be there can be put in a prominent box, including a photograph of her. The crosshead and copy in the box should read something like this ...

"Meet Mae West at Blinkers Park!

Famous movie star Mae West is coming to Blinkers Park all the way from Hollywood this Saturday, just to meet you and your family. She'll be signing autographs from 2 to 4 p.m. So make it a date ... and don't be late!"

And that's all you need to say about her. If you feature too strongly on the celebrity at the expense of using the space to promote Blinkers Park, you'll lose the families who can't make it on the day, but might otherwise go along there another time. Always remember who's paying for the ad, and who's paying the celebrity. You're hiring Mae West to promote Blinkers Park; not to promote herself.

Testimonial advertisements

Testimonial ads use a genuine case history of a satisfied existing user of your product or service to promote it to others. These ads are a very good way of proving to your readers that your product/service works well, especially now that many countries have brought in legislation to ensure that all such advertising is true. Legislation like this has been widely publicised and most members of the public know that advertisers can't make false claims. Any testimonial in an ad has got to be for real.

Terrific. So why don't we see more testimonial ads? Where's the catch? The catch is that the value of testimonial ads has not escaped very many advertisers in the past. Testimonials have been done to death. Legislation to make it squeaky-clean or not, the public have become very sick of ads which proclaim in bold letters ... "Just Look at What These Satisfied Customers Have to Say! ... Mrs. A. Bonkers of Birmingham Can't Wait to Buy More Doggo for Her Puppy!" (followed by a quote from her letter) ... and so on. We have all seen this type of advertising a thousand times, and are *you* impressed by it? Honestly?

There is another dubious factor about testimonial ads, which links back to what we said earlier about the consumer's question: "What's in it for me?" Bland, complimentary comments from other users of your product/service don't really underline what your promise is to the reader; only what you've done for somebody else. And the reader doesn't care about somebody else.

Testimonials can be useful, though, provided you approach them with care and honesty. Put yourself in the reader's shoes; what is there in a testimonial from another user that's going to have an effect on me? Is the testimonial strong enough to truly mean something to me? And once you have extracted the testimonial from your existing user, have you ensured that the benefits outlined in it are pointedly turned to me, the reader?

One good way of getting the right sort of testimonial from an existing user is to ask him or her what advice he/she would give to a prospective buyer of the product/service. Say you're selling support hosiery aimed primarily at middle-aged women, and you're running an ad in suitable women's magazines ...

> " *'Any woman who works as hard as I do will be much more comfortable in STAND-UP support stockings'*

... says Mrs. A. Bonkers from Birmingham, sales assistant in a large department store."

The headline, though a testimonial, refers to the reader. You could also include a photograph of Mrs Bonkers at work in her department store, ideally smiling encouragingly at the reader. In the body copy, you then make sure the rest of the ad is totally about the reader, leaving Mrs Bonkers behind as soon as you can ...

"Do your feet and legs ache after a long day at work? If your job means you're on your feet all day, like Mrs Bonkers, you need as much support as possible to help keep you feeling comfortable ... hour after hour. That's why STAND-UP support hosiery ... " and so on.

Writing testimonial ads should be treated with a certain amount of cynicism, and respect. If you can get good testimonials – the right type which refer to the reader of the ad – they can be useful. But always remember the most important criterion of all, and that is the benefits you need to put over to the reader. If you bear that in mind when finding, interviewing and putting together your testimonials, they can work well for you.

A final word about interviewing to obtain your testimonials. If you're doing it yourself, use a tape recorder and then get the interview transcribed verbatim. When you're talking to the interviewee, try to ensure that the questions you ask do not call for a mere "yes" or "no" answer. Phrase questions in a positive way, without trying to put words in the interviewee's mouth as this can create hostility.

Bad questions
"Do you like STAND-UP support hosiery?" (can be answered with a "yes" or a "no".)

"Please could you say that STAND-UP hosiery are the best you've ever worn?" (putting words in the interviewee's mouth, which can create hostility. May well be answered with a "no").

Good questions
"What are the main things you like about wearing STAND-UP support hosiery?" (should bring out a list of good points about the benefits of the product. If you just say *"what do you like about"*, as opposed to *"what do you like about wearing)* the?, interviewee might start talking features – colours, fit, etc. You're looking for benefits, remember? Also, this question is not likely to create hostility, because both you and she know that she already uses the product.)

"If I did a job like yours, what advice would you give me about the benefits of wearing STAND-UP support hosiery?" (should get interviewee to say some relevant things about you, in this case standing in for the reader).

Whether you take your testimonial quotes from users' letters or from an interview transcript, always, always write to the person concerned clearly stating what quote you propose to use, and asking them to confirm in writing that they're happy for you to use it. In the UK, all testimonial givers have to sign a statement which ensures that what they say is genuine, and that no one has made it up for them in return for payment. Rules like this may vary from country to country. This is not only good housekeeping, but it can also mean that you are legally covered should the interviewee ever get difficult, or should someone make a complaint about the ad. If you're in any doubt about the legal implications of testimonials, check with your lawyer before you publish anything.

Property and other classified ads

Although we lead this section with "property ads", the following is equally applicable to many forms of "classified" advertising undertaken by both large and small companies; so even if you're not in the property business, read on.

Property advertisements are probably among the most badly written examples of advertising copy in the world, and are therefore the best example we can choose to illustrate a better way of writing words that sell. Most estate agents (or real estate brokers in North America) write their own descriptive copy for ads in local, regional and even national publications and, in fairness, this is often necessary as details of property are not normally available until the last minute – there isn't time to call a professional in. But there is time to learn how to put the copy together well, and once you've learned the basics of how to do it the process of doing it well doesn't take any longer than it does to do it badly.

Most people who have bought a house in the last ten years will remember the jargon used in ads – this varies from country to country, but in the UK includes such awful clichés as *"Des. Res."* (desirable residence), *"in need of some modernisation"* (falling apart), *"established garden"* (wildly overgrown), *"ideal first home"* (minuscule and shabby), and so on. Property ads have to be much more feature orientated than do other types of advertising. This is because first, anyone reading the ad has already thought of the benefits as he/she is thinking of moving house, and second, in many instances the features of the house are its benefits anyway. The shorthand of property-speak is acceptable, too, because most prospective purchasers understand it and expect it. However, this is still no reason why you should not put the shorthand and jargon together in a readable way that sells. Perhaps the best way to illustrate how to improve on copy style is to quote a real example of a house being sold by a friend of Suzan St Maur's some years ago. It was an old cottage in a lovely location some thirty miles out of London, England, and the ad went into one of the UK's leading Sunday newspapers. First of all, here is how an estate agent would have written it ...

"THREE BEDROOMED GEORGIAN COTTAGE located at XXXX Green. Accommodation comprised of two reception rooms, modern bathroom, fitted kitchen. Oil-fired central heating. Covered car parking. Established garden. London 30 miles. £XX,000 freehold."

Boring, and about as emotive as a hob-nailed boot. It also includes a mistake which many estate agents fall for; if you must use the word "comprise", (old-fashioned and lumpy) accommodation "comprises" – it doesn't "comprise of". It's okay to break grammatical rules in ad copy, but you need to know the rules before you can break them effectively. Although the ad tells you all the necessary features, it doesn't give you a hint – not even one word – that suggests the character of the place. If it were an old three-bedroomed house in a row with fifty others that look identical, there wouldn't be much personality to pull out of it. But in this case, the cottage was unique – yet many estate agents would have ignored that. Anyway, here's how Suzan St Maur's version went ...

"AN ORIGINAL ROSE-COVERED COTTAGE overlooking XXXX Green where (well-known Victorian novelist) lived, just 30 miles from London (XX motorway). Warm, rich Georgian brickwork encloses exposed oak beams ... sitting and dining rooms ... three bedrooms ... bathroom ... big, country kitchen ... carport. Large cottage garden with roses, orchard and lawns. Central heating plus two open fireplaces. Offers over £XX,000; phone XXXXXX 12345."

Ah ... you can see yourself there now, can't you? Curled up by a crackling fireplace with a cup of cocoa and a muddy, smelly spaniel at your feet? Admittedly, St Maur's ad was longer. But the 'phone never stopped ringing all day, and by lunchtime on the Sunday the owner had had four offers all well over the asking price. The moral of this story is that although a property ad has to be factual and consist of wall-to-wall features, you can throw the odd benefit in even if the space is very limited. An emotive adjective here and there will do; obviously property ads must be 100% true, because in some cases the ad copy can be considered as part of the legal specification. But no one could dispute *"warm, rich, Georgian brickwork"* because that's exactly what it was. It was also absolutely true to say that it was *"an original . . ."* because the place was 100% Georgian, and similarly it was covered with three huge climbing rose plants that smacked you in the face every time you opened a window or door.

You *can* think benefits into property and other classified ads. Let's take another example, this time for a used car.

> 1. *"VOLKSWAGEN BEETLE FOR SALE; 80,000 miles. Red. Bodywork in need of some attention. Engine and other mechanics in good running order. Five new tyres. Offers over £XXX."*
> 2. *"GOOD HOME WANTED FOR LOVEABLE BRIGHT RED VW BEETLE: old family friend for 80,000 miles sadly must be sold. Bodywork needs some attention, but she runs really well and all tyres are new. Offers over £XXX."*

Which car would intrigue you more?

Recruitment ads

The principles of writing recruitment advertisements are much the same as for any other type, but there is one point which does differentiate them quite considerably. Most other forms of advertising are trying to sell something, and that's all. Recruitment ads are trying to sell a position in a company, but they're also asking the candidate to sell himself/herself to you.

Some companies get overly carried away with this notion and create ads that are so patronising and downright rude, that they would be lucky to get a response from a chimpanzee. Fortunately many companies are guided by recruitment consultancies who carefully steer them away from this, but ads like the following still occasionally appear ...

> *"COULD YOU PROVE YOUR SELLING ABILITY TO US?*
> *Bloggs Bearings, the largest ball bearing manufacturer in the UK, is now at the leading edge of its market ... with a turnover of £X million per annum and a well-deserved reputation for the finest sales operation in the industry.*
>
> *There now exists a vacancy for another sales executive to complete the team of efficient, effective people we employ. The successful candidate will have to prove his or her ability to excel in a particularly*

tough environment, and meet the demanding quarterly targets without fail.

Applications are invited from men and women aged 20–35, with several successful years' selling experience behind them. Write to the Personnel Director, telling him why you think you're capable of making a worthwhile contribution to the leading ball bearing manufacturers in Britain.

(Address here.)"

Doesn't exactly make you want to reach for your pen, does it? The way you write your recruitment ads says a lot about your company, not only in the actual messages, but in the style of writing as well. You need to aim your writing style at the sort of person you want to attract. You also need to tell the reader a lot more about what you're going to do for them, although you should say what the pressures are going to be and what you expect of them. But these can be seen as positive points.

Take another example; a recruitment ad for a secretary. Here the tone is much chattier, because we want to attract a bright, lively, person with a sense of humour and a practical ability to run an office full of frenzied corporate video production people. Although the job will not involve actually making movies, there is a certain kudos to be portrayed in working for a company that makes these programmes, so we use that to flag the reader. The person may get involved in the film-making process at some level, so we're not being dishonest in suggesting the part that they might play. We also need to make it clear, right away, that the job is secretarial.

"ARE YOU A SECRETARY WHO CAN HELP US MAKE MOVIES?

Here's your chance to help look after a busy, 10-strong team of people who make business television programmes and films for a variety of interesting clients. We need a good secretary who not only knows how to type, but who can run our office, look after our administrative work, and generally keep our creative people sane!

You'll work in attractive offices in London's West End ... use the latest word processor and other high-tech office equipment ... and occasionally, get the chance to come out with us on location shoots. The hours are often long. But you'll enjoy the opportunity to run things your way – organise the functions of a busy office – and meet some very interesting people. You'll also be in charge of a small team of audio typists, and organise the best ways for them to work.

We don't mind how old you are, as long as you've got some useful experience. And you'll need a sense of humour. Making movies is hard work but it can be fun as well. The salary is good, and we offer private health insurance plus five weeks' holiday a year. If you think you've got what it takes, we want to meet you! Give Karl a ring – 01. XXX. 0000, and have a chat with him. He'll tell you all you want to know about us – and ask you all we want to know about you.

(Name of contact, company, address and telephone number here.)"

There aren't many people who wouldn't get the picture about this job. Without actually saying it in so many words, it gets over the message of what the job involves; hectic, demanding, needing a self-starter and someone who can roll up their sleeves and take charge. It suggests that the successful candidate will need initiative, leadership qualities, and an ability to take flak from time to time. But it also suggests that the person will be part of a friendly team, and will be respected for what he/she does. While it doesn't try to hide the disadvantages of the job, it makes them sound interesting – and for the right person, they would be. At the same time, by highlighting the disadvantages in this way, it rules out the people who just want a nine to five job with no significant responsibilities.

The most important thing to remember about writing ads of any kind is to get on the reader's wavelength. The most important thing to remember about writing recruitment ads is not only to get on the reader's wavelength, but to instigate a wavelength that attracts the sort of person you want. Not only do you need to convey the details of the job but also its personality and that of the company. And, you need to make the best of what you have to offer, while at the same time not lying; lying will only result in the wrong candidates applying for the job. Be truthful in recruitment ads; be lively; talk to the person you want; and don't bore him or her with too much about the company itself. The fact that your company is the fastest growing in its field will be interesting, but only in respect of what it can offer the employee.

Remember, the better the selling job you do in recruitment ads, the better the quality of candidate you will attract. And although widespread unemployment has altered the nature of recruitment in recent times, you still can't afford to be patronising and pompous. No one worth his/her salt wants to work for a stuck-up organisation which considers it is doing people a favour by employing them.

POSTERS

Writing copy for posters is a bit like writing a press ad with headline, illustration and pay-off or baseline, but no body copy. Naturally, your headline here must be good enough to stand on its own, and because it is on its own with the illustration the two must work together even more closely than they do in a press ad, although good press ads always display a very strong partnership between headline and visual anyway.

Of course, you do see posters that contain a lot of copy in addition to the basics mentioned above; some even contain long body copy. A lot of what good poster-writing is about is in studying where the poster is going to be displayed, how big it's going to be, and in what circumstances people are going to see it. You don't need to go into much research to find out how people are going to read a newspaper or magazine, watch television, or listen to radio. Naturally there are variations within these media (for example, drive-time radio, peak-time TV, daily newspapers, recreational magazines) but those variations are pretty well documented and quite easy to interpret on the basis of common sense. Posters are another story; you can create a poster of one size, but the viewing circumstances for those identical posters can vary enormously.

So before you start writing for poster copy, you need to think about where the posters will be placed. Large posters at railway stations can contain more copy, because people waiting for trains have time to look at them and read all the words. If your target audience is commuters, they may not have time to read all the copy at one time, but they'll catch up on the rest the next day. A large poster by the side of the road should not contain many words because drivers won't have time to do more than glance at it. However, if your poster site is within viewing distance of a set of traffic lights, drivers will have more time to read. And so on.

If you are planning a widespread poster campaign, you obviously can't create a different version for every poster site. But you can isolate the common denominators among the sites you have chosen, and bear in mind the average length of time readers will have to absorb your message; this will have an effect on the words you write.

Unless you're creating a poster that is designed to entertain readers as well as sell something – for display at railway stations, bus stops and airport waiting rooms – you're better off sticking to strong but simple words. The idea behind both words and pictures should be powerful enough to catch the imagination, as well as the eye. Busy, cluttered posters make good backgrounds for graffiti, but don't get noticed half as much as one strong illustration with a few well-chosen words completing the picture. Even at very local level, a poster can still benefit from simple creative thinking: take the example of a poster for a typical English village fete. This is how it goes normally ...

"ST BINGO'S ANNUAL SUMMER FÊTE

Saturday, June 23rd, 19XX

2.30 to 5.00 pm

Tombolas
Cake stalls
Games
Children's dancing display
XXXXtown Brass Band
Draw for holiday and other prizes
Grand opening at 2.45 by the Duchess of XXXXshire."

And this poster will appear on roadsides, as well as in areas where people can read all the words. Now, let's divide the posters into two categories; those which should be used in places where there won't be much time to read them, like by the side of the road and in people's windows, and those which can be read at more leisure – like at the bus stops and in local shops and stores. First, the poster which will be read on the hoof (or tyre).

"A GREAT DAY OUT FOR YOUR FAMILY ... WITHOUT GOING OUT OF XXXXTOWN!

ST BINGO'S SUMMER FÊTE

SATURDAY JUNE 23rd

STARTS 2.30 ... DON'T BE LATE!"

Not every driver will see all the words at one time, but local people will have more than one opportunity to see the poster, unless they're going away on holiday or emigrating, in which case they won't be around for the fete anyway. And this approach is much more benefit-led. Alright, local people normally like to support the activities of their community, but bear in mind that the fête is still likely to be in competition with going shopping, taking the children out to a theme park and watching football on television. So a little "sell" in the poster may help to catch those who would otherwise contemplate doing something else. Now, let's see how we can improve on the poster which people will have time to read. The structure should be similar, to double up on the message passing drivers will get.

"A GREAT DAY OUT FOR YOUR FAMILY ... WITHOUT GOING OUT OF XXXXTOWN!

ST BINGO'S SUMMER FÊTE

It's always a terrific day out for the family at St Bingo's annual fête. This year, it's going to be bigger and better than ever ... with the XXXtown Brass Band playing all afternoon and for the first time, the St Bingo Sunday School dancers' new formation display. And there's lots more, too:

Three tombolas

Games for parents and children

Cake stalls

Locally grown fruit and vegetable stalls

Bring and buy stalls

... plus a grand draw – you could win the first prize of a dream holiday for two, in romantic Paris. The Duchess of XXXXshire will open the fête at 2.45 ... so come early – don't miss a moment of the fun!

IT'S A GREAT DAY OUT ... AND IT'S RIGHT ON YOUR DOORSTEP!

ST. BINGO'S SUMMER FETE

SATURDAY JUNE 23rd. STARTS 2.30 ... DON'T BE LATE!"

The poster copy introduces an element of sell, without losing the local touch – hard, slick advertising-speak would be out of place in a poster like this. Many posters of this type display their information in a series of bullet points. However, assuming readers will have time to absorb it all, there's no reason why you can't put at least some of the information in the style of body copy prose, with bullet points here and there to give emphasis. This way is much more readable; long lists of bullet points aren't very inviting.

Another useful job posters do is to target readers travelling towards a certain destination. On the way out to airports from city centres, you'll often see posters advertising airlines, duty-free shops and so on, geared entirely towards people on their way to the airport by car, taxi or bus. All over the world you'll see posters by roadsides advertising something of potential interest to drivers – the words *"last petrol before M98 motorway – OILGAS garage two miles"* or *"SLEEPTIGHT'S ... the finest motel in XXXtown ... five miles ahead"* are common in many countries. This facility of poster advertising is of special interest to local advertisers, either to encourage local business or to catch passing trade. Say you're running a restaurant. First, how could you encourage local trade with a general poster, but aimed primarily at the more sophisticated commuters who can afford to eat out regularly? Your illustration is of a Spanish guitarist singing his heart out by a colourful display of Spanish food ...

> *"TONIGHT, DRIVE HOME TO DINNER IN SUNNY SPAIN ...*
> *RIGHT HERE IN XXXTOWN*
> EL SALMONELLA ... A DELICIOUS TASTE OF SPAIN IN JOHN STREET."

You might decide to appeal to the daytime traffic as well, including people going shopping in the city, or going into the city for an evening out ...

> *"WHY DRIVE TO THE CITY WHEN YOU CAN ENJOY THE*
> *BRIGHT LIGHTS OF XXXTOWN?*
> EL SALMONELLA ... A DELICIOUS EVENING OUT AT JOHN
> STREET'S TASTE OF SPAIN."

Naturally you can't put in opening days and times, telephone numbers, and so on, but then you may well be running ads in the local press and radio which give details of that. The poster just gets people thinking about your product/service ... implants the idea, and reinforces the fact that the restaurant is local by giving the name of the street. You could use a similar poster at the local railway station, to catch commuters returning home from work in the city. The structure should remain the same, although you can add some copy for the commuters who are waiting for trains in the morning. However, many people will decide to go out for a meal on impulse, especially if they have just come back after a hard day's work. In this case, they won't hang around to read the small print – so you need to make sure they can get the idea at a glance ...

> *"TAKE SOMEONE SPECIAL TO DINNER IN SUNNY SPAIN*
> *TONIGHT*
> *... RIGHT HERE IN XXXTOWN.*
> *El Salmonella's Restaurant: John Street, XXXtown"*

or perhaps ...

> *"COULD YOU DO WITH A LITTLE SPANISH HOLIDAY*
> *TONIGHT?*
> *Delicious Dining in XXXtown's Own Corner of Spain ... El Salmon-*
> *ella, John Street."*

Now, let's put something together for passing trade; we assume that XXXtown is on a main road which carries a lot of holiday-makers on the way to or from their destination, plus business people going to or from conferences and meetings.

> *"FOR A DELICIOUS MEAL, DRIVE STRAIGHT ON TO*
> *SPAIN...*
> *Right Here in XXXtown: El Salmonella's, John Street"*

or alternatively ...

> **"DROP INTO SUNNY SPAIN FOR A DELICIOUS DINNER ...**
> **RIGHT HERE IN XXXTOWN**
> *El Salmonella's Restaurant, John Street – Turn Left at the Next*
> *Lights."*

WRITING FOR SALES PROMOTION

Sales promotion is complicated to define, because it covers a number of different activities. However, one way of looking at it is as any activity which sets out to boost the sales of a product or service in addition to, and/or in parallel with, the mainstream advertising for that product/ service. There is a certain amount of cross-over these days between sales promotion and PR, although, generally speaking, sales promotional ads and other pieces of communication have to be paid for by the advertiser, whereas much of PR consists of getting publicity without paying for media space or time.

Sales promotion activities tend to have a shorter lifespan than mainstream media advertising campaigns. This is because many sales promotion projects are designed to increase traffic, especially in retail outlets, by using an incentive device to encourage customers to buy a particular brand of product or service. Often, the idea behind this is to build up customers' purchasing habits, so that when the special incentive is no longer there they will still continue to buy that brand. The types of product which benefit from sales promotion are wide and varied, but seem to share one or both of the following common denominators; comparatively low unit cost (suggesting a lesser degree of premeditation by people who purchase them) and widespread competition (selling in a market place where there are many similar products). Examples include fast-moving consumer goods (FMCG) like food, washing powders, beverages, toiletries and so on, petroleum products and, increasingly, newspapers and periodicals.

Incentives used in sales promotion are as varied as the products they promote. They can consist of anything from spot-the-ball competitions to money-off coupons, from tokens to collect and submit in return for gifts to one-off giveaways, from prize draws to live product sampling. All of these create a need for some fairly original thinking. You see a great many offers that are incredibly complicated, and a great many more which are good promotions in themselves but totally unrelated to the product they're supposed to be promoting. But our job here is not to try and tell you how to devise promotions; there are a number of good books on the subject and offices full of experts who get paid to do just that on the part of advertisers. We would offer two pieces of advice to advertisers thinking of creating their own promotions, though; keep them simple, and make them relevant.

Earlier in this book, under the heading *Advertising Campaigns*, we described a simple promotion for a restaurant, offering customers a romantic evening out; and what better way to enhance a romantic evening out at a restaurant than by giving couples a free bottle of wine? That is simple and relevant. And once customers are in the restaurant, you hope that they will be so favourably impressed by the place that they'll come back again and again.

You could tailor that promotion even further, if you wanted to. For example, you could place an ad in a weddings feature of the local newspaper, saying that you will give a free bottle of wine to couples celebrating their engagement at your restaurant. Or, ditto, for couples celebrating their wedding aniversary, perhaps with a bunch of flowers to take home afterwards. These promotions are also simple and relevant.

Another important criterion you need to observe when creating sales promotions is legality. Competitions and draws are governed by laws in most countries, and you would do well to check with your lawyer before spending any money on something of this nature. In Britain, the British Code of Sales Promotion Practice is administered by the Advertising Standards Authority, and all member organisations agree to stick to the rules it sets out. The Code contains a number of guidelines which cover things like stating what "free" really means, stressing the required proof of purchase and closing dates, ensuring that advertising for the promotion does not continue if stocks of giveaways or products should run out, and so on. Although this system means that the sales promotion industry is self-governing, in effect, people who have a complaint about a promotion by a member organisation can contact the ASA who will investigate it on their behalf. If they agree that the complaint is valid, they will tell the advertiser to do something about it.

Whether your particular promotion is governed by law or code of practice or not, you should add "clear and properly structured" to your list of priorities along with "simple and relevant". Even if there are no official bodies around to rap you on the knuckles, a poor promotion, or one which does not live up to its promises, can become very bad publicity for your company.

Another way in which your promotion can backfire is if your distribution is inadequate. If your company spends a lot of money on advertising a free gift promotion, or a scheme whereby consumers have to look for a pack with a special label, you must be sure that there are plenty of gifts which will get sent out promptly, or that packs with the special labels are available in the stores. Although this isn't necessarily the problem of the person who writes the sales promotion copy, it is worth their while to consider just how effective distribution will be. If it transpires that distribution may be less than perfect, you can work a compromise into the written material – for example, *"Send your tokens off now – there are only 500 free widgets to be won"* or *"You'll find our special packs in all larger branches of Fillyerfridge Supermarkets"*.

Broadly speaking, the writing you need to do for sales promotion activities can be split into two main stages. First, there is the advertising stage, where you announce your promotion to the public. (This may include television and radio commercials as well as press and print ads. However, we've categorised sales promotion under press and print ads, as this forms the most significant part of sales promotion writing.) Second, there is the material you need at the point of sale to remind people of what they've already seen and heard about the promotion, and to encourage them to go ahead and make the purchase. Naturally, these two stages must be very closely co-ordinated, both verbally and visually, so the overall message is transmitted throughout all the media you use.

Before we look at each stage in more detail, let's focus on the co-ordination between advertising and POS (point of sale) stages, and how important it is. Say a newspaper, which is one of two or three similar newspapers in a large urban area, is running a competition where the first prize is a new Ford car. The competition runs over one week, with readers having to collect one question each day and fill in the answers in an entry form which they cut out of the paper on the Saturday. The idea behind this would be to get people to buy the paper every day for a week, and so get them into the habit of reading the *Daily Rag* rather than its competitors. The paper will probably run television and radio commercials the week before, announcing *"win a brand new Ford Siesta in the Daily Rag's 'Drive to a Fortune' competition ... all next week!"* They will also run ads in their own paper the week before. The message will be echoed at the point of sale, that is, news-stands and newsagents, with a display card or shelf sticker which says roughly the same thing. During the week of the promotion, the message changes to *"don't miss your chance to win a brand new Ford Siesta in the Daily Rag's 'Drive to a Fortune' competition ... all this week!"* The competition will also be heralded in a large flash across the upper front part of the paper's front page, so it can be seen when the papers are in racks on a news-stand or on a newsagent's shelves. The same message and graphics will be used to announce the competition details themselves, within the body of the paper.

Basically, co-ordinating a sales promotion message across a variety of media is much the same as translating a sales message into an advertising campaign. In fact, writing the words for sales promotion follows much the same guidelines as those for writing ads, leaflets, and so on. However, there is one main difference in the approach you need to take. If you're just advertising a product or service, you should focus your attention (and the reader's) on the *benefits*, leading the advertising material with the most important benefit your product/service has to offer. With sales promotion, though, you're dealing with a dual message; that of your product or service, *and that of the promotion itself.* And the second half of that equation, the promotion, can also be benefit-led; not only does the product do something useful for readers, but the promotion does as well.

If you look at many sales promotion campaigns, you could be forgiven for thinking that sales promotion is about plugging the offer or incentive, never mind the product/service. Some advertisers (and some advertising agencies, too; naughty naughty) get so carried away with the tremendous interest they think they will create with their offer that even the name of the product/service – never mind its message – gets buried under a heap of "free" this and "win" that. What happens then is that the promotion sells all your competitors' products. So one very major consideration in advertising a promotion is to make sure that your product/service and its message get over loud and clear; and this ties in with our earlier points about relevance and simplicity. If the promotion is relevant (eg, a free coffee mug when you send off four special labels from Stay-Awake instant coffee jars) and simple (*"buy one can of new Doggo petfood, get one free"*), it is a lot easier to retain strong *brand identity* in the advertising material you create. And it is also a lot easier to work in a good, strong, benefit-led selling message.

Let's look at how a sales promotion campaign might work for Doggo petfood, which has been relaunched with added flavour and vitamins. For a start, we should consider what the mainstream "consumer" advertising is doing, in the headline concept at least ...

"New Doggo tastes better ... and it's better for your dog".

Now, we need to adapt that idea so that we still give an impression of the benefits, and also get over the benefit of the promotion.

"New, better-tasting Doggo – better for your dog and better for your pocket ... WITH THIS MONEY-SAVING OFFER!"

Not exactly award-winning headlines, but they illustrate the difference in emphasis you need to consider between straightforward consumer advertising and sales promotion.

Body copy in a sales promotion ad needs to be hard-sell, but it also needs to tell the reader exactly how to go about benefiting from the offer in as clear and uncluttered a way as possible ...

"New, better-tasting Doggo – better for your dog and better for your pocket ... WITH THIS MONEY-SAVING OFFER!

Your dog will love new Doggo, with its improved flavour and texture. New Doggo's not just tastier, either; it's better for your dog, too, with added vitamins and minerals to help keep him healthy and lively.

And right now, new Doggo's even better for your pocket ... with this great offer. For every large can of Doggo you buy this week, we'll give you another large can absolutely free!

All you have to do is look for the Doggo display at your nearest Fillyerfridge supermarket. And remember, you'll get one free large can of new Doggo for every large can you buy. But hurry; this offer closes on January 20th.

New Doggo ... tastes better, and it's better for your dog."

Now, how about the printed material which goes into the point of sale? This has to echo the message of the advertising, to remind people of the offer if they've already noticed the ads. But it must also stand alone, because many people may not have seen the ad. (Anyway, some promotions are only conducted at the point of sale and don't use support advertising at all.) And because there are probably half-a-dozen other special promotions going on in the supermarket at the sane time as yours, you need to make your message very clear and noticeable. You also need to make your message short and to the point, because a harassed shopper double-parked outside a store, rushing and struggling to load a trolley with the week's groceries while keeping two bored children out of mischief, has a pretty short attention span.

In the case of the Doggo offer, there's no need for any complicated printed material, as there's nothing much to explain. All you need is a nicely designed display, with a large and eye catching sign which says something like ...

New, better tasting Doggo ... buy one large can, get one free!

You could also do a free leaflet, which could be displayed in a rack by the main display. This would be about dog nutrition in general, and how Doggo is better for your dog because ... There could be a sign over or by the rack, saying:

> *"FEEDING YOUR DOG FOR HEALTH AND VITALITY ... WITH DOGGO. Pick up your free leaflet here".*

COMPETITIONS

Probably the most important thing to remember about competitions is that in most countries they are strictly governed by the law. In the UK, it is illegal (as this book goes to press) to run a competition that involves entrants in buying something and providing proof that they have, without getting them to do something that needs a certain amount of skill. Obviously one way of introducing an element of skill is to make the questions difficult. But this has two main drawbacks; one, your idea of difficult questions may not be other people's, and you could be in legal trouble if there is any dispute over this. Two, if the questions are that difficult, you're going to put a lot of people off the idea of entering in the first place. The solution is what is known as "tie breaker"; one of those lines reads ...

> *"Using your skill and judgement, please complete this sentence in no more than 15 words: APART FROM ITS ADDED VITAMINS AND MINERALS, DOGGO PETFOOD IS BETTER FOR MY DOG BECAUSE*
>
> ....
> ....
> .... *"*

In legal circles, a tie-breaker like this is usually considered to need enough skill to meet the requirements. However, because people are free to write what they want, they are not likely to be put off by a tie-breaker as much as they would be if they had to spend three days at their library researching the answers to your questions. Normally the tie-breaker is accompanied by a line that says something like ...

> *"In the event of a tie for first place, the judges will look for originality, creative thinking and understanding in the tie-breaker sentence."*

Provided your questions are pretty easy – and they should be – you'll find that most entrants get them right and "tie" for first place, so your judges will have to use the tie-breakers to select a winner. And there really *is* a lot of skill and judgement needed to write good tie-breakers. In the UK, entering commercially run competitions has become something of a national sport. There are societies and associations of competition entrants, and magazines and other publications that publish a great deal of information about competitions currently in operation plus a selection of winning tie-breakers. Competitions, especially if they offer good prizes, attract a lot of attention from these sporting folk, who might even buy more of your product than normal into the bargain.

If you want to run a prize draw, then there can be no obligation on entrants to buy anything at all. This fact has to be made very clear in any promotional material concerning a draw.

The laws concerning competitions and draws vary from country to country, but in nearly all industrialised nations there are some relevant rules or laws. In the UK, get yourself a copy of the Gaming Act, which will tell you in detail what the rules are. The British Code of Sales Promotion Practice also has some guidelines about competitions..

Basically, the guidelines consist of some useful pointers based on common sense. They recommend that you should check with a lawyer before publishing anything about a competition, which makes good sense. They also point out the need for you to make absolutely clear all the necessary information, including simple rules that are easily understood, what the prizes are and what they're like, what – if any – restrictions there are on who may enter, what and how many products entrants need to buy to qualify for entry, when the closing date is, and the fact that only entries received by that date are eligible (in other words if the entry gets lost in the mail, that's not your problem – even if the entrant can prove the entry was posted.)

Now, for the good news. Although competitions are quite heavily controlled – certainly in the UK – they can also be very good value in promotional terms, provided that you publicise them well. Competitions on a national scale require very heavy, expensive publicity if they're going to work, but then they are likely to attract a lot of PR spin-off especially if they're interesting and unusual. The ways in which you promote competitions are the ways in which you promote anything; ads, direct mail, radio commercials, even TV if the budget will permit. Naturally you would only use the broadcast media to flag the audience's attention, and give details plus entry forms in the print. Or, you may decide to direct people to your retail outlets to pick up an entry form there, and so increase your traffic.

Competitions themselves, just like any other form of sales promotion, should be simple and relevant. It's always a good idea to try to theme your competition to something about your company or your product, and to include your company or product name in the title. There's no point in spending a fortune on a competition if it doesn't sell at the same time, or at least focus attention on your corporate image and/or your brand name ...

"WIN AN ALL EXPENSES PAID WEEKEND TRIP TO LONDON'S CRUFTS DOG SHOW

> *... with the DOGGO PEDIGREE CHAMPIONS COMPETITION!"*

or, how about ...

> *"WIN A DREAM FISHING VACATION IN THE BEAUTIFUL BAHAMAS ... IN THE SUNNY SARDINES CATCH-A-FISH CONTEST!"*

Another point about competitions is that they need to be worth entering. Competitions for a knitting wool company that offer an exciting leaflet on how to knit sweaters as first prize will not attract many entrants, and may even have a detrimental effect on your company's image by suggesting – probably with justification – that the company's run by cheapskates. If your first prize is a holiday, it may be possible to enter into a joint arrangement with the holiday company and/or airline so that they pay for some of the cost, in return for a share of the publicity. However, multiple sponsors of a competition are not a good idea, because more than one or two names in a promotion will confuse potential entrants and dilute the branding so much it will hardly be noticed at all.

As with other types of sales promotion, you're dealing with a dual message in competitions. In fact because a competition needs a lot of explaining in all printed material and in broadcast commercials as well, you're likely to have to suppress any hard sell on your company/product. That's another reason why it's so important to include your company/product name in the title, and theme the competition to something that's relevant. With a competition, like anything else, you must sell the benefits rather than the nuts and bolts. It is important to state in the headline of any print ad or in a prominent place in a commercial that it is about a competition, and competitions must be won. However, once you've made that point, you can stress the benefits of the first prize; the way you will *feel* on your dream fishing vacation in the Bahamas ...

> *"WIN A DREAM FISHING VACATION IN THE BEAUTIFUL BAHAMAS ... IN THE SUNNY SARDINES CATCH-A-FISH CONTEST!*
>
> *Imagine yourself strapped into the fighting chair on a luxury motor yacht ... pitting your wits and strength against the powers of the ocean ... relaxing in the tropical sun with a cool drink in your hand after a thrilling day ... this, is the first prize you could win in the Sunny Sardines Catch-a-Fish contest! Two glorious, tropical weeks in one of the Bahamas finest hotels ... first-class air travel there and back*

... day trips in a luxury motor yacht fitted with all the latest fishing equipment ... it's the dream vacation of a lifetime for any fishing fan. All you have to do is ... etc. "

You write a summary of the entry requirements here. Elsewhere in the ad you should put the list of requirements for entry, and also a description of the first prize and any secondary prizes. If the entry form is actually in the ad, then – in the UK anyway – you must include the rules of the competition and an accurate description of all the prizes. You must also put in any alternative prizes, such as cash instead of the holiday.

Prize draws must also be very good, and very worthwhile entering, if they are going to work. Organisations like the *Reader's Digest* run particularly spectacular draws, with first prizes of large amounts of money, expensive cars, and so on. Usually this type of draw is promoted by direct mail, and is connected with a sales pitch for a book or other product. Naturally, (in the UK at least) you don't have to buy the product to enter the draw. However, direct mail, provided you use a sufficiently large envelope and can afford the cost of print and postage, allows you to send out quite a lot of sales information about the product in addition to the documents connected with the draw. Normally you should send out a covering letter which sells the product and talks about the draw as well; often these letters will run to about four pages. But people do read them, and a lot of products get sold this way.

The approach you need to use for promoting prize draws is much the same as that for a competition: the dual message. However, bear in mind that draws are very tightly governed by law in most countries; even more so than in the case of competitions. So, again, a good talk with your lawyer is essential, if you decide that a draw is for you. In addition, the prizes you need to offer have to be very appealing, hence expensive, so you will need quite a big budget.

CHAPTER 7

SELLING ON BROADCAST:

Radio and television advertising

Many of the broad advertising principles we have outlined earlier in this book apply to broadcast ads as well. Your research, your approach, and getting the "idea" are all the same, suitably adapted, of course. The big difference comes in the actual writing of the ad; the difference between the printed word and the spoken word. And there are differences between the ways in which press and broadcast ads are perceived.

In our chapters on writing speeches and scripts you'll find a lot of advice on how to write for the spoken word but, although much of that is equally applicable to writing commercials, there is one main difference here.

Let's look at the print/broadcast difference in perception first. The good news is that people are more likely to take notice of your radio or television commercial than they are of a press ad. That's for a number of reasons; one is that it's more difficult to get away from a commercial, because it means you have to physically and/or mentally switch off. Even if you look away from the television set, you still hear the sound track. If you're listening to a radio programme, you're not likely to bother turning the sound off for a couple of minutes during the commercial break – you'll listen through until your programme comes on again. Another reason is that a commercial is not fighting for a reader's attention; while a commercial is playing, there is nothing else going on within that medium. With a press ad, unless it takes up a whole page of a publication, there are likely to be other items of interest around it, to which the reader's eye can easily stray.

The main difference between commercials and speeches or scripts is time; now for the bad news. In a corporate video programme you have a good number of minutes in which to put your messages across. In a commercial, you only have a few seconds. You have no time to develop an argument and back it up with interesting information. You have got to come straight to the point.

Naturally, it is essential that you create commercials around benefits rather than features, just as you would with any kind of advertising material. But because you've got to get your point across quickly and effectively, all commercials should put over *one* idea . . . one main benefit or group or benefits . . . and that's all. One strong, straightforward thought will stick in listeners'/viewers' minds; a complicated concept will simply make them mentally switch off.

Before we go any further, it's worth pointing out that much as you may be itching to write the international advertising campaign of the century, beware of radio and television. Broadcast commercials – television in particular – cost a lot of money in terms of air time and production. So if your company is planning to spend a considerable sum on these media, it really is worth hiring experts to create the ads for you. The most commonly chosen type of expertise comes from advertising agencies, but there are also a number of freelance specialists and production companies who can help generate good scripts.

Many commercial broadcast stations have in-house production people, including copywriters, who will advise you on the right creative input for your campaign in exchange for a fee. This is not to say that you couldn't come up with the right ideas, or the right words; it is possible that you might. But experienced experts can save a lot of your time and money in the long run. And just because you don't physically write the scripts doesn't mean that an informed appreciation of how to do it isn't a good idea. To judge the quality of scripts, you need to know the difference between a good approach and a bad one first.

If you do want to try your hand at more complicated commercials, there are a number of specialist advertising books you can read; and, in some major cities, there are courses you can attend. Nonetheless, there's nothing to beat the expertise you acquire while working in a large, successful advertising agency for a few years; that's how most writers of big international television campaigns started, and is probably the only safe way of learning the skills required.

However, many companies will buy air time on local or regional broadcast stations to promote a local/regional product or service. Television stations often offer special rates for local advertisers, and special deals on short-length slots of, say, seven, ten or fifteen seconds. With these lower-cost, geographically restricted commercials, you do not need to create a major advertising campaign, but merely to put your message over in as memorable but simple a way as possible. These are the sort of commercials you can write yourself, provided you know the basics, and get good results; so we'll look at these more closely.

One problem many advertisers inadvertently let themselves in for is in trying to adapt a press ad idea into a radio or television one. Although it is true to say that you should always write copy for the press in the way that people speak, remember that this is not necessarily the same as spoken speech. Conversational prose is different; it can bend more rules than spoken speech can, because with it you are only dealing with people's eyes, which can respond to cryptic one-word sentences, abbreviated word forms and odd words that trigger further thought. Ears are another ball game; they respond best to speech that sounds as if it is occuring naturally. Odd words and jarring phrases in spoken speech can have a counter-productive effect, because people hearing them begin to think about the words rather than the message. Yet, all too often, you'll listen to a radio commercial or the sound track of a short television commercial and realise that all the advertiser has done is to lift the copy straight out of a press ad. Radio or television (sound track only) commercial scripts like this are about as effective as a slap in the face . . .

> *"VOICE OVER: A romantic evening for you both . . . at El Salmonella. Special offer this week . . . free bottle of wine for every dinner-for-two. Table d'hôte menu from £7 per head. À la carte main courses from £4. Booking advisable. El Salmonella restaurant, George Street, Johntown, just 200 yards from the Town Hall. Telephone Johntown 12345."*

Now, you may think the above example is exaggeration for the sake of emphasis. But all you need to do to see otherwise is to tune into some local radio or television stations. This sort of commercial does get transmitted. Many is the harassed voice-over artiste who gets asked to read a script like it, and tries valiantly to make it sound better. They usually fail. So how about this for a radio ad, or for a television commercial that shows a still photograph of the romantic restaurant interior?

> *"VOICE OVER: Now there's even more reason for you to take that special someone to El Salmonella . . . this week, we're giving away a bottle of wine to every couple . . . turning your evening out into a romantic occasion, absolutely free! And with our table d'hôte menu, your dinner for two at El Salmonella can cost as little as £14. So 'phone us and book your table now . . . at El Salmonella. We're in the telephone directory and Yellow Pages."*

Spoken speech of any kind should flow smoothly. There can be short, punchy sections, but no abrupt stops and starts. Each sentence should lead on from the previous one, and the words should balance out well. When you are at the lower end of the learning curve in the writing of spoken speech, it's a good idea to read your script into a tape recorder, then play it back. Often you'll hear little imbalances and hiccups which are not apparent on paper. Bearing in mind the fact that commercials have got to be very, very concise and flow smoothly, you can begin to see why writing them is not as easy as it looks. A useful tip, is to write your main message down, not worrying about word lengths (see below). Then, gradually, refine your script and tighten it down, removing all the superfluous words and thoughts. To try to write very concisely right away will result in a stilted, jerky script; by whittling a longer version down to size a little at a time, you should be able to retain the balance and smooth flow that you need.

The last lines of these two examples also flag up another general point about local/regional advertising; addresses and 'phone numbers. Realistically, there is no way you can get viewers/listeners to memorise a 'phone number, or even an address, unless it's very simple. Yet all too often local broadcast ads contain the full address and a choice of telephone numbers. This is a waste of valuable air time. You're far better off getting the viewers/listeners to remember the name, then look up the details; if your selling proposition is strong enough, they will. Strong branding . . . plus, identifying the "promise" with your product/service . . . is essential, especially when your commercial is likely to be surrounded by other commercials also yelling out names. Naturally, you don't want to overdo the product/service name, because this will irritate the audience. And if for some reason you feel you must put some information in about addresses and telephone numbers, keep it as simple as you can.

Word lengths are another point worth mentioning. Most beginners in the commercials writing field over-write by about 200 per cent. Radio and television commercials are normally read at an average speed of one-and-a-half words per second. It doesn't take a degree in mathematics to figure out that this means 45 words in a 30-second slot; no more. Naturally, many people in real life speak somewhat faster than that; most notably horse-race commentators and American auctioneers. Never fall for the temptation to cram as many words as you can into the few seconds you're paying for; more words do not mean more sell. Just as with press ads, where white space around the words can sell as hard as the words themselves, so "air" can around the spoken words of a commercial. A powerful message, delivered in an unhurried, masterful way at the rate of one word per second, is a lot stronger and more memorable than a hysterical voice yakking away without taking a breath.

The last general point on radio and TV commercials is about comedy.

Everyone thinks they can come up with funny lines and ideas, and usually they're right – for themselves. The trouble is, writing lines that will make other people laugh is different; not everyone shares your sense of humour. Writing comedy, like writing children's stories, always seems easy until you try it. In fact, those two writing forms are the most difficult of all to do well. So our advice to you is to avoid comedy in commercials; it's a skilled dramatic craft, and not one you are likely to learn while holding down a full-time job in another discipline.

Copy clearance

In many countries, radio and television commercials have to be cleared by an independent "watchdog" body for ethical, moral and commercial appropriateness, before they are allowed to be transmitted. In theory, the official bodies are just as happy to listen to or look at a finished commercial as they are to read a script, but from your point of view it is madness not to get your commercial cleared at script stage. If the official body should want something changed, you may have to re-record or re-shoot (in the case of television) the whole thing. Always check on copy clearance with the broadcast stations you use (or the production company, if you use one); they will normally arrange for your script to be submitted to the appropriate organisation for approval. You should always allow as much time as possible for this to be done, although these bodies understand the pressures of the business and will usually turn your script around promptly.

RADIO COMMERCIALS

A lot of people – including some professional copywriters – feel that radio is a restrictive medium in creative terms. They believe that it is somewhat one-dimensional, with no pictures to strengthen the selling message. What these people don't realise is that sound need not be one-dimensional. When you listen to radio drama, the lack of pictures can be more than compensated for by the inclusion of sound effects; cleverly used, these can encourage you to form your own images in your mind, and create an atmosphere where you can almost imagine that you're right there, in the thick of the action with the characters. On a much smaller scale, the same is true of radio commercials.

The other great advantage of sound, or rather sound production, is that it is very cheap in comparison to the production of still and moving pictures. Sound effects can be hired literally off the shelf in most good recording studios and radio stations, for a small charge per effect. Such places normally have libraries with hundreds of different effects ready-taped on cartridges, with any sounds from a bumblebee in flight to a Roman chariot race to choose from.

What you must remember, though, is that a cluttered sound track will be detrimental to what you're doing. Don't try to put too much in; use your sound effects to set up the benefit you're selling rather than to underscore words that explain it. Let's see how this can work in practice; first, the cluttered approach . . .

> "*SFX: Crowds walking along street, followed by crack of thunder, then heavy rainfall. Woman cries out angrily. Running feet, rainfall, occasional cracks of thunder. Continue under . . .*
>
> *VOICE OVER: If you get caught in a sudden downpour, there's nothing so irritating as getting soaked . . . especially when you're on your way somewhere important. The answer? A KEEP-DRY pocket umbrella . . . folds up so small you can keep it in your pocket, briefcase or bag. And it unfolds in a few seconds to keep you dry and comfortable . . . whatever the weather. So next time it looks like rain, make sure you've got your KEEP-DRY handy. KEEP-DRY pocket umbrellas . . . for people who like to be home and dry.*"

With all that racket going on, the listeners are going to find the voice over annoying and superfluous. It is better to space all the effects out, and add in a few lines of character dialogue so the story-telling is split between them and the voice over. A continuous droning voice over is sometimes necessary, but extra character voices for radio don't cost a lot more and really help to bring the commercial alive. How about . . .

> "*SFX: Crowds walking along street.*
>
> *SFX: Sudden crack of thunder, followed by heavy rainfall, fade under . . .*
>
> *WOMAN: Oh, my hair! I'll look a mess for my meeting!*
>
> *MAN: Sorry, darling, but my umbrella's so bulky . . . didn't bring it today . . .*
>
> *SFX: Rainfall and crowds walking hurriedly; fade under . . .*
>
> *VOICE OVER: Isn't it time you bought a KEEP-DRY pocket umbrella? Folds up so small you can keep it in your pocket or bag.*

SFX: Rainfall, crowds walking hurriedly, then umbrella being raised and clicked into place. Fade under . . .

DIFFERENT MAN: Here, Marion. Use my Keep-Dry.

WOMAN: Thanks, John. You're always ready for anything . . .

VOICE OVER: KEEP-DRY pocket umbrellas. For people who like to be home and dry.

SFX: Final crack of thunder. "

Of course, sound effects can be very useful to add a little zest to a straight voice over commercial, without added character voices. Let's say you're selling weekend breaks in a country hotel, and you plan to put your commercials out during the drive-in/drive-out periods on weekdays to catch business people on their way to and from work.

"SFX: Traffic jam, engines revving, horns hooting, etc. Fade out under . . .

VOICE OVER: If the city life is getting you down, how about a break this weekend? Here at Restview House, we're doing all-inclusive weekend breaks with swimming, golf, tennis and horse riding nearby, all from just £85 for two nights. Restview House is about an hour's drive from Johntown.

SFX: Fade up traffic jam noises as above.

VOICE OVER: . . . yet a lifetime away from the bustle and crowds.

SFX: Birds singing.

VOICE OVER: Restview House, near Fredtown. Look for our ad in your local paper. "

The last line of that voice over brings us to another relevant point about radio commercials, and what we said earlier about not putting in your entire address, telephone, telex and fax numbers. If you are running press ads at the same time as radio commercials, use them to reinforce the message on radio *and* give listeners the details they need. Remember, all you can realistically expect to do in a radio or television commercial is to get over one main message, and in this case it is the fact that Restview House can give you the peace, quiet and recreation you need. If that message is lodged, interested listeners will either look you up in the telephone book or look for the ad. And even if they don't consciously look for it, the fact that they have heard the commercial will make them take extra notice of it when they come across it.

Radio commercials should be laid out as we've illustrated above.

There are no hard and fast rules; the main objective is to set the script out so that all the interested parties can clearly understand what you intend should happen where. And that leads us neatly into production; not a subject we need to examine in detail in this book, but one which is certainly relevant to writing words that sell, as this is the next step after your writing is done.

Local and regional commercials can be produced in more than one way. For big national campaigns, they are usually done by a specialist production company, of which there are normally several in every major city. There are obvious advantages to this, as your commercial will be made by experts who are very experienced at radio and know how to get the best results, how to "mix" the sound so it works well through small mono or stereo radio speakers. However, these production companies tend to be expensive; worthwhile if you're spending a lot of money on a big radio campaign, but perhaps a little wasteful if you're only running one commercial on one station.

A more efficient, and usually less expensive, way is to ask the radio station to do it for you. Most local radio stations, as we mentioned above, have their own production facilities and will produce the script for you. They will add in all the sound effects, music from a library if you want it, find and direct the character voices and voice over artiste, and so on. You may, of course, be a bit restricted. For an all-in price, you may have to settle for their choice of voice over artiste rather than Lord Olivier, and you may find their sound effects library a little lacking if you want the genuine noise of a charging wildebeest in your commercial. But for the straightforward stuff, the local radio station will normally provide you with good value, and do a very good job.

TELEVISION COMMERCIALS

Once again, it is worth saying that television commercials are usually very expensive to produce and buy air time for. Unless you are very sure of yourself, it's better to leave the creation and production of these to the experts. But, as with radio, many advertisers use television on a local or regional basis with inexpensively produced commercials, which are not national campaigns and therefore don't involve such a major exercise. These are often written and produced by experts, as well, but can safely be tackled by an amateur who knows the basic ways to approach the project.

A typical example of this sort of advertising is the seven/ten/fifteen second "card". The visuals consist of one or two still photographs, with a voice over – usually provided by the television station – saying a few words. Writing the script for commercials like these involves exactly the same techniques as writing for radio, except of course you must be sure that the words work with the visual and that you don't waste precious words on telling viewers what they can already see. Sound effects and music should be kept to a minimum in these ads, because in such a short timespan you want viewers to concentrate on your selling words only. And, as with radio, never try to cram too many words into the slot; a gabbling voice over will lose your impact for you.

Where you use more than one or two visuals, you should reduce the number of words. Many copywriters believe that the more you have to show, the less you should say, and vice versa. Let's say your company, Bridal Gowns Unlimited, is taking some 15-second spots on a local TV station. If you show one picture of a beautiful bridal gown, you need to explain verbally that you've got a whole range to choose from at many different prices and they're all there, waiting for you to try on. If you show five different bridal gowns, you merely need to say that BGU has all you need for your wedding outfit . . . at a price to suit you best. This principle also ties in with the other notion that you never tell viewers what they can already see.

The great benefit of any audio-visual medium, television commercials included, is demonstration. Even if you're using stills, you can use this advantage well. Supposing your company sells second-hand sports cars. If you show a picture of the exterior of your showroom, you're merely showing viewers that your company sells cars. If you show a picture of someone driving a beautiful sports car down a country lane on a sunny day, you're showing viewers a little of how it feels to own one of your products. That's a far more enticing benefit than the fact that they can buy a car in your nice showroom.

Moving pictures are much more complicated, as this involves filming or videotaping which gets expensive. Home movies are definitely out, as the quality of film or tape shot by well-meaning amateurs may look alright as you play it back on your own equipment, but it is guaranteed to look tacky once transmitted over the airwaves. In some countries (UK included), broadcast stations will not transmit film or tape that has not been shot by properly qualified union crews, so amateur productions are just not viable. If you want to go to the expense of commissioning film or tape to use in a television commercial, it is also well worth the expense of doing it properly; a poor job will make your company look amateurish. It is sometimes possible to produce footage or tape for a commercial at the same time as you're shooting a corporate videotape programme, and, provided you warn the production company first, allowances can be made for this and money saved. Just ensure that the corporate production company uses union crews and post-production (in the UK and other countries where such rulings apply), otherwise your commercial may not be cleared for transmission. The creative team at the production company will also be able to write a good script for the commercial, or help you to do so.

There really is very little we can add to this section on television commercials, because all the basic principles have been explained in the sections on press ads and radio commercials. This is, of course, based on the assumption that most readers are likely to use television advertising in the context of simple visuals and voice over narration. Commercials involving dialogue are a bit different; we cover the ways in which to approach dialogue in the chapter on video and audio-visual scripts. As you can imagine, writing dialogue for television involves very concise, brief lines that get straight to the point. You have no time to set up your character; he or she must identify him/herself immediately. That is one of the reasons why many characters in dramatised commercials seem so stereotyped; the house-wife, the new housewife who is also a career person, the smooth young business executive, the sophisticated girl-about-town. What they say has got to be very direct; just as there's no time for you to establish the character within the dramatic framework, there's no time for the character to do it either. Dramatised commercials are also known by some copywriters as "slice of life" . . . but the cynics might also say that they are the thin end of the dramatic wedge.

If you want to try your hand at dialogue for commercials, the best way to start is by watching other people's television ads. Listen carefully to the words the characters speak, and take careful note of the circumstances in which they say them.

Sometimes, characters don't say anything at all; they just act out a short scene, with music and/or sound effects behind, and convey it all through action. Ironically enough, this sort of script must still be "written"; you, the writer, have to determine exactly what character does what when, and where. Of course, you must bear in mind that any filming or taping that involves dialogue will naturally involve actors, the actors must be directed by a good director. All this adds up to extra expense.

But let's look at the prospect on a local/regional basis, and see what we can do with those second-hand sports cars, using a simple location and two actors. (Note script layout for commercials; pictures in the left-hand column, sound in the right-hand column.) First, an example of bad, lumpy, unemotive, low-sell, dialogue . . .

VISION	SOUND
Long shot of bright red sports car coming towards camera. Car pulls up near camera, stops. Two men get out and lean on car, patting it appreciatively.	SFX: Engine noise.
	MAN 1: I like this car. I think I'll buy it. What did you say the terms were when you buy a car at Honest Ed's Motors?
	MAN 2: Only ten per cent down and then easy repayments over three years, Sir.
	MAN 1: Sally, my wife, will love it. Of course, she'll be impressed by the economy of the payments.
	MAN 2: At Honest Ed's Motors, we try to pelase everyone, Sir. So, you'll take it?
	MAN 1: Yes.
	MAN 2: If we go back to the showroom now, I'll draw up the papers.
	MAN 1: Good, Shall we go?
The two men get in the car and drive off past the camera. We superimpose the name and logo.	VOICE OVER: Honest Ed's Motors. Sports cars that please everyone. "

The benefits are woolly and ill-defined; no real people would actually speak like that in real life, and the whole script lacks selling power. Let's try again, with the same budget but a different approach, better dialogue, and a touch of gentle humour . . .

"VISION	SOUND
We open with a close-up of a man in the driver's seat of a sports car. We gather he is driving fast along a country lane, as he is concentrating hard, changing gear, turning the steering wheel, etc.	SFX: engine revving, changing gear, etc.
	MAN 1: (TO HIMSELF) Nothing like a spin on the open road! Hope Sally'll like it . . . wonder how much it'll cost?

The camera pulls back to reveal that he isn't on the road, but in the showroom. A grinning salesman walks over to him . . . he's still half in his dream world.

MAN 2: *All Honest Ed's sports cars are just ten per cent down, with easy repayments over three years, Sir. And I'm sure Sally'll love it.*

The customer in the car looks at the salesman, bemused at first, then smiles sheepishly.

SFX: *Fade out*

MAN 1: *I'll take it!*
MAN 2: *But wouldn't you like to take it for a test drive first?*
MAN 1: *(THOUGHTFULLY) I already have . . . (REALIS-ING) Oh. Good idea! (LAUGHS).*

The salesman gets in the car, and smiles at him. The camera pulls back even further, to show doors open beyond the car. The engine starts up with a healthy roar, and they drive off. Name and address of company superimposed.

VOICE OVER: *Honest Ed's Motors. Used sports cars that bring back your dreams without breaking the bank.*

Both scripts would be relatively inexpensive to make, involving one day's shooting on location with the two actors, assuming that Honest Ed provides the vehicle. In the second version, we still get over the main selling points, but promote the benefit much more heavily. The benefit in this case is that one of Honest Ed's sports cars can make you feel good about driving again, without costing you a fortune. By showing how the dream can come alive for the customer, we are saying, indirectly, that you the viewer will feel just as good as the character in the commercial. Another great advantage of moving pictures in an advertising context is that you can get viewers to identify with the characters . . . empathising with them, wishing they could feel the same way, or sympathising with the problem they have . . . which is then solved by your product/service. It's possible to do this with illustrations in press ads, too, but in a rather more artificial way. Television is a voyeuristic medium, as we see with some of the more successful soap operas which allow us into the boardrooms and boudoirs of all sorts of intriguing people. Commercials can do the same, although only as moving snapshots.

Essentially, writing dialogue should be approached in the same way as writing voice over narration. And that is by writing down the entire playlet that you have dreamt up, irrespective of how long it is. The chances are that even if you try to aim for, say, 30 seconds, you'll have written about 60. It takes years of practice before you can write a first draft that is about the right length. So, then set about paring your script down, removing not so much unnecessary words as unnecessary *thoughts;* natural-sounding dialogue can't get away with being as verbally economical as voice over narration. People use *ums, ers, buts, wells, ands, maybes,* and so on as links in natural conversation and it is important to keep such links in your dialogue. Voice over sections don't need to have all these conversational links, but narration is a different style to that of dialogue. Narration should flow well but viewers don't expect narration to sound like something the bus conductor would say. They expect narration to be informative, crisp and, in the case of commercials, hard-selling, without the personalised nuances of natural speech.

CHAPTER 8

SELLING DIRECT:

Direct marketing

DIRECT MARKETING

Direct marketing is probably the most intensive form of promotional writing, because in some ways it is the closest you're ever likely to get to your potential customer without physically standing next to him or her. Direct marketing is the easiest and most accurate type of advertising to monitor, because you know within a short time how successful it has been by the number of orders you receive.

With general, media advertising, you try so far as is possible to speak to your audience in a personal, direct way. But with direct marketing, it is one to one; just you, the potential customer, and the piece of paper that acts as the vehicle between you. Because direct marketing and especially direct mail is much more accurately targeted than general advertising, you can get to know your audience much better beforehand. Unlike the research you do for general advertising, where you have to loosely define the different groups of people who are likely to be interested in your product, with direct mail you already know who those people are. This is because the list of names to whom a direct mail piece will be sent is, or should be, decided upon before you start writing anything. With mail order, it is not so much the audience that is easy to define (you may even advertise in the same publications as you would with a general advertisement); it's more a case that you need to put up a very definable flag for readers, so they know exactly what you're selling very quickly, and are drawn into the ad. Mail order advertising is also very much more price-orientated, because you are asking people to cough up money and buy your product *now*, by mail, rather than suggesting they might like to try it next time they're out shopping. Although many purists would argue that price is a feature, not a benefit, a good price is definitely a benefit ... or at least you can turn it into one.

Direct marketing of any kind has to be very hard sell, in comparison with general mass-media consumer advertising. Everything hinges on getting the reader to fill in the coupon, write out the cheque or credit card number, and send it all off. (Some direct marketing just gets the reader to send off for more information. But because that implies a reasonable degree of commitment on the part of the reader, even without paying any money, you need to sell just as hard.)

Another point about direct marketing that leads on from the earlier ones is that because you are asking people to get involved in the purchasing process now rather than sometime later, you need to tell them everything they need to know now. Naturally, you lead off with a main benefit or group of benefits, just as you do with general advertising. But with a product or service that they can physically go and inspect in a shop or office building, they can learn all the details they need to know, by themselves, before making a purchase. With direct marketing, they can't go and touch and feel; all they have to make their decision on is the illustration, and the words you write. So you have got to tell them rather more than you would in a general ad. This means longer copy, and more developed ideas.

So, what special qualities do you need to write good direct marketing copy? John Yates, one of the UK's most experienced direct marketing and direct mail writers, has this to say ...

> The most important quality is a strong selling sense. People either have a selling flair in them or not. I have always told young writers, when they've said they want to be copywriters: How do you feel about selling? Could you go out and sell? Because all you are as a copywriter is a salesperson in print. I've said that for a lifetime and I believe in it one hundred per cent.
> ... If you're a writer in the direct marketing business, you've got to love selling ... you've got to have it in your blood. You've got to get up in the morning and feel the enthusiasm which is absolutely essential ... you've got to be able to quickly look at a product and see its sales points, and be able to put those points across in good selling copy.

And that's it in a nutshell; writing copy for direct marketing is almost like a written version of a face-to-face sales pitch. If a salesperson makes a cold call, he or she is likely to follow a pattern of selling that starts by outlining the main benefits, reinforces those with some good hard back-up information, fills in with additional features described in terms of their benefits, and ends by attempting to close the sale ... to get the customer to say 'yes'. Direct marketing copy has to follow the same pattern, and close the sale by persuading the prospect to take action immediately.

DIRECT MAIL: SELLING THROUGH THE POST

In most industrialised countries, direct mail is the third largest advertising medium, after press and television. In the UK alone, the most recent figure of money spent on direct mail advertising, quoted by the Post Office, at over £500m per annum. In Britain, the Post Office says that over one-and-a-half billion pieces of promotional material are sent through the mail every year. This averages out at six items per month for every British household. (In Switzerland, the volume of direct mail shots going through the doors of every home is four times that of Britain.)

Now, £500m worth of advertisers in Britain alone can't be wrong; direct mail works. It is also remarkably cost-effective, not only because you can monitor your success very accurately, but also because it is cheap to produce in relation to the coverage you get; it's a case of design, print and postage as against let's say film production and television air time. The other great way in which direct mail gives you good value is that there is far less wastage; with press and television advertising, even by choosing the right publications for press ads and the right times of day for radio and TV, there will still be a large percentage of the audience not in the least bit likely to want to know about your product/service. This is probably because they're the wrong age, the wrong gender, the wrong professional or socio-economic group, or whatever. With direct mail, the selection and compilation of mailing lists has become a respected skill, and for good reason. A well-prepared mailing list ... up-to-date, with every name in the right socio-economic, professional, gender, age and whatever other type of group that's most likely to want your product/service ... will give you a far higher percentage of genuinely interested parties.

In the chapters on general advertising, we say that you should get to know your audience before you write to them. In the majority of cases it is more a case of getting to know who they are. With direct mail, you already know who they are because they have been identified in the list. Now, because you want them to commit themselves far sooner to your product/service than they would with general advertising, you need to get to know them very well indeed. This then allows you to position your product or service in a way that strikes a chord with their own special requirements. John Yates again ...

> If you're selling a dental tool, you have to understand the basics of dentistry, so at least you understand what the dentist is looking for. Is he/she looking for something that's going to save time? Is it something that's going to make the job easier? Is it just cost-effectiveness? No, it's going to be a lot of other things as well to do with his/her job,

and you must apply that premise to every single profile and every single target that you write to, before you write a word of copy. You've got to get inside them ... imagine you're standing next to them in a pub talking to them.

Of course for copywriters like John Yates, who write direct marketing and direct mail advertising on a hundred or more different products every year, the research phase is a bit different to that of someone in industry who only has one product or range of products to sell. If you're selling dental tools, for example, the chances are that you'll already know a great deal about dentists' needs without having to undertake the research that a professional copywriter would. But that only applies to readers of this book who work in specialised market places. If you're selling a diverse range of products by direct mail you will need to become familiar with everyone who is likely to be interested in the range, however diverse it is. And there will be variations according to the nature of your offer, regardless of the fact that the product is the same. Say you sell cars. The customers and contacts on your mailing list will be fairly wide and varied. And an offer you make via direct mail, offering a discount on new cars purchased before a given date, will attract a different group of potential customers to that which would be attracted by the announcement of a new model; so you've got to fully understand the differing needs of each target group.

Another point which you have to consider is the circumstances in which your target audience will receive a mailshot. Will you send it to their offices, or to their homes? People who receive a mailshot in their offices will have very little time to devote to reading it. They will only read it at all if it grabs their attention very quickly, and then reveals "what's in it for them" very quickly, too. The whole message has to be very concise, and get them to the action at the end in as short a time as is reasonable.

Mailshots sent to people's homes are a slightly different story. In the home environment, there isn't the pressure on people to read and absorb as quickly; they can read through a longer mailshot at their leisure, over breakfast, or in the evening. But because the home mail-reading environment has its distractions, like television, newspapers, housework, children, letters from Auntie Maud and so on, your mailshot has to be more entertaining in nature. Here, you need to use illustrations, good pictures of the product/service you're selling, and lead the reader through the (longer) copy in an interesting and inspiring way. Once you've hooked the reader's attention, you can take your time – within reason – to tell them everything worth knowing about what you're selling, provided your copy is lively enough and interesting enough to hold their attention right to the end.

Planning direct mail

With press ads or commercials, most people agree that one insertion or one spot on radio or television is inadequate, if you want to get your message over effectively. With general media advertising, you can repeat the same ad or commercial a number of times, on the assumption that you'll catch people who haven't seen or heard it before, and that those who have will be reminded of your message. Many advertisers, and especially those embarking on a major advertising campaign, will also do a series of ads or commercials, so that there is some variety in the campaign. These will either look at the main selling benefit in three or four different ways, or will each concentrate on a different benefit perhaps targeted at one specific segment of the market. But for the advertiser running a small campaign, one press ad/or one commercial repeated, say, ten times, can be very effective, as the message is sufficiently general for the repetition to serve as reinforcement.

With direct mail, however, your message is not (or should not be) general. In addition, each mailshot received by the reader is far more likely to be read thoroughly than one insertion of a press ad is to be read, or one broadcast commercial is to be fully absorbed. Yet one mailshot on its own is not going to achieve as good results as a number of mailshots. So, the most effective way to get the best out of a low-budget direct mail exercise, is to use a campaign consisting of at least two mailshots; ideally, three. And all three must be different, phrased as if the reader has already taken notice of the previous pieces, while at the same time reiterating the main selling points.

Here's how John Yates approaches a three-shot direct mail campaign:

> The first shot could well be what I call an impact piece of some kind, which really does knock people for six and give them facts they need to know. Not all the facts, though, because the idea of direct mail is that you put the bait on the hook but don't tell people everything ... What you have to do is tell them enough to excite them enough to fill in a card, or telephone you to get a salesperson round there quickly.
>
> The impact piece should put the story over in a very dramatic way. Also, you should give a strong offer, because an offer is vitally important to direct mail. It's often the offer that gets people to pull out a pen or reach for the telephone and without it, you're going to be a dead duck.
>
> Shot two can then be a smaller piece which is a reminder mailing; possibly an illustrated sales letter. I've believed in illustrated sales

letters for a lifetime and I'm still getting fantastic results now. People make the mistake of sending a mailshot out on their own house stationery year after year, and wonder why they're not getting terribly good results. If you dramatise your message by using an illustrated heading, and bring your company name down to the base of the letter, you'll find that very much more effective.

Shot three can be something like a giant "telegram", a short, sharp impact piece, or another illustrated letter of a different type. The third shot should repeat the main points you made in your first impact piece, possibly bringing in a different or altered offer, which has got a freshness about it.

An offer, by the way, is a kind of secondary hook to get readers to purchase. If you're selling an expensive coffee table book, for example, your mailshot will be about the book – and the offer might be a free personal organiser, calculator, or other similar product that readers get if they send off for the book within seven or fourteen days. The offer is normally introduced towards the end of a mailshot, to add impetus and a "sting in the tail".

Writing for direct mail

One of the most important things to remember about direct mail is that in many ways it is an invasion of the reader's privacy. You, as the advertiser in the mailshot, have inveigled your way into the reader's home or office, so you have to be very quick in putting over why the reader should not throw your mailshot straight into the wastepaper basket. With press or broadcast advertising, you can afford to be more subtle; there, the reader/viewer/listener has actually got a choice whether to take notice of you or not. And human nature being what it is, the fact that there is a choice is likely to lessen any hostility someone might feel at being "advertised to". With direct mail, however, there is a potential hostility which must be overcome at all costs within the first couple of lines.

Most readers will recall the vast number of mailshots you see which are covered in blaring headlines and crossheads, screaming messages and pictures, all of which make you wonder what on earth the mailshot is trying to sell you. Often, you have to search all the way through the documents before you discover what the deal is. If, that is, you have the patience. The vast majority of readers will not bother to search very far, but consign your expensive literature to the bin before they even know what you're selling. They will only read on through the literature if they already have a good idea, and are interested in it.

So, the most important criterion in any direct mail exercise is to make your message known right away, and make it clear. John Yates agrees ...

Imagine if somebody writes to you and they send you a straightforward offer and it grabs you in the first sentence with "How would you like a free holiday in Bermuda?" or whatever ... "all you've got to do is tick this card". That's telling them good and telling them quick, and I still believe that clarity is the keynote of good communication in direct mail. People today are living in an even more complex world than 20 years ago; they are moving faster, they haven't got time, and therefore good direct mail must be clear and simple, quickly and easily understood. People want to know what you're selling; what's in it for me.

So, having established that your message – in the form of the "what's in it for you" element – must be made clear right at the beginning, what are the main guidelines to writing good direct mail?

Assuming that virtually all direct mailshots include a letter, and that the letter is the most important part as it usually gets read first, let's concentrate on that. Other pieces included in a mailshot are likely to be in the form of brochures, leaflets and fold-out documents, which are covered in the general advertising and brochure chapters. Sales letters, as they're called, are letters just like any other; personal communications between you and the recipient. The one main difference between sales letters and personal letters, though, is the role you play. In a personal letter, you write in your own style about what you want to say; in a sales letter your focus is totally on the recipient, and you write in the style that he or she will identify with most readily – regardless of your own personal style. Because of this, your style will vary according to who is going to receive the letter. If you're writing to a householder, you will speak in a relaxed and amiable way, or as John Yates puts it, *"as if you were standing next to him or her in a pub"*. If you're talking to a doctor or company chairperson, though, your style will be more formal. More of that later.

Staying with the "average" person – for example a housholder – for the moment, though, here is some more useful advice from John Yates ...

> A sales letter should be short, with short sentences and short words. I don't mean staccato style all the way through; you should change your style. For instance if you have a couple of short sentences, then you should put a longer sentence, with a bit of balance and variety to it. Always create variety and tempo but generally speaking, keep to the point ... people do not like long and boring letters ... they like to be spoken to in the way that a friendly person in a store might talk to them. Remember that we are all warm, and we are all human ... therefore communication in letters should be warm, in a style that is friendly without being too friendly.

Another important point to remember is that you need, in your first line, to show the reader that you are in sympathy with his or her needs. If you can attract their sympathy right away, you will encourage them to read on. Naturally, you don't want to say anything that is hard to believe, or that smells of an advertising cliché; merely to put over a simple statement that suggests you've done your homework and understand what their requirements are.

That brings us to yet another point; the "you" angle. The reader, much as he or she may be a nice person, doesn't really care much about you or your company. So starting a letter with "we", or dwelling on "we" in any way other than one in which there is a direct benefit to the reader, will kill your mailshot. John Yates agrees ...

> The most important thing to remember above anything else in my opinion is the "you" angle. It's an old cliché, old hat, and it's been mentioned so many times that it's got hairs on it ... but it really does amaze me even today that companies seem to forget that nobody is interested in their company or how long they've been going. So starting copy with "we" is an absolute killer. You've got to translate everything in terms of "what's in it for me". You must start your letter with "you", and keep the "'you" angle right the way through it. The "we can do this, we can do that", is a dead duck; a complete switch-off ... no one is interested.

The final main point to remember about writing sales letters is, that you should not let the facts get lost or concealed by selling language. This may sound ridiculously obvious; but even in some very expensively produced, widely circulated mailshots you have to look pretty hard before you'll find any hard facts. Readers aren't stupid; they're not going to be interested in your product or service unless a) they know precisely "what's in it for them" right at the beginning, and b) why that's in it for them. The only believable way in which to answer the "why" part is to tell the truth, and tell it straight, with facts that readers can latch on to. In a way, the selling part acts as a vehicle to take readers from the facts in isolation, to how those facts will be of benefit to them.

Combining these four points – choosing the correct style, getting the reader on your side by showing that you're on his or hers, concentrating on "you" rather than "we", and giving them facts – let's have a look at an example. Suppose you're launching a new window cleaning service in your area, and you want to mail local householders.

The first criterion is to forget about all the things you're paid to think about. The fact that you've got twenty window cleaners in bright new T-shirts carrying brand-new equipment and driving around in brand-new vehicles may be very important to you, if only because it has cost you a lot of money. But those facts are of no interest whatsoever to your readers. The only way in which they may be of relevance to them, is as a substantiation of what they're really going to be interested

in; a good, reliable, cost-effective service. That's what's in it for them.
Let's start with the wrong way of writing to a householder

> *"Dear Sir,*
> *We are proud to announce the new See-Through window cleaning*
> *service in the XXXtown area. Our 20-strong team of cleaners has*
> *been fully trained to ensure an efficient and thorough service to*
> *householders, at very attractive, cost-effective rates.*
>
> *We also offer discounts to groups of ten or more households wishing to*
> *have their windows cleaned at the same time. Further details of this*
> *discount facility are available on request.*
>
> *If you would like more information on the new See-Through window*
> *cleaning service, please contact our offices.*
>
> *Yours faithfully,*
>
> *I. Glass*
> *Chairman"*

Not exactly going to set the world on fire, is it? And it's certainly not
going to get much interest, unless someone's windows are so dirty that
they can't see through them at all and they're incapable of cleaning
them themselves. Let's look at the goofs in detail

> *Dear Sir,* (First mistake. Quite a few householders are women.
> This is also too formal an address for householders; it's OK for
> a sales letter to business/professional readers, but could hardly
> be considered friendly.)
>
> *We are proud to announce the new See-Through window cleaning*
> *service in XXXtown area.* (Wrong again. You may be proud to
> announce it, but to say so sounds old-fashioned and corny.
> The reader doesn't care if you're proud about it or not.
> Remember, the reader doesn't even care about you.) *Our*
> *20-strong team of cleaners has been fully trained to ensure an efficient*
> *and thorough service to householders.* (How many cleaners does it
> take to do one house-full of windows, unless you're talking
> about Buckingham Palace? One? Two? To tell householders
> that you've got a team of 20 trained cleaners will make them
> think they've got to pay a fortune for the service) *at very*
> *attractive, cost-effective rates.* (Nonsense, says the reader. Cost-
> effective is what businesses talk about when they're trying to

justify high prices. I only react to facts; how much would an average three-bedroomed home cost?)

We also offer discount to groups of ten or more households wishing to have their windows cleaned at the same time. (Fine. But the way this is phrased it could be meant for groups of householders in Zimbabwe. What about me and my neighbours?) *Further details of this discount facility are available on request.* (You'll tell me about the rates if I ask you nicely. Am I not important enough to merit a bit more information now? Where are the facts?)

If you (Aha! You remembered; you are writing to me after all!) *would like more information on the new See-Through window cleaning service, please contact our offices.* (Here we go again; why should I? Who, at your offices? The canteen manager? I feel as much like contacting your offices as putting my head in a gas oven. If you want me to buy from you, you could at least make it easy for me.)
Yours faithfully,

I. Glass
Chairman (Gosh. A real chairman, writing to me? What does he or she know about cleaning a few grubby windows in a townhouse? Don't you have a sales manager? Or a customer relations manager?)

Let's try to write the letter in a way that's going to arouse interest and new business leads.

Dear Householder,
A CLEAN, CLEAR VIEW FROM YOUR WINDOWS ... AT A COST THAT CLEARLY MAKES SENSE ... FROM SEE-THROUGH WINDOW CLEANERS.

Window-cleaning can be a time-consuming chore for you ... messy, dirty, and even dangerous. Paying someone else to do it can help; but can you always rely on them to turn up regularly?

Now, though, you can leave the problem of window-cleaning to us. See-Through window cleaners have just set up a new, professional service in your area ... to clean your windows as often as you want, on a regular basis. All you have to do is tell us how often you want your windows cleaned ... once a fortnight, once a month, or whenever ... and one of our fully trained cleaners will be there, every time you say.

And you don't pay more because we're professional. An average three bedroomed home costs just £X.00; a terraced, three storey town house around £Y.00.

GET TOGETHER WITH YOUR NEIGHBOURS AND BRING THE COST DOWN EVEN MORE!

Talk to your neighbours about See-Through window cleaners ... and get together to have your windows cleaned. For ten or more homes, on a regular basis, we'll give you a discount of 20% each – that's only £Z.00 for an average three bedroomed home. Twenty homes or more get a massive 50% discount each; an even more worthwhile saving!

LET US GIVE YOU A FREE QUOTATION ...

Let us show you how economical it can be to have your windows cleaned professionally by See-Through. Just mark and post the enclosed reply-paid card, and one of our representatives will call at your home within the next few days to give you a free, no-obligation quotation.

And – if you want your windows cleaned right away, call our customer service department on our quick service number. We'll send one of our trained cleaners to your home within 24 hours.

Let See-Through give you a consistently cleaner, clearer view from your windows ... at a cost that clearly makes sense!

Yours faithfully,

CLARITY GLASS
Customer Service Manager

The letter is longer, because you can't expect readers to pick up telephones or send off cards unless they know enough about your product/service. However, it contains a headline and two crossheads, so the overall message can be seen at one quick glance. And the style is crisp, without long, boring sentences and long words ... friendly and conversational, without being overly familiar. The offer of a free, no-obligation estimate is towards the end to give readers an extra nudge. Although we can assume that a mailshot like this would be run on a fairly low budget, it would be worth commissioning someone to produce a small illustration – a cartoon, say – to illuminate the headline and make it more appealing. The company name should go at the top of the letter, near the illustration and the headline, and the address and telephone numbers should go at the bottom, in a prominent typeface.

The reply-paid card should be simple:

> *YES! I am interested in having my windows professionally cleaned by See-Through.*
> _____ *Please ask your trained representative to call at my home in the next few days.*
> _____ *Please telephone me and tell me more.*
>
> *NAME:* _____
> *ADDRESS:* _____
> _____
> _____
> *TELEPHONE NUMBER: (day)* _____ *(home)* _____
> *TYPE OF HOME: (Please tick)*
> *large detached* _____ *small detached* _____ *semi-detached* _____ *terraced* _____ *flat* _____ *maisonette* _____
> *other* _____

Another good idea would be to include a separate card which readers could keep handy, stating See-Through's telephone number. Some readers may not be interested now, but they may have a need for your service in the future. An attractive card that can be propped up on a kitchen shelf or kept in a utility file or drawer might well make you some more sales in the long term. How about this?

> *"WINDOWS DIRTY? CALL THE PROFESSIONALS ON*
> *0123.456789*
> *SEE-THROUGH WINDOW CLEANERS ... FOR CLEAR, CLEAN*
> *WINDOWS AT A COST THAT CLEARLY MAKES SENSE."*

Let's have a look at the letter in detail.

> *"Dear Householder,* (Good. Non-gender specific, and informal without being too friendly. Addresses like 'Dear Friend' or 'Dear Fellow-citizen of XXXtown' are so corny that they make Europeans burst out laughing. Even North Americans, who are usually less cynical but nonetheless street-wise, are unlikely to get a nice warm feeling from addresses like that. On either side of the Atlantic, the only warm feeling corny addresses generate is when readers toss them into the fireplace.)
> *A CLEAN, CLEAR VIEW FROM YOUR WINDOWS ... AT A*

COST THAT CLEARLY MAKES SENSE ... FROM SEE-THROUGH WINDOW CLEANERS. (There's no reason why you can't have a headline in a sales letter. It attracts readers' attention, and focuses their minds on what's to come. This headline gets over the "promise"; what's in it for them. It also outlines the benefit to them of clean windows; at the outset at least, you're not selling clean windows, but what you can see out of clean windows. A suitable illustration will reinforce this benefit. Even if they don't read any more than this, recipients of the letter will remember the name, what you do, and what's in it for them. This could even have useful implications if you're advertising elsewhere – in the press or on local radio, for example. Hearing or seeing the name again will ring a bell with potential customers.)

Window-cleaning can be a time-consuming chore for you ... messy, dirty, and even dangerous. Paying someone else to do it can help; but can you always rely on them to turn up regularly? (Here, you're setting up the problem ... using the you angle to tell readers that you understand their view of window cleaning. It shows that you've done your homework, and that you sympathise with them. It's fairly factual, because you don't want to exaggerate or dramatise the issue; that lacks credibility and will affect your upcoming sales message.)

Now, though, you can leave the problem of window-cleaning to us. See-Through window cleaners have just set up a new, professional service in your area ... to clean your windows as often as you want, on a regular basis. All you have to do is tell us how often you want your windows cleaned ... once a fortnight, once a month, or whenever ... and one of our fully-trained cleaners will be there, every time you say. (This puts some meat on the bones of what's in it for them, still featuring the "you angle" very heavily. Your own selling points, e.g. the trained cleaners, your professionalism, etc, – are turned to the benefit of the reader.)

And you don't pay more because we're professional. An average three-bedroomed home costs just £X.00; a terraced, three storey town house around £Y.00. (Double hit, here. You reinforce the fact that you're professional, and by implication better than the student who cleans windows between lectures and disco outings. You also give some hard facts to substantiate your claim that your service represents good value; merely saying that prices are low isn't enough. People are smart enough to know that the advertiser's idea of a low price probably isn't the same as theirs.)

GET TOGETHER WITH YOUR NEIGHBOURS AND BRING THE COST DOWN EVEN MORE! (The first crosshead to underline this major selling point. Note you should say "bring the cost down even more", not "bring the cost down". If you don't add the "even more", readers will think the cost was very high to start with. Also, we're using action verbs; much more compelling than if you were to say "big discounts for ten homes or more".)

Talk to your neighbours about See-Through window cleaners ... and get together to have your windows cleaned. For ten or more homes, on a regular basis, we'll give you a discount of 20% each – that's only £Z.00 for an average three-bedroomed home. Twenty homes or more get a massive 50% discount each; an even more worthwhile saving! (More substantiation, more facts. In the first example, it's worth working the individual cost out to make the point quickly. With the second example of 50% off, most people know that means half price so you don't need to rub their noses in it.)

LET US GIVE YOU A FREE QUOTATION ... (Here comes the offer, and the action bit; what you want them to do. You want to make the next step as easy and attractive as possible, and getting a representative in there to give a quotation will also help you to sell the whole service. Although some managers might groan at the thought of spending valuable sales time on hundreds of free quotes, realistically speaking most of the readers who send off the card will be interested enough to try the service at least once. Again, in this crosshead we've used the "you angle" more interesting to the reader than "Free quotation".)

Let us show you how economical it can be to have your windows cleaned professionally by See-Through. Just mark and post the enclosed reply-paid card, and one of our representatives will call at your home within the next few days to give you a free, no-obligation quotation. (A substantiation of the offer and what you want them to do next.)

And if you want your windows cleaned right away, call our customer service department on our quick service number. We'll send one of our trained cleaners to your home within 24 hours. (Don't forget there might be quite a few people who do want to act right away. Make this easy and attractive for them, too. And make sure the quick service number is stated loud and clear on the letter.)

Let See-Through give you a consistently cleaner, clearer view from

your windows ... at a cost that clearly makes sense! (A final recap on the main message, reminding readers of the benefit attached. We've also added "consistently", because that recaps on the secondary selling point of having your windows cleaned on a regular basis.)
Yours faithfully,

CLARITY GLASS
Customer Service Manager (A real person, who sounds like a logical person to write to you. She's "management", so she should know what she's talking about, but she's not so high up in the clouds that she can't identify with what it's like to live in an average three-bedroomed home with dirty windows.)

Business-to-business sales letters

If you compare a business sales letter with a consumer equivalent, the two will look superficially quite different. But the basic ingredients are the same; choosing the correct style, identifying with the reader and his/her needs, concentrating on the "you angle", and dealing in facts. Using the analogy of a film, the characters and locations change but the plot remains the same.

The style of a business sales letter must not be friendly; cordial is a better word, if a rather old-fashioned one. Business people would not accept a buddy-buddy sales pitch from a live sales person in their office, because they would find it disrespectful and irritating. A sales letter is, in effect, a written sales pitch. If you want guidance on the tone you should use for a sales letter, go and speak to the best sales representative in your organisation (assuming the subject of the mailshot is one he or she knows about) and get that person to do a "live pitch" to you. You'll soon pick up ideas on how to translate that into selling copy.

Long words aren't so much of a problem, provided they are easily identifiable to the reader, and provided they're the best way of expressing that thought or fact. Obviously you'll need to research the reader's needs, and have an understanding of his or her problems – although to talk about problems is usually unwise, because even if business readers genuinely have a problem they don't particularly want to be reminded of it. A positive approach – that is, meeting needs or providing improvements, not solving problems – is much more successful.

The "you angle" remains exactly the same, no matter what type of sales letter you're writing. In a business sales letter, you may talk about "you and your company" or "you and your colleagues", rather more than you do about "you", the individual, but the concept is identical.

The importance of facts is even more acute in this type of writing than it is in consumer communications, because of the short time you have in which to convey your message. Earlier in this chapter we talked about the difference between the environments in which sales letters are received – business and domestic. When you mail people at home, the chances are that they will have more time to read a rather longer mailshot. However the business reader probably doesn't have more than a couple of minutes to spare – and that's assuming he/she has been grabbed by a good "promise" so early on in the letter that he/she doesn't throw it away after ten seconds. So the business sales letter has got to be short and to the point, with the minimum of sales padding. If your facts are good, state them clearly, succinctly and positively, and then let them speak for themselves.

With a business-to-business mailshot, it is a good idea to enclose a separate document which describes your product or service in detail. This allows the reader to get the overall message very quickly, and then go back to the other document – usually a brochure – later, when he or she has more time. In effect, the sales letter is seen as a "covering letter" to accompany the document, and should just highlight the main "promise" – the "what's in it for me" – the offer, if there is one, plus any other special or tailor-made information that's not included in the general copy of the other document. So, if you were mailing companies about a new service, your letter might begin by putting over the benefits of that service in the first half, then conclude by telling readers about a special introductory offer, with a discount for new customers signing contracts within X weeks. There should always be clear instructions at the end of the letter as to what to do next. There should be a prominent telephone number, with a real person's name to contact, and a reply-paid card that will act as the invitation for your representative to call. Realistically, you don't make many direct sales as a result of a mailshot campaign; what you do is *"put the bait on the hook"*, as John Yates says. If all your mailshot or series of mailshots achieves is to get the reader to send off the card, you've succeeded; you can then hand over the next stage of responsibility to the sales person.

To go into another long comparison sequence of the right way and the wrong way of doing business sales letters would be duplication, as most of the points we made in the consumer letter examples are equally relevant here. But there is one point which deserves demonstration, and that is in "business language". (Jargon and style in a general context have been covered earlier in this book.) With a mixture of influences ranging from the letters produced by accountants, lawyers, bank managers, business schools and pompous senior managers who judge the height of their prestige by the length of their words and sentences, a style of "business language" has developed on both sides of the Atlantic. Many aspiring management people assume it is the correct way of approaching most forms of business-to-business communication, including sales letters, and impresses readers with their professionalism.

"Business language" includes all the management-speak clichés, pseudo-computerese, bad punctuation, split infinitives, absent punctuation and meaningless jargon that have ever been invented. Yet you still see it ...

"Dear Sir,
It has come to our attention that there is a growing need within the (reader's) industry for a degree of management expertise and commitment to quality in toilet cleansing that has hitherto not been achieved.

The firm of Bleache, Brush, Scrubbe and Pollish was established in 1403 and has over the years developed a unique methodology in the cleansing of toilets all over the globe with particular concern for companies in an on-going industrial situation. BBSP focuses on providing customers with a quality-assured service with close monitoring of the exponential flush factor which has become a key management concern particularly over the last 200 years since the launch of the market-led porcelain product with user-driven flush system input which has impacted heavily on human resources and cost/profit ratios within the overall industrial scenario.

As a result of major new developments in BBSP's research and development laboratories the BBSP service is poised to launch into a new era of toilet cleansing for industrial-oriented customers allowing users to enjoy a previously inconceivable standard of comfort, hygiene and security of utilisation creating considerable cost savings and increased environmental productivity in the workplace. This exciting new innovation is at the leading edge of toilet technology and will spearhead the way forward of BBSP's upcoming sales thrust program, generating a more user-friendly toilet market environment within the parameters of a fully computerised self-trigger flush situation.

We feel sure that all the major players in the (reader's) industry market sector will be eager to learn more about the challenges and solutions that lie ahead in the toilet cleansing arena and are therefore proud to announce a major international symposium on the subject to be held in the new Conference Centre at Boguecloisette just ten miles south of Paris France in April next year. The symposium will include comprehensive presentations on methodology, R&D seminars, management briefings, an open forum for debate plus of course extensive demonstrations and opportunities for hands-on experience. The symposium will be chaired by none other than Professor I Moustafa Tinkel, the world's foremost authority on total quality assurance in ergonomic toilet design and its computer-aided manufacture. An invitation and speaker list is enclosed for your perusal and an early response is requested as the demand for places at the symposium is considerable at this moment in time.

Thanking you for your attention we remain,

Yours truly,

W.C. Flushing
Chairman and Chief Executive

Need we say more?

Mail order: selling off the page

Drawing the demarcation lines between the different parts of the direct marketing picture is difficult, because there is quite a lot of crossover from one to another. Mail order, in theory, is exactly what it says – ordering by mail. So it is a form of advertising which requests the reader to clip the coupon, fill it in, and send it off with the required amount of money to the advertiser (or place an order over the telephone quoting a credit card number), effectively buying the product there and then. You are literally "selling off the page". Direct mail is often mail order as well, when the reader is given the opportunity to buy the product in this way as the result of receiving a mailshot. But if the mailshot only suggests that the reader marks and posts the card to get more information or request a sales person to call, then strictly speaking that isn't mail order.

All of what we say in the chapter on general media advertising is relevant to mail order. Obviously, though, mail order advertisements are normally restricted to print of one kind or another – usually press ads or direct mail. The one main differentiating factor about mail order ads is that you're trying to get the reader to act immediately, whereas with general press ads you don't necessarily expect them to rush out and buy your product/service there and then; the action you want the reader to take is likely to be spread out over a longer period. The more urgent emphasis needed for mail order should be reflected in the way you write the copy.

One interesting point you'll notice if you look at mail order ads is that they tend to be more feature-orientated than general press ads. This should not be to the detriment of selling benefits, of course; but, if you want readers to buy the product/service, they will need to know all the relevant facts about the product in order to make their decision to purchase. Rather as is the case with direct mail, you should look upon mail order advertising as the written version of a live sales presentation to a customer. This will include benefits plus a description of features. The trouble is that with mail order ads you do not normally have very much space in which to get over all the information. Mailshots are not so much of a problem, particularly in consumer mailings, because you can include a brochure or fold-out piece which gives chapter and verse on the product's benefits, features and everything else. Mail order advertising space is as expensive as any other form of print space, and that explains why many mail order ads are positively crammed with words – advertisers trying to tell readers as much as possible, in as small a space as possible.

Mail order ads also tend to be much more price orientated, especially when they're selling products or services at a relatively low unit cost. It is only when you look at ads selling encyclopaedias or gold jewellery that you'll find the purchase price buried somewhere down at the bottom of the space.

Mail order ads are also much more "hard sell" in nature, because they need to motivate the reader not just to think about buying the product/service but actually to make the decision immediately. Even ads for prestige products like fine porcelain or books sell like crazy in every line of copy, although they don't use such market-stall phrases as *"hurry – order now, while stocks last!"* or *"your special chance to buy this amazing widget cleaner at half price!"*

Naturally, tangible products being sold through mail order should be illustrated in the ad, and the headline should tie in with the illustration. Photographs are far better than drawings, for the obvious reason that they show the product far more like it is in real life than a drawing can. And it's worth investing in some good quality photography for mail order ads, because the better you can make your product look, the more readers are likely to want to buy it.

One major pulling point in mail order ads is *"send no money now"*. This means that readers can send off the coupon duly completed and have the product for a limited time – usually seven to ten days –

before they are billed for the money. This has obvious advantages, particularly in the mail order selling of clothing, shoes, and other items which have to be tried on for correct fit, etc. It also overcomes the disadvantage some readers may perceive in effectively paying for something before they've seen, touched or felt it. Much of the mail order advertising you see in the UK contains this benefit; and if the advertiser doesn't include it nowadays its absence might well be seen as a disadvantage.

In terms of writing the copy of a mail order ad, the only practical advice we can offer you – other than that described in the general advertising chapter – is to write as concisely as possible, while still keeping your copy benefit-led. Let's say you're selling an item of clothing; a long cotton dress. Here are its features ...

- **Original African design**
- **Multi-coloured pattern**
- **100% machine washable cotton**
- **Loose fitting**
- **Available in three sizes**
- **Ten day free approval (send no money now)**
- **Price £20.00**

The space you've booked for the ad is in the colour supplement of a middle-to-upper market national Sunday newspaper, and the size is a half page upright. You have timed the space booking to appear in the spring, when people are beginning to think seriously about their summer holiday. Your first consideration is to show the dress, as it is bright and attractive. You will need to commission colour photography, and hire a model. Rather than just show the dress, though, you should get the photographer to shoot it with a few props; let's say the model holding a long, cool drink in her hand, leaning on a balustrade gazing out over a moonlit evening. (This can all be done with props and lighting in a good photographic studio; you don't have to pay for everyone to fly out to Kenya.) There should be some luscious green plants around the place, too, unless the colour of the plants is likely to clash with the colours of the dress. Although some potential purchasers may be men, buying the dress as a gift for a woman, it is reasonable to assume that the vast majority of interested parties will be women who will actually wear the dress. So you should target your ad at them. The style of the dress is likely to appeal to women over 30, as it is fairly classical in design and not high fashion.

Your headline should now reflect the implied benefit of the sophistication of the dress and its suitability for the jetset life, but at a low, attainable price.

"CAPTURE THE MAGIC OF AN AFRICAN EVENING ... IN PURE, COOL COTTON"

This should be followed by a sub-heading which says,

"FOR JUST £20.00, including P & P."

Body copy should be very tightly written and include all the main selling points, written with benefits in mind.

> *"This 100% machine-washable cotton dress is perfect for warm summer evenings, wherever you are. The lively, bold colours and shapes – an original design especially created for XXXXXX Mail Order Ltd. by African artist YYYYY ZZZZZ – go beautifully with everything ... whatever your mood, whatever the occasion. And you'll feel cool and comfortable in this elegantly flared, unfitted shape.*
> *So order your cool, cotton creation of African magic now ... in plenty of time for those long, lazy summer evenings. Three sizes fit all; small (8–12), medium (14–16), and large (16+)."*

Now, we come to the coupon; a very important element of the mail order ad. This is where all the details of payment should be; and above all else, you must make everything clear. As with every other form of advertising, it's essential to make it easy for the customer to purchase; a complicated or cluttered coupon will encourage readers to turn the page, even if they do quite like your product. If you're going to use the "send no money now" approach, then that should lead your coupon copy; if it is cheque/credit card or telephone ordering, then head it with a line that says something like *"Two easy ways for you to order"*. A line saying *"Ten days free approval"* should also be fairly prominent.

Whatever happens, make sure you set out the ordering procedure in a simple and logical way, not only to encourage readers to go ahead but also to make life easier for your staff who will have to process the order. Where there is a choice of colours and sizes, make these easy to identify, and also allow enough space for readers to fill in the necessary information. Too many mail order coupons assume the reader is capable of reading and writing in miniature and allow ridiculously small amounts of room for the coupon copy and spaces. Presumably, these advertisers want to use as much space as possible to sell the product, and think that the coupon is a necessary evil that can be squashed in a corner somewhere. What they forget is that no matter how much readers may like the product, the coupon is the only means by which a reader can buy it and therefore put money into the advertiser's coffers.

One very strong influencing factor in the way that coupon copy is put together is the law. There are a number of laws governing mail order advertising and sales in most countries, both in terms of the mail order set-up and concerning credit and payment arrangements. Obviously if you're running a mail order business anyway you'll be aware of what you need to do, but for companies using mail order on an incidental basis it is very sensible to check with your lawyer or the local official bodies what the rules are before you write your copy. Just remember that however much legal jargon may be attached to the rules of mail order advertising, you do not normally have to reproduce it verbatim in your ad. It is nearly always possible to write in the necessary disclaimer terms with the "you angle" in mind. Don't forget to do it; remember, every word of a mail order ad must sell.

Mail order catalogues: Descriptive copy

In some ways, a catalogue is like a printed version of a store or shop layout. Just as they are in a store, items in a catalogue are displayed according to their category and importance. There is the disadvantage of the catalogue in that customers can't touch and feel the goods, or try them on. But there are advantages, apart from the obvious ones that apply to catalogue shopping in general. One advantage is that you, the advertiser, can control the way in which readers "shop around" in your catalogue (up to a point), by grouping products together and allocating appropriate space and drama to those you want to sell most of. In a shop or store, customers are free to walk around and look at what they want to see, whether it is displayed on a gondola in the middle of the store or stuck in a corner somewhere.

Another advantage of catalogues is that you can draw customers' attention to what you want them to notice, by including good headlines and copy. Space is at a premium in catalogues as they are usually very expensive to produce and every square centimetre must sell like mad. So body copy should be factual, short, descriptive and lively. Where you can bring in the benefits aspect, though, is in headlines and crossheads, and in the first line or few words of the descriptive copy that accompanies every product story.

Good headlines will serve to flag readers down, and suggest benefits arising from the group of products shown on a page or double-page-spread. For example ...

"The Perfect Christmas Gift for the Teenagers in Your Life"

"Sweaters in Fashion Colours to Keep You Warm and Cosy"

"Enjoy Elegant Swedish Crystal at Sensible British Prices"

"Turn Your Cooking into French Cuisine with These Smart Casseroles"

"Bed Linen You'll Love to Dream In"

... and so on, manage to get over what the products are while working in a benefit or two at the same time. These headlines take up a little more space than the following ...

"Gifts for Teenagers"

"Sweaters in a Choice of Fashion Colours"

"Low-Price Crystal Ware from Sweden"

"French Casseroles"

"A Large Range of Bed Linen"

... but they sell a lot harder, so they're worth the extra space.

Similarly, a few extra "benefit" words can precede descriptive body copy. Although they may increase that block of copy by 10% or so, they reinforce the sales message and lead the reader into the description of the item in a positive frame of mind. Lead-ins like ...

> *"Here's a great way to start your day each morning*! This fully-guaranteed automatic alarm clock wakes you up with lively music – not a harsh buzz. Comes with long-life battery and mains attachment. Price £X.00."

or ...

> *"The skirt every woman dreams of* ... elegant, smooth A-line skirt in 100% machine-washable brushed cotton, with fully adjustable elasticated waistband for added comfort. Comes in pale blue, rose pink, or primrose yellow. Length approximately 36 inches. Sizes 10 to 18. Price £XX.00"

... add a worthwhile bit of extra sparkle to the copy, without cluttering it up unnecessarily. The rest of it in each example is tightly written, stringing all the main features and facts together in a readable way. Obviously, with compact copy like this you can often dispense with verbs and other non-essential parts of speech, but try to vary the style so you're not writing staccato sentences right the way through.

Although the purpose of body copy in catalogues is to inform, you should try not to bore people or bamboozle them with lots of cryptic, one-word sentences, one after another.

Other copy in catalogues takes in the information pages, which tell you how to go about ordering, what the mail order company's total services are, and the all-important order form.

Information pages should be well-written, a main headline across the top of each page or double-page-spread, and crossheadings through the body copy to break it up and lead readers through each section. This way they can glance at the page or spread and know roughly what it's about. If they're only interested in one particular aspect – ordering by telephone, for example – they'll feel much happier if they can go straight to the section with the crosshead *"Order by telephone for even faster service"* than if they have to wade through three columns of other information before they find a reference to it.

Order forms are the *bête-noire* of most mail order organisations selling by catalogue, and it's true to say that trying to design one for a couple of hundred products with different sizes, colours and prices is usually a nightmare. Copywriting skills don't really come into this, but words do; and our recommendation is that, whatever complications you may suffer at your end, *keep the order form simple for the customer to use*. As we mentioned earlier when referring to mail order coupons (which are small order forms), you want to make it as easy as possible for customers to buy your product. A complicated order form with dozens of boxes to tick and code numbers to fill in will put some people off. Remember, in many ways your catalogue is competing with stores and shops; and when you buy something in a shop all you do is go to the counter, produce the item and the money, and within seconds your purchase is wrapped and in your hands.

CHAPTER 9

PLEASE READ OUR BROCHURE:

Brochure writing

BROCHURES: SELLING OR TELLING?

Although every medium we talk about in this book contains words that sell in one way or another, most types of brochure sell in a more subtle way. Small leaflets and "leave behinds", used largely in sales promotion and direct marketing, are really longer versions of print advertisements and should be structured as such. The principles of print ad writing apply equally to these formats; good selling copy, material broken up with strong crossheads that crystallise the main selling points so the reader can grasp the whole message by just reading the crossheads, and so on. That last principle applies in some ways to longer brochures, but these days the brochure has become almost an art form in its own right, and the standard advertising approaches are not necessarily appropriate. Brochure writing and design are specialised disciplines.

There is also something of a dual role which a brochure performs that makes it different from hard-sell advertising material, where your writing must be very direct and focus sharply on the "you" angle. With a brochure, you can afford the luxury of talking rather more about "we" as well. Brochures tend to be read in somewhat less competitive circumstances. Advertisements compete with each other, and with editorial matter; sales promotion leaflets with a thousand other displays in a supermarket; mailshots with personal letters and the telephone bill. These media have precious little time in which to do the selling job. Brochures, particularly if they look prestigious, are likely to be taken more seriously and in comparitive isolation, and consequently have more time in which to do the selling. So the brochure can tell as well as sell; but that's where the difference between brochures and other media ends. However much advantage they might have, brochures must still intrigue the reader and hold his or her attention if their contents are to be absorbed and retained.

Setting the Scene

Here is a striking example of how not to intrigue your readers. The following is taken from a real capabilities brochure – the first line of the first paragraph on the first page ...

> *"All our feeding heads are fitted with telescopic pistons on both lifting and forwarding suckers. The stroke of these "search" suckers can be as much as 47mm giving extremely good tolerance on wavy piles of material."*

These detailed characteristics of the company's search suckers are the first thing the reader encounters. A brief history of the company appears on the final page of the brochure. It concludes with this enigmatic comment ...

> *"To handle the extensive activities of a progressive company, a staff structure has been built within it. Based in London, the company has good access to the world markets for its products. Current expansion of its production facilities are expected to bring about further inroads in foreign markets."*

Apart from some obvious difficulties with grammar, the writing suffers from at least two ailments common to many brochures. First, it adopts a tone and voice that seem to have emerged from some weird notion of what a corporate brochure ought to sound like – grand statements involving structures and global markets coupled with descriptions of minute product details. Second, its purpose in life is poorly defined. Is it a product brochure? Is it a corporate capabilities piece?

The end result leaves the reader puzzled. What do they mean when they say, *"to handle the extensive activities of a progressive company, a staff structure has been built within it"*? It sounds as if, not very long ago, Bob and Bridget were running the show out of their caravan until they hit it big with those searching suckers and had to hire a secretary and a salesperson.

Compare this with the opening of a recent capabilities brochure from a major aerospace organisation.

> *"XXX Aerospace is one of the four largest aerospace groups in the world and, by any technological or commercial criteria, by far the most succesful and influential aerospace group in Europe.*
>
> *Our heritage spans the entire history of aviation from the earliest pioneering years. Today we have an unequalled range of research, design, development and manufacturing programmes and share in collaborative partnerships with industry leaders in over 20 countries."*

This opening quickly locates the reader and delivers some background, and does it all in a highly positive way. It's unfair, perhaps, to compare a huge aerospace concern with a small manufacturer of printing equipment. But there is no reason why their brochure couldn't have begun this way ...

> *"ZX Ltd designs and manufactures computer-controlled paper-feeding devices for the printing industry. In the three years since we were founded, our ability to incorporate electronics into mechanical printing equipment has brought the company rapid growth and expansion.*
>
> *We began with a staff of four. Now we employ over sixty people including designers, machine tool operators, computer programmers, managers and sales staff.*
>
> *We will continue to focus on the specialised paper-feeding market whilst adding new capabilities to provide a broader range of services to our customers."*

The lesson of this example is that a brochure reveals a great deal about a company, but not always what you, as the writer, may think you're revealing. How you say what you say, what you don't say, how what you say looks – are all as important as the actual printed words.

Most readers today have seen enough corporate literature to distinguish instinctively the professionally produced, well-designed brochure from the awkward and amateurish. When expense is an issue, it is better to produce a simple leaflet of just a few pages – and do it well – than to attempt something more grandiose without enough resources. That can only result in a hotch-potch of writing, photography, graphics and objectives.

THE PRIMARY BROCHURE VARIETIES

To avoid getting this embarrassing and potentially expensive egg on your corporate face, you need to determine just what your brochure is about.

Annual Report and Accounts. Publicly traded companies are required to issue an annual report and accounts. The accounts are there for the benefit of shareholders who have an understandably strong interest in how their investment is doing. The report is there to present the management's view of the important events and trends of the year past. Many corporate managers consider these documents to be the most unread pieces of writing ever produced. Unread or not, however, they're produced regularly and much care and resource is lavished upon them.

Some privately held companies also issue annual reports although they're not required to do so. These are usually intended to be digested by financial and industrial analysts, customers and the company's employees.

Next to advertising, writing an annual report is perhaps the purest form of corporate good news delivery. The report must always convince the reader that – even when times are tough – everything is under control. There may be "disappointments" or "changes of direction" or "shortfalls" but there are never "mistakes" or "problems" or "disasters". And, usually, any disappointments or shortfalls are the result of "changes in market conditions" or because of the negative impact of some other positive move . Here is an example from a recent report and accounts of a major British bank:

> *"Although Merchant Banking made a post-tax loss of £14m during its first full year as a separate business unit, this mainly reflects the impact of absorbing the development costs of a number of new activities, particularly our primary gilt-edged market-making company, and the expansion of our international securities business. "*

Whether this division was expected to make a loss during its first year, or whether it spent much too much money on these new activities (and it sounds like the gilt-edged market-making company was really a drain on cash), is hard to tell. To absorb the costs of development and expansion activities sounds positive and reasonable – and may well be. You wouldn't expect the bank to write: "We underestimated the costs of start-up by about £14 million and, therefore, lost our shirts last year."

Changes in staff and organisational structure must also be presented in the best light. Even if heads have been rolling at HQ, such bloodshed is usually referred to as a restructuring or refocusing of human resources. Financial services companies have been through a period of great change over the past several years. This is from the report and accounts of a British building society:

> *"Prudent management of resources has always been fundamental to the Society's operation. 1985 was a year in which we restructured our senior management at our central offices in (NAME OF CITY) to produce a leaner decision-making body which more readily focuses on the needs of the market place; this is reflected in the report. "*

This is a quintessential example of good news delivery. The only clue that the restructuring involved redundancies (and we can't really be sure that it did) is the word *"leaner"*. But the unpleasant reality of out-of-work senior managers is balanced by the rosier picture of *"prudent management"* and *"focuses on the needs of the market place"*. Of course, the question does arise – if the building society has always been prudent in managing its resources, how did it develop such a fat decision-making body in the first place? But few people will care to ask the question. And besides, companies have very little use for history. What's important is today, and tomorrow.

> *The year ahead will be one of business opportunity and a period of intense preparation for the exciting possibilities ahead. We are looking forward to it.* (Building Society.)

> *As we face the challenging prospects for the 21st century, we can be confident that our present programmes and our research for the future will keep XXX Aerospace in the forefront of the world's high technology markets and well placed to continue our success.* (Aerospace organisation.)

> *Creating long term value for our shareholders depends upon winning in competition with others. We remain confident of our ability to meet this challenge and to make further progress in 1987.* (Bank.)"

Although there are new challenges and stiffer competition, corporations always remain confident and forward-looking. There is nothing wrong in that.

Corporate capabilities and image. Large organisations usually produce a brochure – several brochures – that include unaudited trading figures and descriptions of the company's activities. These brochures do not have the report element of the report and accounts, in that they don't include discussion of particular events, except where appropriate. They may not appear annually either, but will be updated only when some significant element of the brochure becomes obsolete.

The purpose of this type of brochure is to give the reader a clear, concise overview of the company's operations, products and services. There may also be an element of something known as "corporate philosophy" included, and characterisations of the corporate culture. Proud chairpersons and companies enjoying record-breaking years are more prone to philosophising and culture-praising than companies in trouble. Perhaps the most overused cliché in the philosophy department centres around the corporate "commitment to people". For example:

> *"The success of our business depends on the hard work, professional skills and enthusiasm of many thousands of men and women who work in the Bank all over the world."*

or ...

> *"The Society will continue to be driven forward by the efforts and abilities of a committed and enthusiastic workforce."*

Of course it would be difficult to argue that any company is not dependent on its workforce and its enthusiastic commitment. However, not only has saying it become a cliché, it also makes the reader a bit nervous that a corporation feels it *has* to say it. It implies that it has some doubts about its truth.

Product brochures. The purpose of the product brochure seems refreshingly obvious; it's meant to present the features and benefits of a particular product or service. However, so many products today are complicated – particularly electronic or computer or financial or insurance products – that simple descriptions are difficult to come by. Few companies make "screws" or "tables" any more. They make multi-purpose fastening systems, or modular tabling units with electronic-facilitating ports.

It's important, as always, to consider your audience. If your product brochure is aimed at people "in the business", your language and approach will be quite different from what you would use for the general public.

It's possible to read a brochure and finish it not knowing what the product or service actually is. Here's a piece from a booklet about a computer software programme:

> *This is a sidekick.*
> *Sidekick is a lot of things, but first and foremost it is always there when you need it. That's because it is right there in your computer's memory all the time until you turn the power off or reset your machine. No matter which other programme you are using – word processor, data base, spreadsheet, TURBO, Pascal, BASIC, or whatever – Sidekick is always present underneath and may be activated with a single keystroke."*

It sounds like electronic knickers – always "underneath" your personal programme. But what is it? Really? If the writing doesn't give you a clear idea of what the product is and can do for you, it can't be doing its job.

Instructional booklets. There is a great unfulfilled need in this world for writers of instructional material. Something about the professional writer does not love the discipline; there's virtually no room for self-expression (which even the most hardened of business writers still harbours the need for) and little chance of glory.

Open any computer software manual, electronic equipment guide or the like and you have a good chance of developing a bad headache and galloping vertigo. Here's a bit of instruction from a facsimile machine manual ...

> *"While key 1 is pressed, the character above the cursor changes. Release one key at the character to be set. If the three key is pressed, the characters are displayed in the reverse way. Character display sequence (progress from left to right and from top to bottom) 2 key makes a space.*

Simple, isn't it?

WRITING FOR THE READER

Few people's idea of pleasure is to sit down and have an exciting read of a corporate brochure (except perhaps rival directors of corporate communications). However, many people need the information contained in brochures, and will allow them a great deal more time and consideration than they would a press ad or sales leaflet. But however much readers need to know what's in your brochure, they would still rather be reading a story or a novel. So the desire for information juxtaposed with the desire not to read leads to a method of reading that has nothing to do with the way you would read a story or a novel. People will read the first page last, or the middle page only. They may start reading halfway down the column. They may read up, instead of down. They may read the shortest page. They may read the picture captions only. So the canny brochure writer writes to accomodate the random reader.

Chunking. The technique of "chunking" sometimes reaches its ultimate expression in the corporate brochure – with text broken into bite-sized bits and liberally sprinkled with graphics and photographs. Each chunk can be consumed easily, in a few seconds. If you're reading while waiting for an appointment with the director of marketing, you can easily read a chunk, look up anxiously at the clock, read another chunk, chatter with the secretary, read one more chunk, and then scramble into the office. This allows you to open the conversation by saying: "I was just reading that you now have 72 shallow draft vessels operating in coastal waters. I think I saw one of them when I was sailing last weekend."

Non-sequential stories. Chunking means that the story you are writing is not, in fact, a story at all. It doesn't have a beginning, a middle and an end. It doesn't have a sequential flow. It's a string of tiny stories, each with its own message. Each chunk is relatively separate and each page or page-spread is also reasonably separate. This approach means that you need to be careful about antecedents – you can't refer to something mentioned on page one, because the reader may have started reading on page 12.

Pictures and graphics. Here, it's time for you to swallow your brochure-writing pride and accept the fact that people will look at the pictures first. They may then read the captions. They will then, if necessary, read the shortest bits of text. If absolutely necessary (if they're still waiting for that appointment), they will read the big chunks of writing. It makes sense to put a good deal of information into the visuals the images and any captions that accompany them. Visuals are more than decoration; they are an effective vehicle for delivering useful, if non-specific, information.

SOME APPROACHES TO THE CORPORATE BROCHURE

There is probably a finite number of ways to approach the presentation of your company's activities in an image or capabilities brochure. Particularly with large organisations, the goal is always to find some structure or design that will simplify your operations and make them memorable in a positive way.

Division. The most obvious structure is by division, or other clearly defined organisational units. Of course, this is also the dullest approach. *"The Business Services Division operates from 12 locations throughout the United Kingdom, employing some 8,000 employees and serving the burgeoning service industries in their areas."* In very large companies, such divisional distinctions are arbitrary and constantly changing. It may even come as a surprise, for example, for someone inside a company to find out that he is employed by the Business Services Division, when he thought he was working for Small Electronic Equipment Group.

Product. This is a useful structure for companies that offer comprehensible or tangible products, as opposed to complex services.

Market sector. This is a bit more interesting, because now you can relate your products to real activities in real life. If your products – let's say the range of B-Type ZX-90 CMUs – are used in the production of major motion pictures, you have a far more interesting story to tell. Companies often use this organisational structure because it gives the reader a warm feeling, particularly if he or she operates in the market sector decribed.

Case study. To show how real companies have used your product or service is perhaps the most powerful and memorable way to organise your business activities – and accordingly, it can be the most difficult to achieve. You may find, for example, that in reality nobody uses your ZX-90 CMU in the way you had thought – they use it a great deal, but only in conjunction with a competitive R4-JX20 with a capacitant reduction unit (CRU). In other words, you're confronted with real life as opposed to your good news version of it. You have to weigh the benefits of the credibility of the documentary approach with the burdens of finding a story you really want to tell. Companies may also be wary of endorsing your products for liability and competitive reasons, and because they may also be required to commit resources to a project which brings them little or no return.

Metaphors. Some companies, particularly companies that deal in services, will present themselves in terms of a simile or metaphor. *"We're like mountain climbers ... always ready to climb over the most difficult obstacles."* Or, *"we're like fine musicians ... sensitive to the nuances of your needs"*. It sounds corny, and can be. The only way such oblique approaches work is if they're produced flawlessly – if the writing, photography, typography, layout, paper, binding are all absolutely appropriate and impeccable – and if the metaphor really works without being pretentious or laboured.

Even then, you seldom find a company doing two such brochures in a row. This is because at the end of the day computer system specialists are nothing at all like fine musicians – they are like fine computer specialists. In our view, it's better to get to the bottom of what your company does and how you do it – rather than try to force a comparison with something wildly different from what you are.

Themes and catchphrases. People in business like themes. To call a brochure "the corporate brochure" or to call a programme "the quality programme" is a bit bland and sometimes cumbersome. If you can say: "We're the New Age" company or that this is the "Push for Profit campaign" – life is easier and a bit livelier. However, most themes used for externally distributed brochures have little, if any, effect. Unlike the straplines that advertising creates – and rams home with lots of exposure in well-financed campaigns – a brochure line will be read once, if at all, and forgotten.

Themes and catchphrases only take hold through common usage, or through a concentrated awareness-building campaign. That's why a friendly little theme on a brochure cover like *"Tomorrow's Infra-red Slicer Components Today"* doesn't carry much weight in the reader's mind. You're better off providing a simple headline that describes what you do, like *"Engineering Thermoplastics for Automatic Applications"*, than dreaming up something that might make people cringe.

Special cases: the multinational group. The current penchant for takeovers and mergers and international adventurism has led to the development of huge multinational corporations and massive holding companies. Writing a corporate brochure for such corporate entities is no small task. The problems are that, because the groups have grown through acquisition and merger – and have often been put together by financial people or entreprenreurs, rather than by people trained in a particular business – they lack a distinct culture or personality.

They may also lack a clear marketing or product strategy, and really be a conglomeration of products and services that have no common thread. If the politics inside a huge company that has gradually grown are dense and complicated, the politics inside groups formed of formerly distinct companies – particularly if there were hostile takeovers involved – are even more complex.

Chunking is often the best approach to such brochures. In other words, you should produce a corporate or image brochure for the holding company, and then a separate piece for each of the divisions or smaller companies.

TRANSLATION

Another consideration when you're producing brochures for British or European companies is translation. Many companies have branches in several countries. Although most staff members and most customers speak English, each country will probably want to produce its own language brochure. This has a limiting effect on what you can do. First, clever concepts don't travel well. Metaphors, similes and humour, in particular, may have the wrong connotations – or none at all – in other countries.

Second, consider the physical space of your words. Many languages, particularly German, require more words to say the same as their English equivalent. And third, you need to adopt a rigorously non-colloquial style. Colloquialisms and regionalisms and metaphors and theme phrases either do not translate or translate in some way that you would prefer they didn't.

WORKING WITH OUTSIDE SUPPLIES

Most companies choose to hire professional help to develop their annual report and accounts, and image/capabilities brochures. Some companies generate their own capabilities brochure; many produce their own product pieces. When you hire professionals, you should be purchasing not only the requisite skills and capabilities, but also a relatively unbiased, objective "eye" – people who can look at your organisation and see its strengths and weaknesses in a way that no insider can.

Do not expect, however, that by hiring a specialist company your responsibilities come to an end. Being a client is no easy task. Your first job is to sell your company, and the particular job in hand, to the producer. Although the designers and account handlers (and writers, should you decide not to write the brochure yourself) who work on brochures should be able to turn out adequate work under any conditions, it will be of a much higher standard if they are excited, amused, attracted or intrigued by the subject matter. A lot of that exciting and intriguing input must come from the client.

Although the best brochure producers will want to fall in love with your company – and find glorious new ways to present it – their enthusiasm will very nearly follow your own. If you can convince these people – usually verbally – about what a great company/service/ product you have – and make them believe it, you will definitely get a better brochure.

That accomplished, there will also be a fair amount of administrative and organisational work to be done; locating information, setting up interviews, conducting tours, finding photographs. The more information and material the producers have to work with, the more detailed and appealing the brochure is likely to be.

A WORD OF CAUTION

It is a hard fact; most people care a great deal less about your company than you do. And, they may even be so hardened as to approach your corporate message with cynicism ... we're sorry, but it's true.

There may have been a time when the corporate entity was viewed as an essentially positive phenomenon. But today, it's fair to say that people mistrust corporations and their motives. This may or may not be warranted, but it happens. As a result, the wise corporate writer does not ask readers to swallow too much corporate glory; tales of our illustrious heritage, our great founder, and our magnanimous contributions to the great good of society are asking for trouble.

In fact, any sense that the company is a great institution in its own right is definitely not the right approach today. Most companies are selling themselves as being in business only to serve customers, to be partners with them, to find solutions for them. There is no longer a sense of "We thought up these great products. We produce them in the best way possible. You want them."

Speak to your readers as you would have them speak to you. Don't shout too much or make extravagant claims. Tell the truth as you know it (while being positive, of course) and then, turn the page.

CHAPTER 10

SELLING LIVE:

Speeches, including live presentations

THE SPECIAL CHARACTER OF A LIVE EVENT

There are several characteristics of speechwriting that are quite different from any other forms of writing discussed in this book.

The performance element. The words will be spoken aloud, not read. The meaning of the words is greatly governed by the delivery of the speaker. Inflection, intonation, pitch, volume, tempo – all these things can greatly enhance (or completely muddle) the intent.

The personal aspect. Most corporate communications are rather impersonal. They often sound as if they are written by a committee (as they often are) rather than by an individual. That means that there are not many idiosyncratic phrases, no regionalisms, few humourous bits. But when someone stands before you, fully visible, and speaks in his or her own voice, you expect a bit of personality. And you expect that personality to belong or seem to belong, to the speaker – not to the speaker's speechwriter.

The environment. As a writer of a brochure, a television or print advertisement, a video or business report, there is very little you can do to predict, allow for or control where, when and how the audience will be reading your words and receiving your messages. In an event, however, you should know precisely the type of surroundings the audience will find themselves in. To listen to a speech in an ornate ballroom at the Grosvenor House in London is quite different from hearing a speech in a tent alongside Wailea Beach on Maui.

The flow. You should also know what has come before and what will follow in most events. It's very important, particularly in sales and management meetings, for everyone to get their stories straight – and avoid contradictions of fact or emphasis.

Sophisticated business people who have experience in organising large customer events tend to prefer working with a single writer, who will write – and rewrite – everything said in the meeting. This ensures a consistency of tone and message. It should also ensure a proper flow – with emphasis on emotion in one section, facts in the next. A good meeting has its fast moments and slow ones, its chunks of emotion punctuating its stretches of factual content.

The Audience. You need a clear view – as always – of the audience, and what its current general mood is. If you're writing for financial analysts, you may know that they are in a sceptical mood towards leveraged management buy-outs these days. You may know that the sales force is nervous, because of recent rumours about reductions in staff and third quarter results. You may even know who the specific individuals in the audience are. This knowledge allows you to be very specific in your comments, if appropriate. The tone can be more personal and pointed than if you are writing for the great, unspecified general public.

Some of the events you may be called upon to write a speech for include ...

Events for internal audiences

Sales and management meetings. These gatherings may take place regularly, as often as every month, or infrequently – every year or two or three. They tend to feature various members of management presenting annual results, new products, marketing strategies, reorganisation plans, making special announcements, awarding prizes, honouring top achievers.

Internal presentations. Usually made by a small number of colleagues to various layers of management to gain approval for specific projects or products.

Company-wide events. Now and again, a company feels it necessary to hold an event to which all are invited: assembly line workers, engineers, sales personnel, managers, everyone. These are often momentous occasions – to introduce a company-wide quality improvement programme, for example, or announce that the company has been sold.

Incentive or award events. These events are meant to motivate people to do better in the run-up to the event, as much as to reward them at the event. They are characteristically light on business content, heavy on emotional issues; praise and exhortation. They often take place in exotic offshore locations (athough many are happily held in Bournemouth or Chicago, Edinburgh or Atlanta) and feature dinner-dances and sunny outings in among the seminars and plenary sessions.

Events for external audiences

Presentations to industry or financial analysts. These are high level affairs, where senior management presents its plans, products, prospects and profit statements to opinion leaders and attitude-shapers. The theory is that these people are reasonably expert in their fields and, if convinced of your messages, will help convince other people that you're telling the truth.

Press conferences, briefings or background sessions. These can range from informal, off-the-record chats with a small group of specialist reporters to huge, glitzy events meant to amaze and impress.

Special events for customers. These can range from a dinner with a small number of valued customers, which includes a few remarks by the chairman, to theatrical extravaganzas complete with big name live entertainment, elaborate staging and media.

Seminars and trade association conferences. Business leaders are often asked to speak at specialist seminars or conferences. They are usually asked to deliver a non-commercial message relevant to the subject at hand: pollution control or materials recycling, financial planning or computer industry trends.

THE KEY MESSAGES

A speech is ephemeral and therefore fleeting. People tend to remember only a grossly simplified version of your total message. (However they will remember any hideous gaffes or embarrassing moments in elaborate and graphic detail.)

It is therefore very important to establish a clear, simple one-sentence summary of your major point. It should be the answer to the question (asked by the absent colleague): "What did this character have to say?" You want to be sure the answer is not, "nothing much". Rather, it should be: "We're moving strongly into the flavoured animal feeds market. Sounds terribly exciting." Or: "Our productivity is down by 6%; we have to work harder". Or: "The sales staff is being reorganised so that we can serve our customers better".

This doesn't mean that the speech should simply repeat the message over and over, until it has been firmly drilled into the minds of the audience. It does mean that everything in the speech should support, reinforce and elaborate upon the message.

Arguably, of course, there are really only two messages. To external audiences, it is: *"we're extremely good"*.

To internal audiences, it is: *"we're extremely good, but we could be better."*

At the same time, you need to be aware of the hidden agenda. Lurking behind the major messages there may be some unstated objective to consider. This may sound duplicitous and sinister, and it may be – but probably isn't. For example, a management presentation which is ostensibly called to present the year's plans to middle managers, may be in fact to show off the strength of managerial talent to potential investors. Or, a marketing presentation to overseas colleagues may, in fact, be a recruitment exercise – designed to lure the high-flyers to foreign shores.

The actual writing of the words for a speech is, you may now have gathered, only part of the task. It does have its differences from any other form of writing, however.

Establishing a voice. Whether you are writing for yourself, or for someone else, you need to establish a voice. This is true of any type of writing. It is more complicated, and perhaps trickier, for speechwriting. People are willing to accept all kinds of different voices in written documents – from quite informal to very formal. However, when someone is speaking, you expect them to sound as if they are speaking naturally. The trick here is that sounding natural may not be the same thing as speaking naturally.

In fact, if you tape record someone speaking extemporaneously and have the comments transcribed, you may be surprised at what you discover. People do not necessarily speak in very short phrases as you might expect. They may speak in extremely long, elaborate and complex sentences. Some people use complicated words, others use only simple ones. Some people love to repeat phrases in characteristic ways. Some people like to begin sentences with subjects, other people like to begin sentences with objects or modifiers.

The point is that natural speech is different for everybody. This is not a particularly startling revelation, but it means that to write a speech that sounds natural for one person will require a different style than that employed for somebody else.

To establish a voice, and to get it right, takes a lot of listening with a good ear. It's a bit tricky, because you don't want to parody the speaker, nor do you want to write exactly as he or she would speak. This is the reason many managing directors have their own staff speechwriter – they can write as that person would speak, as second nature.

What is most important of all is to establish a voice that you – or the speaker, if it's not you – will be able to deliver comfortably. One good way to achieve this is to tape record yourself, or the speaker, talking through the main messages of the speech, as if he or she were actually delivering it. If you're the one who will deliver it, write down the key points or flow of your speech (see below) and then talk through them as if the tape recorder were your audience. If the speaker is someone else, get them to go through the same exercise imagining that you're the audience. Then get the tape transcribed. What will result may be muddled and confused and full of "ums" and "ers", but it will give you a number of strong clues as to the voice you should use to write the speech.

When establishing a voice, you will also find yourself bucking the great tide of the larger corporate voice. This is an unmistakable voice, vocabulary, syntax and phraseology that builds up in any organisation over time. Nowhere is it written down. There are no printed rules. But anyone who has lived in the organisation longer than a few months will recognise it. Even if they can't write it themselves, it is amazing how accurately attuned their ears will be to variations from the norm. They may not like the corporate voice, but they will feel comfortable and safe with it. The trick for the speechwriter is sounding fresh enough to grab the attention of the audience without sounding so different as to alarm the listeners – and make them wonder if they are in the right meeting.

ATTITUDE AND TONE

There is one school of thought which says that if you're trying to deliver a simple message you should aim all your comments to the lowest level. "Speak with a sixth-form vocabulary" ... "Write for the moron". This is a cynical and defeatist approach. It is to confuse being simple with being simple-minded. If you pitch all of your thoughts at their most basic for comprehension by the least supple minds, you'll probably not connect with the people you really want to reach.

If you think of your audience as uninformed on a particular topic, but not ignorant, you'll find yourself treating them with respect. To consider them ignorant is negative and rude. It implies that you consider your audience inferior to yourself. Uninformed simply implies that they have not had the interest or opportunity to learn about what you can tell them.

The arrogant speaker considers his or her topic to be the most absorbing topic in the world – engineers and scientists tend to fall into this trap most often. They become completely immersed in the behaviour of supercooled gallium arsenide which has been exposed to sunlight. This is probably extremely interesting, and some members of the audience will consider it so, for its own sake. Most people in business situations, however, will want to know what this has got to do with them and why it matters. So you need to explain clearly all the points that may be of confusion to your audience and then explain – again – what desired action you want them to take.

The opening. The old adage about telling the audience what you intend to tell them is another way of stating the importance of locating the audience. You know what you're going to talk about, or at least you should. Your audience does not. So the opening needs to attract their attention, and locate them in time, subject and space. This is only polite. It allows the mind to select the proper file, to locate itself, to prepare itself to listen. There is simply no way around the need for a clear opening. You wouldn't approach someone you had not seen for some time in the street, and simply plunge into whatever topic you had on your mind. Neither should a speechgiver. Have a little sympathy for your audience.

This doesn't mean that the opening must be dull. It should have a bit of humour, a touch of mystery, a personal note. You're attempting, right at the start, to make contact with the audience. You don't want them to sit placidly, performing the role of audience, as the speech is read out – the speaker dutifully performing the role of speechmaker. A strong opening that makes contact will have a positive effect on the audience. They will join the event. If you fail to make contact at the start, it's very difficult – if not impossible – to make it once you're into the heart of the message.

One speech began like this ...

> *"Tonight, I'm going to talk about the operating results for the year, the introduction of the new ZX90 CMU ... and the knees of a young boy."*

What? What do the knees of a young boy have to do with the operating results? The effectiveness of this opening was that it accomplished its two tasks elegantly – it announced the topics to be discussed and made contact, by intriguing the audience. (It turned out that recent corporate fortunes were like the skinned and scraped knees of a young boy in summer – they hurt, but were indications of experience that would help the corporation/boy grow.)

TALK IN SCENES/TELL A STORY

The principle of chunking – breaking the writing into small units – is as appropriate to speechwriting, as it is to the other types of writing we've been discussing. It is perhaps even more important in a speech –

because not only does it focus the attention of the audience on one current thought, but it focuses the attention and energy of the speaker as well. It's best if the scenes are, in general, quite short – two to three minutes long for each scene. You should be able to state the point or key message in one simple sentence.

Each scene should flow into the next. People are surprisingly logical (although each in his or her own way) and have a natural desire to make connections between one thought and the next. The goal of the speechwriter is to get everyone mentally nodding their heads as each scene rolls by, so that when you reach the final scene, which contains the summary message – it will seem to be the inescapable result of a closely reasoned argument that they've been agreeing with all along.

The flow should really be reducible to a series of simple statements that closely follow your outline. For example, suppose that the managing director is making a speech to all the employees of a large company. He has some difficult news to deliver. The flow might go like this ...

1. We're going to talk today about some exciting new prospects for our company.

2. We know that business today is changing rapidly.

3. We know that the growth of electronics, in particular, has had a major effect on the nature of Component Module Units.

4. This has led us to develop the new ZX9-E CMU which incorporates a special systems element for electronic connections.

5. We are so excited about the potential of the ZX90-E that we have decided to expand into new markets.

6. The most exciting market for the new electronic style Flange Covers happens to be in Southern Greenland.

7. We believe that, by concentrating on the South Greenland market, we shall double our growth in the next three years.

8. If we can achieve this goal, we shall be in an excellent position to expand, raise salaries and offer profit-sharing opportunities to all employees.

9. That is why we have decided to relocate our corporate headquarters and all manufacturing operations in Southern Greenland.

10. Because you are so important to us, we wanted you to be the first to know about this change.

11. This change of operations does not mean that there will be mandatory redundancies. We would be delighted to move the entire staff to Southern Greenland.

12. Naturally, for those of you who do not wish to relocate, we have a generous separation programme.

13. For those of you who can make the move with us, we look forward to a great new period of prosperity and growth.

14. We believe that, in this changing business world, we are making the right move at the right time.

15. Thank you very much.

In short, the hidden agenda here was to break the bad news that the company is moving to Southern Greenland. The managing director might have chosen to start off by saying something like: "I'm sure you've all heard the rumours that we're moving to Southern Greenland. Well, they're true." This is a very difficult opening to recover from.

Again, there is nothing but good news. No matter what.

SOME SPECIFICS

Transitions. Although audiences like scenes, they like them to form a flow they can follow – a train of thought they can follow, that begins at the beginning and sweeps – with occasional peaks and valleys – inexorably towards the end.

Many speakers mistake flow for "making smooth transitions". They make these so called smooth transitions by writing such things as, "Now, let us turn to the all-important subject of ..." This is, in effect, a device for locating the audience – partway through the speech. The trouble with it is that it is tedious. And no one, except an enormous bore, speaks that way in real life.

The great advantage of speaking before an audience is that many transitions or changes of tone or thought can be made in ways other than words. A pause. A breath. A slight shift of the body. A new tone of voice. A quickened or relaxed pace. These are the most effective transitions. Announcing your intention of turning to whatever does the trick, but it is pretty lame.

Repetition. You need to repeat things in spoken speech, more often than in writing that is read – for the simple and obvious reason that there is no text for the audience to refer to. You need to keep antecedents very close and, whenever modifying or referring to a previous thought or subject, repeat it so that there's no doubt what you're referring to.

Lists. Speakers like to tell audiences that they have three points to make, or twelve actions to describe, or seven major issues to discuss. This often has the effect of causing great anxiety on the part of the audience: "Let's see. If he has seven points to make and spends seven minutes on each one, that's forty nine minutes. I'm bored already."

The Power of Three. There is some deep, ingrained, and unknowably powerful inner urge to speak and write in threes. It may have religious origins, it may be something even older than that. But it's amazing how many times the key points to be made are three in number, or the outstanding qualities of the award winner are also three. Would-be speechwriters are often advised as to the power of threes; and to use repetition coupled with threes is considered an absolutely surefire rhetorical device. (Alfred P. Doolittle of *My Fair Lady* fame said: "I'm willing, I'm waiting, I'm wanting to ..." and Henry Higgins remarked upon the natural fluidity of his speech.)

However, because people expect cadences of three, they can also have a lulling effect. It's the figure of speech and the known delivery that causes audiences to stop listening and start humming. There is virtue, therefore, in breaking the known and established rhythms – of going to lists that contain two or four items.

A CENTRAL IMAGE OR ANECDOTE

Think about any speech you can remember, and you'll probably find yourself thinking less about what the speaker said and more about how he or she said it. You may remember a gesture the speaker made. You may remember a general tone of voice. But you may also remember a phrase, or an anecdote that seemed to contain the essence of the speaker's message. If you can create one or two word pictures that capture the central message of your presentation, you have a good chance of capturing the imagination of the audience in a lasting way.

Skilled speakers will often begin their speech with such a word picture or anecdote, and keep returning to it throughout the speech ... each time adding new meaning and new interpretations to it. Clergymen seem to have mastered this technique particularly well – probably following on from a traditional religious inclination to speak in parables from which clear moral lessons can be learned. You can tune in to BBC Radio's *Thought for the Day* and hear this technique practised more or less brilliantly every morning. The guest will often begin with an innocuous tale of, let's say, meeting an old acquaintance in the supermarket and, before you know it, we're on to a lesson of charity or world peace.

The speaker who began with the image of the boy with skinned knees exemplifies this technique. Such images have a mnemonic power that's as effective as it is inexplicable. To ramble on about objectives and plans and results and actions, never stopping to say, "entering this new business is like diving into cold water; after the shock it's invigorating ..." or, "our new car is so quiet you can hear the clock ticking – and it's digital" is never to bring your subject alive.

WRITING TO SLIDES

In some companies the process of speechwriting is closely allied to "doing the foils". That is to say, the speaker sits down and creates a set of slides or foils that will then form the structure of the speech. This has its plus and minus points. The plus side is that what's really happening is that the speaker is creating an outline. The bad part is that the foils tend to become the presentation and there's no room for emotion, scenes, or speaking in pictures. In the worst case, it means that the audience could just as well set up a projector and go through the foils themselves. It's also cheating. It is removing the burden from the speaker and putting it on to the slide projector.

Slides have a mesmerising effect on an audience. The slightly darkened room and the steady, soothing whirr of the projection equipment create an atmosphere that's placid, verging on the soporific. If you can deliver your speech without slides, do so. It's brave. It makes you work harder. People will remember it. If you think you must have slides, be sure you're using them for a good reason. There are a few ...

Text to reinforce a point. It does help to clarify your messages if you reinforce the spoken words with the key words. You have to be careful, though, that the words on the slide match your words exactly. They seldom do, given the exigencies of slide production and the tendency for speakers to keep changing their text.

However, every little discrepancy between slide and text will worry the audience. They'll wonder which is correct. Their brains will work hard to rectify the mismatch. By the time they've given up, you're a paragraph further into your speech and they're trying to catch up.

The worst mistake that speakers make, and they make it all the time, is to put too much text on the screen. This means that the audience must now decide whether to read the text or listen to the speaker or do both. Since we know that both can't be done effectively at once, it leaves the audience exasperated. An exasperated audience is not the most receptive audience.

Photographs. Using photographs, of course, can often save you time and energy in describing concrete objects or locations. If you're planning to relocate to new headquarters in Marlow, a few photographs will save you quite a few minutes of verbal description time.

Graphics. Many business people in responsible positions have boiled their management philosophy (or life philosophy) down over the years into a simple graphic that can be sketched quickly on to a napkin, or reproduced with some grandeur as a full colour slide. The graphic may show the overlapping nature of design, engineering, manufacturing and sales. It may represent the what, the how and the why of people motivation. It may show business as a triangle or as interlocking rings. In the world of high technology, a whole visual language has evolved with boxes and arrows and dotted lines and puffy clouds.

Charts and graphs and non-photographic representations of intangible ideas are vastly over-used by speakers. When they're used, they should be very simple, showing one thing at a time. A projected chart showing the five-year results of six major competitors in two markets is too complicated. A chart might compare the results of two companies in a single year, but no more.

So watch slides; they can overpower both you, as the speaker, and the audience. In the business theatre industry, in which both the authors work a great deal, slides used in this context are called "speaker support". And that's what they should be; supportive. They should enhance what you say, say things for you only when it's simpler to show something rather than describe it verbally, point out relevant facts and figures – not list them all. Provided you use slides to support your speech, they will have a beneficial effect. If it turns out that your spoken words are supporting the slides, what's the point of giving a speech at all? Don't let the tail wag the dog.

CONCLUSION: THE BIGGER MESSAGES

No matter what the stated subject matter of your speech, you'll also be delivering messages to your audience that are just as important but have nothing to do with the topic at hand. And the audience will be looking for information that you might not have expected to deliver.

Speechmaking is performance. How you say what you say may not be as important as what you say, but it will greatly effect how what you say is perceived. As people listen to a speaker, they are analysing and assessing the whole package. They will assess how the speaker moves. ("He can't be very enthusiastic about this new programme, he hasn't used a single gesture yet.") They will assess how the speaker sounds. ("His voice is quavering. He must be nervous. He can't be terribly important".) They will study how the speaker looks. ("She's too tanned and expensively dressed, she can't be working hard enough for the amount of money she earns.")

They will, in fact, listen to your words. ("It was very clear. He seemed to get lost in the middle. I didn't like that business about new reporting procedures.")

In short, they will be judging – not just your speech – but what your speech and its delivery has to say about your position in the company and the soundness of the company in allowing you to present your ideas.

In any speech delivered by a manager of reasonably elevated position, the audience is looking for a reading on corporate health. "How do this speaker's comments relate to the general position of the company? If he has launched a major new advertising campaign, does that mean we're desperate for more sales, or does it mean we have plenty of money to spend on image-making?"

Corporate health is often demonstrated – and consciously so – by the amount of money and attention lavished (or not) on the settings and staging of conferences and meetings. If the annual marketing meeting involves a five-star hotel in a sunny destination and features a well-known television linkperson under 60 years of age, you can assume, with justification, that the company is doing well. Or that management believes that the company is about to do well. Both are healthy signs. If the sales conference is held in the community centre down the road from the company's offices, you get the message with equal clarity.

And as we've assessed above, your audience, especially an internal one, will also be looking for signs of the corporate health of the speaker. "Does he seem to be moving up? Is she showing signs of moving out? Should I attach my star to her department? Do I risk offending a future MD if I ask him a rather direct and challenging question?"

Speeches are about cultural adjustments, about admonishment and reward. But they should always be positive (no matter how negative the hidden agenda) and never deliver conflicting messages. Negativism is more disturbing in a live performance than in any other corporate medium. There's something shocking about a speaker being negative or off-putting in person. This is why most companies, when the news is bad, will choose not to hold a meeting at all until things have improved. Why get together and be miserable? Communal events should be, by nature, positive events.

One major company held a party to congratulate itself on winning a large contract. At the same event, a new cost-cutting programme was announced ... along with some stern admonishments. It was a clear case of mixed messages, one of which was negative. The message of the party was, "you're good". The message of the new policy was, "you're bad". Although the intention may have been good, the reaction was, understandly, bad. And the motivational mileage that might have been enjoyed from the good news was totally cancelled out by the bad news.

However there does come a time when something that is perceived as bad news, really is good news. This is where good speeches and presentations can turn a negative perception into a positive one. In the example that follows (a real speech by the chairman, with the names changed) a major, massive, UK nationalised business had decided to reorganise itself from a structure which had been around too long into a leaner, more customer-led service industry. There were two potential negatives to dispel here.

One was the fact that the chairman (a talented man who had been knighted for his many earlier contributions to British industry) was new to the organisation and there were general fears that he was a) going to walk all over the excellent work done by his predecessor and b) that he knew little about selling. (The audience was the company's sales force.) Two, was the natural British suspicion and cynicism about change – particularly in a nationalised industry where change is an even more sensitive issue than elsewhere. The changes which had been announced earlier in the conference were, in fact, very good news for the sales force, and there were no redundancies planned. However, the chairman needed to reinforce the good news, and prove his commitment to the sales force. The speech was written after the chairman had "talked through" the content with Suzan St Maur, who was to write the speech, and contained many of his own ideas and metaphors. Here's what he said ...

"CHAIRMAN: Good afternoon, everybody.

Before I go on to talk about our business in hand, I would like to start by assuring you that I'm *not* the kind of chairman who smiles down on his flock, and trots out the platitudes. My involvement with your activities is much closer to home than that.

It might interest you to know that I started my career as a salesman. My first job was as a management trainee with COMPANY X, fundamentally working in sales. And my first management job was as a district sales manager, followed by that of Northern divisional sales manager, sales controller, general sales manager, and sales director. I also ran one of the largest sales forces in the country, at COMPANY Y ... with over 1500 sales people in my team. To this day I firmly believe in the old adage that *nothing* happens until somebody, somewhere, sells something.

And although it was a while ago now, I can still remember very well how it *feels* to be out there at the sharp end. So, I admire the work you do and I am a strong supporter of the sales force.

But now, to business. And *our* business in the past has been an operational culture, not a marketing and sales culture. That is changing. PREVIOUS CHAIRMAN, in launching decentralisation and bringing in a dedicated sales force, set us off in the right direction. His considerable efforts began this vital process of making the NAME OF COMPANY customer-driven, concentrating on service excellence and dividing the business up into its pieces, so that problems could be attacked more vigorously. We still have a long way to go. But my intentions are to make certain that these necessary changes are firmly imbedded, and that we move even faster to get ourselves reorientated for our improved way of doing business.

What I'm definitely *not* intending to do, is to try and change the course PREVIOUS CHAIRMAN set out on, as I agree with what he was trying to do. Perhaps the best way to describe my role following on from his is that, if you like, he managed to get the Jumbo Jet out of the hangar and moving the first difficult few yards down the runway ... when you wonder whether it will ever take off. My job is to keep the throttle wide open, get the Jumbo off the ground and up to cruising altitude, and pilot it successfully on to its destination.

Decentralisation is a key part of that piloting. One of its major benefits has been to introduce stronger management accountability throughout all the disciplines of operations, finance, sales and marketing, to ensure that we recognise the needs of our customers far more. And, that we tailor our products and services to meet those needs. We're far from perfect at it yet, but we must get better every day.

Now, I remember when I was a salesman thinking, 'are those buggers up at the top *ever* going to come up with some new products?' Well, you'll be pleased to hear that this is *still* a question that I'm asking today. Only now I'm in a stronger position to give good answers as well as ask the questions. And there will be some very good answers emerging over the coming months, as you have heard indicated by the managing directors of the two divisions. This is both in terms of product development, and the ways in which it is being put across to customers ... crucially important in my salesman's view, as this, at the end of the day, is what you have to sell.

Although you represent the dedicated resource, if you like, I am making it clear to *all* management in both DIVISION A and DIVISION B, that *they* have got to get alongside the customer as well. I am expecting *them* to have close contact with customers, as well as with their teams.

If we are going to be truly customer-driven, we can't achieve that with just a narrow band of contact. It has got to be a matter of *everyone* participating with equal enthusiasm, and visibility.

Of course, you will remain the 'shock troops' of that, but I know from personal experience that you need support and help from the whole organisation. And it is only if the whole organisation thinks more about the customer, and becomes more customer-driven all the way through, that you will have the right environment in which to be the most successful. So as I see it, it is my responsibility to help you in this way, and make sure each one of you gets the support and help that you need, all the way up to the top.

And needless to say I am totally committed to making sure this happens now, in a number of ways ... through raising the profile of sales within the organisation, reducing the hierarchical structure, creating more open, more flexible management, and generally giving positive signs for change. I even get time to talk to the media occasionally, as you might have noticed, to let *all* our customers know that we're a healthier, fitter, and more responsive animal.

So I stand squarely behind decentralisation. I know that many people still feel uncertain about this. However, there was no doubt whatsoever that the job had to be done. We were just too big and cumbersome to manage as a monolithic whole. Now that we are committed to decentralisation, we must do it thoroughly. I don't believe in being 'half-pregnant'.

Whilst we shall all continue to be part of THIS COMPANY, and draw strength from that, each division will be run as much on a stand-alone basis as possible. That means carrying through the process of separation, to give us a sharper cutting edge. And this is going to work to everybody's advantage; particularly yours. Rather than lose the impetus of our business in a diluted effort involving DIVISION A and DIVISION B together, running the risk of falling between two stools, during the course of this year the two individual divisions will receive a much sharper focus. You will have totally dedicated management. And for the first time in the history of THIS COMPANY, sales will be represented at the top, in both DIVISION A and DIVISION B. This will obviously give sales much greater prestige within the organisation, with all the benefits that are then bound to follow.

This is a definite and positive step forward; it's going to make your roles more clear cut, and more successful. These new roles will be something you can really get your teeth into; roles which will give you more scope, and more straightforward commitment to your own personal career development.

Of course, you could accuse me of giving you a perfectionist view of life; saying too much of how things should be in an ideal world. And we all know that real life is never as perfect as that. But we must have some *vision* of where we're trying to go, and some concept of what is the ideal. Now, obviously we're going to fall short of that ideal, so we need to set ourselves the greatest possible vision, and the most stretched objectives that we can. This way, we can unlock people's creative talents, *your* creative talents, to help drive us on towards the most demanding goals ... something that's badly needed in THIS COMPANY. And I'm encouraged to hear that you have already made an impressive start by forming your own mission statement; I'm pleased to see that once again, a sales team has set the good example for the rest of the organisation to follow. But as you know by now, I am a little biased where sales teams are concerned!

So far, I seem to have been placing a great deal of emphasis on how much work there is yet to be done. But I must point out to you that I am enormously gratified to see just how far the operation has actually progressed so far. Giant steps have been achieved in what, for an organisation the size of ours, is a very short time. Having seen this, I have tremendous confidence that, through continuing change, we will go successfully on to new and greater heights.

But as you've already heard at this conference, change is a word that can generate mixed emotions ... especially amongst the faint hearted. However, as experienced sales people, you are well used to working within a background of change. Up until recently, though, the reality has been that THIS COMPANY *hasn't* changed. And that was a major problem. What is happening as we speak is that there is more of a coming together; because THIS COMPANY *itself* is beginning to change radically. Now, this may worry some people, but in no way should it disturb you. You, as sales people, are used to working within a changing environment, as I just said. In fact, that is all part of the stimulation and challenge of sales in the first place. What's more, most of you will have already felt the *benefits* of the change which is taking place within our business; and there is more to come.

Of course, you won't be surprised to learn that recently I've heard a number of rumblings here and there, to the effect that things are changing too fast. However, I make no secret of the fact that I don't believe it's fast enough.

Reorganisation is a positive, productive part of our lives. And speaking as a former salesman, I've been reorganised more times than I've had hot breakfasts. Consequently, I know that deep down, good sales people *enjoy* the onward and upward motion that change brings about, provided of course that adequate support is on hand, in terms of resources and training. And as you've heard during this conference, all the support you're going to need, is already well in hand.

Alright, we may complain about change from time to time. But the truth, between these four walls, is that we are all far more likely to be bored by *lack* of change, than we are to be temporarily inconvenienced by fast-moving progression.

So, my final commitment to you here today is this personal promise; you will *never* be bored again, in THIS COMPANY.

The way ahead may not always be easy, but it is the *only* way ahead for us. And it is the right way ... positive, exciting, challenging ... the right way for us all to create a prosperous, secure, and successful future.

Thank you all very much indeed."

CHAPTER 11

SELLING ON SCREEN:

Video and audio-visual scripts

One of the keys to writing for the screen media is to understand which medium you're writing for ... and how it differs from the others. This is true despite the general belief held by many business people who are not media-literate, that the various forms are essentially the same. This notion has given rise to all kinds of strange media hybrids; the most notable being the "video film". There is also the "slide film" and, as a useful catch-all category, "the movie". There is nothing wrong with clients or media users confusing the difference between the media, so long as the writers and producers do not. But if you are to tackle the writing of scripts for the screen, you should know which is which, and what each can do. So, let's take a look at the major forms.

Film, or motion picture

Corporate programmes are not often shot on motion picture film these days. 16mm movies used to be the standard for corporate programmes, but today videotape has taken over. Film is still shot regularly for television commericals (usually 35mm film, which is larger and has a better image quality) and for the occasional corporate programme. Film has a very different look to that of videotape; it is a photographic process, rather than an electronic one. Film can accept higher contrast ratios which means that, lit and shot properly, it can have a more beautiful, finely detailed look – rather more like a painting of a scene ... videotape, using the same metaphor, would be like a snapshot of the same scene.

Film used to be the easiest medium for screening, too. But now, the 16mm film projector seems clunky, old-fashioned and difficult to use in comparison with the videocassette player. Most 16mm motion pictures have an optical soundtrack system which delivers less than wonderful sound reproduction. Prints are expensive, and the production process can be a bit more complicated and time-consuming than that of video.

The primary advantage of film, in the corporate world, is that it can be easily projected as a large image; from six to twelve or fifteen feet, for 16mm. Although video can also be projected, it doesn't keep its image quality. Even with the best and brightest video projectors, the image tends to lack sharpness and vividness of colour. With the coming of high definition television (HDTV) sometime in the not-too-distant future, that limitation should be overcome; but for now, any motion picture which needs to be projected looks a lot better if it is shot on film.

Videotape

Videotape is the present corporate rage. It is so easy to shoot, so much fun to edit, and so easy to distribute and screen, video is over-running corporate life ... and perhaps, life in general. In fact the current trend seems to be to shoot everything that might have some value eventually to somebody in the long run, sometime. This means that there is a great deal of video being shot that no-one will ever look at; just like all that home video which is mouldering on shelves across the nation.

A disadvantage, or at least a concern when you use video, is that as it is an electronic medium there are technical advances and improvements being made all the time. The obvious danger for writers and producers is to want to use every new video technique that becomes available ... without regard for whether they suit the subject. There is a tendency for video programmes to follow fashions as they come and go, incorporating all the latest whistles and bells and special effects with images zooming around all over the screen. To be fair, a few well-chosen video effects can liven up otherwise dry and stilted information, particularly when you need to convey it in graphic or caption form. But fashions being what they are, video producers will often overlay perfectly interesting and self-sufficient videotape material with so many special effects that viewers can't find the message at all. So beware video producers, and particularly editors, bearing expensive gifts of ADO, Quantel, and all the other computerised machines that generate anything from mosaic dissolves to flying presenters.

In the past, producers always complained that videotape was harder and more expensive to edit than film. And in the past, this was true; film merely has to be cut up and stuck together again in the correct order (a gross simplification, but nonetheless accurate) whereas videotape is edited electronically. This means copying what you want from the raw material tape on to another tape which becomes the master, which sounds simple enough. Where it begins to get complicated is when you want to change a section in the middle of a video programme that has already been edited. In the film equivalent, you cut it again and stick it together again. With videotape, you have to start all over from scratch. However, video editing equipment today has been made far more accessible and affordable, and the editing process has been improved so much that the job can be done quite fast. And the editing of film, which appears simple in "cutting" terms, involves a number of photographic processes which can be time-consuming – particularly when you wish to add in special effects.

For your purposes, however, the decision as to whether your best medium is film or tape can often be influenced by other, more practically based, issues. If you are producing audio-visual material from your company's in-house department, for example, your decision will be made on the strength of what equipment the department has, or finds most cost-effective to use.

Perhaps the most useful, and most far-reaching purpose of videotape is as a playback medium, rather than for origination. Film or stills projectors can be tricky to set up; a videocassette player is relatively idiot-proof. If a programme has to be shown in a number of different locations, a videotape is probably the easiest way of doing it. However, if you're planning to send videocassettes to different countries, you need to be aware of the different television standards in use, and have the tapes converted accordingly. Before we look at the writing process itself, let's just touch on the close relation of moving pictures; "AV", or slides.

Slidetape

Slidetape is a single 35mm slide projector operating in synchronisation with an audio tape player of some kind. Slidetape is not used too much these days, as it's seen as somewhat old-fashioned. Its main limitation is the single projector; when the slide changes, the screen is temporarily drowned in blackness. The great advantage, though, is the quality of its image ... sharp, with vivid colour. Slides are also reasonably easy to produce, easy to duplicate (although you lose some quality in the process), easy to replace, and easy to handle. They're also much less expensive to produce than film or videotape.

Single screen multi-image

The improvement on the slidetape, is the multi-image show. This consists of more than one projector pointing at one single screen area. The advantage here is that your images can dissolve, or cross-fade, when changing from one to another, avoiding the embarrassing black hole you get with a single projector. It makes for a more continuous presentation with the capability of a varied pace ... with short, sharp cuts or longer dissolves. Single screen shows tend to be based on two, three, six, nine, or even twelve projectors, although in theory there's no limit on how many you have. The more projectors you use, the more creative freedom you have to create special effects; using three or more projectors you can simulate the effect of an image rotating, getting larger or smaller, multiple images, collages and so on. This is done by carefully photographing artwork on slide (or generating it by computer) and then using another computer to control the projectors and their lamps when they're operating the show. The problem with multi-image programmes is that they require a great deal of skill to produce, a trained projectionist and a lot of expensive hardware to show, and a lot of money to make.

Wide screen multi-image

Here's where the expense involved in producing multi-image begins to make a little more sense. The typical wide screen multi-image show consists of two screen areas side by side, with a third screen area in the middle, overlapping the other two. Each screen area has at least two projectors on it, and can have many more. The strength and glory of wide screen multi-image (sometimes, confusingly, called multi-screen multi-image) is that it creates a very large area, with a very bright picture of high image quality. The sound track, on magnetic audio tape, should also be of high quality and complexity. The justification of the expense here is that wide screen multi-image shows probably give you the finest quality of image, and the most impact, for a large audience ... better than projected film, and much better than projected videotape. For marketing and motivational purposes, wide screen slide shows can create a very powerful, emotive impression on very large audiences. But, as we said, you need a deep pocket.

The differences

Despite their differences in quality and ease of use, all the corporate visual media have one major characteristic in common. Their primary goal in life is to deliver non-rational, non-specific messages. They are more about mood and image, emotion and impression, than they are about information and fact. And this is often the first mistake made by people who set out to produce a corporate programme; they ask the medium to do a job it isn't meant to do.

When people watch corporate media, particularly video, they have a natural tendency to compare it with what they see on television. Compared with routine broadcast television, corporate media may often be as well-funded and as well-produced. The corporate show, however, won't be about murder, sex, human relations, or great historical events. It will be about the glory of computer networking or precision milling or overnight delivery. In other words, the basic subject is a bit lacking when it comes to drama and the stuff of human emotion. This is why writers and producers of corporate media are constantly looking for structural techniques which will add drama or humour, pathos or at least a glimmer of human interest where none seems to exist. In comparison to advertising, corporate media don't stand much of a chance; the amount of money spent per second on a television commercial can be vast. A 30-second television commercial may easily cost twice what a ten minute corporate video programme costs to make. With that kind of money in the kitty, the commercial producer can make most things look exciting and dramatic.

The answer is not to try to compete; but understand the capabilities you have within your own budget. To tell you how much money actually buys what would be impossible, as costs vary from country to country and from month to month, in our rapidly evolving audio-visual age. But any good corporate production company, or individual producer, should be able to give you the guidelines you need.

Over and above the cost problem, there are other differences to consider. Most corporate programmes have a running time of anything from four to fifteen minutes. There are longer programmes around, but no good producer would recommend anything running for much more than fifteen minutes; research shows that audience/viewer retention begins to fall off after that, and collapses altogether after eighteen minutes. However, the vast majority of corporate programmes are much longer than commercials; so, the visual and structural styles used in advertising tend not to be as useful for the longer form.

The corporate programme is rarely seen more than once. In its few minutes of running time, it must work on both the mind and heart of the viewer. It is probably not in competition with any other visual presentation, particularly from a competitor. It stands alone. Remember that concepts used for television commercials may well not work with a longer time slot than 30 seconds. (In fact, some concepts that are intriguing for 30 seconds can become quite nauseating if you drag them out for any longer.)

So, if you're about to write for the corporate media, it's important to resist any temptation to emulate the style of your favourite, current television commercial, or, for that matter, the superb movie you saw last week. The corporate media are different, but they are media in their own right and, provided that you see them as such, you'll be successful in writing for them. These issues are discussed in more detail later in this chapter, but for now let's summarise the two main types of media like this.

Film and videotape can offer you all the drama and wizardry of feature movies and television, provided you've got a lot of money. But with normal corporate-sized budgets, you can use the documentary approach, drama (including comedy), or a mixture of the two. Just remember that the more locations you need to shoot, and the more actors you need to hire, plus the more elaborate sets you write in, the more it's going to cost. Whatever you do, don't try to make do with Mickey Mouse sets – or actors for that matter – if you can't afford to do it properly. And never use amateur actors unless it's for very minor roles. If your budget is limited, use a simple, straightforward approach and do it well, rather than try to improvise on no budget. A poorly made programme will reflect badly on you, your company, and your image.

Slidetape whether it is single projector or multi-image, does not have the advantage of "lip sync" – where people speak on screen and can be seen to do so. But you don't have to stick with the tried and tested format of a voice over narration and music to accompany the pictures if you don't want to. You can include sound effects, and also clips of vox pops or interviews with non-scripted people; see below for details. The effect of these is not as direct as it would be if you were able to see them speak, but it adds a slightly surreal extra dimension. Sound recording is cheap in comparison with video or film, so don't spare the horses – or your imagination.

BEFORE YOU WRITE THE SCRIPT

The basic steps you need to take before you start writing an audio-visual script are the same as you would for any other document or form of advertising. We cover this subject fully elsewhere in this book, so let's start right in with how to go about writing your script. But before you do that, it's worth taking a look at an intermediate stage between initial research and brief, and the first draft script.

This is called a **"treatment"**. You'll also hear it called a "synopsis", but this tends to be a shorter version ... just a single-page outline of what the programme is to be about. A treatment goes further. In some ways, you could look on it as the prose version of the script; rather like the short story from which a screenplay is developed. Because an audio-visual presentation is intangible until it is completely finished, most people have a very difficult time visualising and hearing what it might be like. Even with a well-written script, so much of the programme depends on the colours, lighting, faces, delivery of lines, pacing, dissolve rates, quality of graphics, type of music and voice chosen that the finished show often doesn't resemble the script at all. But in the corporate sector – and in television and movies too there are usually a number of people who have to know roughly what the programme will be like, because their approval/co-operation/money is required if the programme is to happen at all. That is why a treatment is necessary; to provide these people with an understandable document that explains what the programme is all about without confusing columns of camera instructions and jargon everywhere to cloud the issue. Another important benefit of a treatment is that it helps you, the writer, to crystallise your ideas ... and helps you work them out without cluttering your own mind with all the shooting paraphernalia that worms its way into the full script. Finally, the treatment helps those who will eventually produce the programme to start planning for it, and to work out roughly how much time and budget will be required.

A treatment doesn't just paint word pictures that describe the finished programme. Apart from saying roughly what appears on screen when, it also attempts to describe the mood that each scene will create. It talks about the nature of transitions, tone of voice, the pace. It describes in a general way the look and feel of the piece, while still leaving enough room for each reader's imagination to supply some detail. Suppose, for example, you're writing a video programme to promote a new office building and you want the first scene to establish the city centre location. The treatment might talk about a montage of images ...

"... quick shots of commuters emerging from the underground intercut with close-ups of characteristic city details: a taximeter ticking over, a newspaper headline, a curtain being opened, a security guard greeting an early arriver.

The music is active and lively, but not terribly melodic ... more a collection of sound effects that help bring each action to life ... a sudden accent with the screech of brakes, a swoop of sound as we tilt up the side of a sheer building face, a quiet tension as we watch a crowd of pedestrians waiting to cross the street."

Although none of these exact shots may appear in the final programme, the mood will probably be similar. That is the idea behind the
treatment ... not to tell the reader exactly what shots will be seen or words
spoken, but to give them a strong feel for the mood and flow of the piece.

In corporate writing and particularly in educational scripting, treatments are also very useful as a melting pot for the information that should
go into the content of a programme. Treatments, because they don't take
anywhere nearly as long to write as scripts do, are the best place for all the
people involved in production to put things in, take them out, move them
around, pull them apart, and so on. The following treatment was in fact
for a broadcast television programme, but as it is exactly like a corporate
programme in many respects – even the budget was low – we have
included it here as an example. The approval process for this project
involved a committee of about fourteen people, of whom only a few had
ever been involved in making programmes before. Consequently to have
produced a script without going through the treatment stage first would
have confused them terribly, and not allowed them to see the information content clearly. In circumstances like these it is well worth the effort
of writing a long, detailed treatment, so everyone is entirely happy with
the content and creative approach of the programme before a script is
written. Making significant changes to a script involves a lot of time –
usually your time, if you're the writer. Making changes to a treatment is
easy. Later in this chapter we'll show you the script that emerged from the
treatment. The actual programme was broadcast on the UK's *Channel
Four* television as part of an Open College educational series. It was produced by Videotel Productions Ltd.

"An Introduction to Tourism in Britain"
Programme One
"What is Tourism?"
TREATMENT

OBJECTIVES

*1.   To provide viewers with an overview of the tourist industry in
Britain today, its impact on the nation's economy, and the job
opportunities that exist within it.*
*2.   To define tourism in its fullest context, and identify the various
groups of people who can be classified as tourists.*
*3.   To illustrate where tourists stay, what they do for leisure,
recreation, (plus business) etc., and how they travel.*

SOME POINTS TO BE COVERED:

*(Please note that these topics are not necessarily listed in order of
presentation within the programme.)*

–   *The great breadth of people and purposes involved in the term "Tourism"; the fact that there are many categories of travellers who are classified as tourists, some of which may not immediately spring to mind. The vast numbers of tourists who visit Britain each year.*

–   *The "league table" positioning of tourism within a) the most successful industries in Britain, and b) the growth industries in both the present and the future.*

–   *The value of tourism to the national exchequer.*

–   *The relevance of tourism to national and regional economies, and the indirect effect it has on other industries, e.g., catering, retail, transportation, manufacturing, etc.*

–   *The multiplicity of career opportunities that exist within the tourist industry; the number of people currently employed in the industry, and the annual growth rate.*

–   *The ways in which tourism breaks down in geographic terms; the foreign tourists who visit Britain, where they come from, and what they do when here; and the UK national tourists, and their preferred activities. Where tourists stay, where they go, and how they travel.*

CONTENT, APPROACH AND STYLE

The objective of this treatment is to provide an harmonious vehicle through which we can convey a number of relevant, although not always closely related facts. What is needed is a linking device; and this we have in the shape of two characters filmed on a beach. They converse between themselves, and also at times with the narrator (who is personified by the camera), in order that they may be seen to be playing active parts in the programme rather than passive parts. By linking all the data back through the simple device of two characters spending a day out at the beach, we can pull the data together and present a more homogeneous flow of information than if we were to present it in straight documentary form. Although there is a certain feel of the surreal to the linking techniques we will use, the information itself will in no way be "tainted" by it, but will come over as hard, interesting facts. It is worth bearing in mind, too, that current television programming – especially that aimed at a younger audience – uses such mildly surreal techniques. This approach will therefore connect our programme with the up-to-the-minute style of non-educational TV, and as such will have a beneficial influence on viewers' receptiveness; a particularly valid point with this first programme in the series.

We begin with the opening titles, plus any necessary information about the series and the course. This can be done with captions and narration over.

The main body of the programme opens with an entertaining visual montage of the old-fashioned, clichéd view of British tourism in the past. Depending on availability of material, we could include such elements as seaside picture-postcards from the early 20th century ... archival film footage of people on the beaches at Blackpool, complete with rolled-up trousers and knotted handkerchiefs on their heads ... thirties' and forties' charabanc tours ... shots of the West End theatres pre-war ... etc. The point of this opening sequence is to ease the viewers, in an amusing way, into the fact that tourism is not generally seen for what it has actually become.

Over this light-hearted montage, the narrator introduces the subject, and asks viewers if they realise the true extent of tourism today ... or do they still look upon it as it was just a few short decades ago? And do they appreciate the large number of job opportunities, for people of all ages, that exist within the industry?

At this stage, we are still looking at our montage of tourism from the past. Now, we see a beach-side billboard showing two life-sized comedy figures, with holes where the faces should be. We have moved from the past, to the present day. Two real faces appear in the holes; they belong to our two characters, who will act as central pivots for the conveying of information throughout the remainder of the programme. When appropriate, it will seem as if they are "conversing" with the narrator, who on these occasions is personified by the camera.

One face belongs to a young man of about 19; the other, to a woman of about 40; the young man's mother. (This is to suggest, ultimately, that employment in tourism is possible for a wide spread of age groups; not just young people.) They look enquiringly at the camera; and the narrator asks them what they know about tourism. They look at each other, smile, then emerge from behind the billboard and stand either side of it. They are likeable, slightly extroverted people, casually dressed in discreet beach clothes, and fairly ordinary in appearance.

They look a bit perplexed, and the young man scratches his head. Then, they say a few lines that typify the popular view of tourism ... e.g., that it consists of foreign tourists visiting the Tower of London, and coachloads of Darby & Joan club members visiting the beaches of Great Yarmouth.

The narrator, "speaking" to them – and of course to the viewers – through the medium of the camera, (the two characters look attentively at the camera as if it were the person speaking to them) suggests they look round at the billboard. This, they do.

Through the medium of the billboard, on which we see a

mixture of stills, live action, etc, to match the narrator's words, we discover that those popular ideas about tourism represent the merest tip of the iceberg. We learn that tourism has grown faster than almost any other industry in the world ... and that Britain is one of the countries where tourism has shot into the lead as the fastest growth industry of all.

After a suitable length of time, the camera moves in so as to fill the screen with the "billboard", and we proceed through the basic truths about tourism. Simple, interesting graphics can be used to pull out the salient facts and figures; e.g., the number of people employed in the industry, the growth of employment, the industry's contribution to the national wealth, the earnings it brings to Britain from foreign visitors, the benefits tourism brings to allied industries, etc.

We then pull back from the full frame images, so that we once again see the billboard and our two characters. They are talking to each other, about the fact that if the tourist industry generates so much in earnings and employment in Britain every year, we can't just be talking about holiday makers alone. The narrator, through the "medium" of the camera, breaks into their conversation, and tells them he/she was just about to bring that point up.

At this stage, the camera moves away from our two characters by the billboard, and concentrates on people elsewhere on the beach. The narrator describes each of the other main groups of tourists, and we see representatives of the corresponding groups in various places on or beyond the beach. (These sequences could well be shot elsewhere, but through editing made to look as if they are on or near the beach.) We see a business person, a group of conference delegate types with sharp suits and lapel name badges, a religious group (say, nuns), a student group, some day trippers, and a visiting family group (say, a young couple with two small children, walking towards and greeting an older couple who could be grandparents.) The narrator points out any interesting facts about these groups – e.g., that business travel represents about 25% of tourism revenue in the UK, the ratio of foreign tourists to UK nationals, the league table of nationalities visiting Britain, etc.

Once again, we return to our two characters. They walk away from the billboard, and sit down on the beach. This is obviously the place they started from, as we see evidence of a picnic, plus all the other accoutrements you would expect ... beach umbrella, chairs, books, even a portable television. They sit down. And on a low table or cloth between them, we notice that there are the beginnings of a game of dominoes. The dominoes are much larger than normal.

Using the dominoes as a link device – their sections are

conveniently the same general shape as that of a television screen – we discuss the elements of how tourists arrive in and travel around Britain; where they stay; and where they go. The first few dominoes, already in place, represent the groups of tourists which we have already discussed. This we see by dissolving through to graphic representations of the groups. Then, we add dominoes; the next few being methods of transportation, followed by places in which tourists stay, followed by activities. At each crucial point, the domino in question is transformed into stills or live action of the issue concerned, and very quickly enlarges to full frame. That way, we can cover a good many subjects quite quickly, not only in terms of describing the activity concerned, but also the career opportunities that exist within it.

Every now and again, we pull out from the domino game, and watch a short conversation between the two characters and the narrator, through the medium of the camera, as before. By now, the two characters are very interested, and ask some extremely shrewd and relevant questions. We learn that the young man is interested in going into tourism, and that his mother would now like to retrain and return to full-time work and is similarly interested in tourism. Occasionally during this section, we touch on less than savoury subjects like long hours, weekend work, etc. But the enthusiastic attitude of our two characters helps us to get these points over in an honest but positive way.

Although in the main our examples (as shown through the device of the dominoes) consist of short visual cameos with narration over, it would be useful to include some longer sections to illustrate major points. These could be drawn from the locations we may visit for other episodes in the series, like Beaulieu, Bradford, Woburn, a hotel, a conference centre, an airport, etc., and could include short interview clips with senior figures in each, describing the nature of the location, how many visitors it attracts each year, and how many people are employed there. This would be especially useful in the case of Bradford, as the facts concerning the beneficial effect tourism there has had on the local economy, not to mention employment, are very interesting. This example, possibly combined with one or two others of a similar nature, will neatly counterbalance the national statistics about tourism's effect on the economy and employment, as portrayed earlier in the programme.

Finally, we return to the domino game on the beach. The game has ended in an amicable draw. Our two characters now sit back, and discuss the areas of employment in tourism they might choose. Every now and again, the narrator interrupts them to point out something they may have forgotten, or to remind them of a particular fact. This sequence is very short, but helps viewers to recap on the main points of the programme. The sequence ends with the characters agreeing that although they've thoroughly enjoyed their day as "tourists", they intend to find out more about WORKING in tourism the next morning. One of them then reaches over to the portable TV set, and switches it on. On that screen, we see the closing picture of OUR programme. We move in on the portable's screen until it fills our screen full frame, and the narrator tells us that we can find out more about tourism by watching the remainder of the series. This is also the opportunity for any other information about the course to be conveyed, and we then close the programme.

The above was a very long and detailed treatment, for reasons we stated earlier. At previous script meetings, the committee (which included the writers of the series) had worked out the main objectives of the programme, but it's always worth restating them at the beginning of the treatment. That makes sure everyone knows what basis you're working on. And once everyone is happy with the treatment, you can move on to the script – confident that time-consuming major structural changes are unlikely, and that all you're liable to have to change are small points of detail.

WHAT THE SCRIPT HAS TO DO

Audio-visual scripts are not meant to be read, which explains why they are hard to read. People who are asked to judge scripts – clients and managers – constantly make this mistake. They want to criticise words in the form they are in. This is understandable, but not acceptable; and in many ways it is why it is so important for people essential to the approval process to assess a production on the strength of a treatment first. Treatments should be readable documents that flow and tell the story naturally. Scripts are not readable documents in the same way, and everyone concerned must be made to realise this. What the script is, is a blueprint for the whole production; and apart from all the technical jargon and instructions you'll find in a camera or shooting script, there'll also be single words, fragments, pauses, periods of silence and many other elements which would not be acceptable in a printed piece.

Because the script is the blueprint for the whole production ... much more than just a few words and music cues ... it is a terribly important document. It lays out the tasks for a whole team of people; graphic designers, camerapeople, actors, directors, musicians, editors. Of course, the development of the script is a collaborative process, involving the client, the production team and the writer. And needless to say the finished product may change substantially from the treatment or even the first draft. However, the script is still the one document that provides the entire team with a starting point, a structure, an approach, a tone, and suggested visuals.

At this stage the full portfolio of elements that need to go into a finished camera script are not as important for you to consider. They can be learnt later. What will help you if you are asked to provide a script for an audio-visual presentation is a few tips on how to go about approaching a programme, and how to put your ideas of words and pictures together in a way that will work. Writing words, and in this case pictures, that sell can be done effectively provided your thinking is correct.

Visual thinking

Before you put any words down on paper, please take careful heed of this one piece of advice. In writing for the audio-visual media, more than any other, you're not just writing words. As television or feature films must have a successful marriage of words and pictures, so must the corporate media. Always, always visualise what you're writing. Even the most straightforward corporate documentary, with a narration and general views and not much else, must still have a strong partnership between what the narrator says and what viewers see. It certainly is not a case of one duplicating the other; never tell viewers what they can already see. Use words and pictures as extra dimensions of each other, and you'll get a good result.

When you're writing a script, you must think of the pictures at the same time. You don't have to work out every shot length and every camera angle; that is the director's job. All you need to have is an idea of what should be happening on screen. One British scriptwriter recently was overheard to say that writers should pay attention to visual content at some stage of scriptwriting, because sooner or later somebody else would have to visualise that script. In our view, that somebody is not somebody else; it's you. You don't do the detailed visualisation, but if you can't work out what viewers should be seeing on screen while someone is speaking your words, then no one else will, either. Writers who use the approach of that British writer are cursed by producers and directors, who struggle to try to make some visual sense out of very pretty, but visually unconnected, words. These people are living in the past, in the days when the audio side of a slidetape script consisted of excerpts from the brochure copy and some poor producer had to find still photographs to match. That is no better than a "magic lantern" show, or somebody talking a bored audience through their holiday snaps, and none of us should be making those awful slidetape and video programmes anymore.

Visual thinking is not difficult. It's just a case of colourful storytelling. If you're writing narration, try to complement words with visuals. And narration doesn't have to tally exactly with what's happening on screen. Narration can also act as commentary ... pointing out issues that are allied to the action on screen, but not necessarily identical. Viewers aren't idiots; their ears are perfectly capable of functioning separately from their eyes, provided there's some logical link between the two. If you're writing dialogue, you need to become the character ... feel what he or she should feel; but more of that later.

To get you going in the right direction, imagine you're telling a story to a small child. Do you describe the big, bad wolf as a cruel, unfeeling individual with deep-seated psychological problems and an innate hatred of people answering the description of young girls wearing small, crimson-coloured headgear suited to equestrianism? If the point of the storytelling is to put the child to sleep, you score a bull's eye. If, on the other hand, you want to stimulate the child's imagination and help him or her to visualise the story, you talk about the big bad wolf with his big, floppy ears, his gleaming, nasty eyes, his ugly black teeth, his slimy, growling voice, and a sickly smile ... making poor Little Red Riding Hood run behind a chair and try to hide from him, trembling and crying with fear. That is visual writing, because despite the fact that you can't see anything but a number of black words on white paper, you can visualise a picture of what the words say.

Determining your approach

Many people involved in corporate video (and slidetape) still feel that the only way to make a programme is to use a documentary, or news item approach. This could not be further from the truth. Television, and to a lesser but still significant extent AV, is an emotional pot-pourri, and for the purposes of your writing work you can virtually take your pick from the wide range of styles you see on broadcast television, provided you bear in mind the differences between this and the corporate media explained earlier. Humour, drama, pathos, shock, threat, sympathy, empathy, stimulation, aggression, are all there for the taking, suitably harnessed to be driven by the message or messages you need to communicate. Of course, you don't have to ignore straightforward "newsy" presentations; but audiences have seen it all before. With a little imagination and lateral thinking, you can do much better.

Although in the early days of corporate video it seemed safer to let audiences identify programmes with what they saw on their nightly news broadcast programmes, nowadays that's the last thing you want them to do. You want them to remember your programme and retain the information it conveys; and if you have to make your audience laugh, cry, cringe, fume, or quake with fear in order to achieve that, then so be it. Don't be afraid to be a little bit daring; that's what makes good programming.

But, and this is a big but, there is always one over-riding factor you need to consider. And that, as we covered earlier, is money. Remember, if you don't have very much to spend on production, forget the ambitious approach; spend what resources you have on making a good, lively, simple programme. There's a lot you can do with one camera and a two-day shoot. That's where the visual thinking and imagination come in.

AV: MORE THAN MEETS THE EYE

With AV, all you have to build on is mute pictures and a sound track. But there's more to those than people think. On the picture side, the most important consideration is to think in terms of sequences of stills ... not one-offs. There is nothing more irritating than a slidetape programme that jumps around from subject to subject. Think visually, in a progression. Think of showing your material in a logical sequence. Just as you would with video, think of establishing shots, followed by more detailed pictures. If you're describing a new computer building, show the outside of it first ... then go indoors and show the new machines.

Stills film is cheap; don't be mean with it. Don't keep one image up on screen for too long; if it's a new computer terminal, show lots of different angles. Show someone using it. Show close shots of someone's hands on the keyboard. Show people's faces ... studying, smiling, consulting with their colleagues. Let the photographer's creative flair loose on the project ... even the most boring metal box can look interesting through a filtered lens, with artistic lighting.

Graphics (charts, diagrams, etc.) are fine, but don't overdo them. Lots of statistics are boring. Use graphics to punctuate a message, to emphasise a point.

If you haven't enough pictures, use a library. There are good picture libraries in every major city and, although library shots aren't cheap one or two can make all the difference. Then, there's the sound track. Sound recording is cheap. Sound effects are cheap. Music (library) is cheap. Use your imagination. As we indicated earlier in this chapter, there's nothing to suggest that you can't have *interviews* in slidetape ... Show a few slow, dissolving stills of someone's face, and play a recording of their voice. The narrator can make it abundantly clear who is talking. Use a mixture of voices to create an effect.

Use sound effects. If you're showing a factory, play some of its noise. If you're showing a motorway, play the sound of cars. If you're showing some archival material of the past, get some sound effects from that era and play them. Most good recording studios have sound effects libraries that contain anything from Concorde taking off to camels spitting in Riyadh. Use them; they'll only cost a few pounds or dollars each.

And there's music. Whether you're working with slidetape or video, a large proportion of the impact of a corporate programme has to come from music. A simple and conclusive demonstration of this is to show a rough edit of a videotape or a rough assembly of a slide show to a client without the music track, and get a reaction. Then show it again with the music track. The difference – even if the visuals are identical – will be pronounced.

Music is laid on as wallpaper. If you're the writer, you can help the producer by indicating the type of music you would like. If you're producing the programme yourself, choose the music (or ask the sound engineer to help you choose it) to match the mood of the programme. And remember, programmes have more than one mood; change the music. Drop it, and start it again (wall-to-wall background music is tedious). Use it to punctuate the words and pictures. Match it to the mood on screen, and to the words spoken. Remember, with modern AV techniques, it is quite simple to programme your slide changes in time to a music beat. Videotape and film can also be edited in time to music, creating a very punchy effect.

All these elements sound very technical. But don't forget that if you are putting a treatment together you need to bear these in mind. And when you write the script, they will have to be included.

VIDEO: THE DOCUMENTARY APPROACH

Let's take an example, where there is a limited budget, and your purpose is to communicate a new product or process to employees. You need to include some sort of address to staff from the chairman, and show how the new product has been developed as well as what it does.

Many such programmes that you see will show a "talking head" of the chairman, straining to read a teleprompter, followed by a voice over reading out brochure copy while a fixed camera is pointed at a metal box. The occasional graphic arrow appears on the screen to point out a particularly interesting widget. After four minutes, the audience is asleep.

There is a tendency among inexperienced or overly enthusiastic corporate people to think that the natural way to shoot a programme is to go and shoot what's there. *"We'll start at reception, because we have a lovely new switchboard, and Bridget is quite attractive, then I think we should proceed through the corridor because we spent a fortune on the new downlighting, then directly into the corporate fitness centre because that demonstrates how committed we are to our people, and from there right on to the machine shop where we really should get the milling and drilling operations of the three types of computer controlled machines ..."*

Wrong. The brutal fact of life is that, apart from a few people, no one in the audience will care deeply about such things as new switchboards or expanded offices or corporate fitness centres, even if it is an internal audience. Its members need to get an image or impression of your message; not the office furniture or, even, the lovely Bridget. Whoever your viewers are, never write programmes based solely on shots of the facilities and labs, offices and lawns.

Next, let's look at the chairman. Many chairmen have developed a bit of an ego over the years. They may fancy themselves as performers. Others may be shy and have no interest in being on screen, but their subordinates think it would be a good idea. The fact is, performing on camera is a very difficult thing to do. The natural reaction for an amateur is to go completely blank. To repeat. To look sideways. To stutter and say "er". So, sticking the chairman in front of a camera is courting disaster, and you should think carefully before doing it. No matter how revered the he or she is to his/her staff, to the viewer the chairman is simply a sweaty, stammering non-actor with a high squeaky voice. But often, you need to include the Chairman in your programme, be it for practical or political reasons.

Getting back to our example: for the same money, how about this? First, get the chairman out of his/her office, and on to the factory floor. Or outside the building, by a big sign that reinforces the company's image. Or if, say, the new product is a car component, sit him/her in a car. On a car. In the back seat of the car, driving along. If he/she can't remember the words, don't let him/her read them – that sounds stilted. Interview him/her, off camera, so your questions act as prompts. If the chairman can remember the words, get him/her to walk around. The camera can follow. By getting them out of the formal environment of the studio or boardroom, most chairmen turn into real, interesting human beings. Not only is that important to you – it is very important to the viewer.

Next, we move on to products. Don't just plonk a product in front of the camera. Don't read out the brochure copy. Get someone in a white coat to lovingly describe the baby he has just borne ... real words, from a real enthusiast, are far more illuminating than any narration script you – or we – will ever write.

If it does something, show it doing it. If it has an interesting widget, don't stick an arrow over it. Get someone to produce a good diagram of the innards of the widget, and cut away to that. Don't just say it cuts fuel consumption by 20 per cent. Show someone driving into a petrol station, filling up, paying, and smiling. Push the cameraman into the back seat of your car and get him to shoot a close-up of the fuel gauge.

Above all, let people and places talk. That's what television's all about. People do not go about their working lives without saying a word. Factories and machines are noisy. Let your viewers see things as they really are – and hear things. Don't shoot mute tape and stick a voice over the top for the whole programme. Break it up with interview clips; and, unless the subject matter needs a lot of explanation, keep them short. Interview people at their place of work, when you can; like the chairman, they're more comfortable – and more credible – there than in some formal boardroom or studio. Let them express the company's views – much better than if it comes from the "voice of God" narration. If they work in a noisy place, get them to talk more loudly.

That's real life. And if you can afford it, get the narrator out from behind the microphone and get him/her walking around your subject matter, talking to the camera.

Now what about something fancier?

VIDEO: DRAMATISATION

The first thing to remember is, don't be frightened by drama. You're not competing with Harold Pinter or Tennessee Williams. Dramatisation is simply the recreation "of a slice of life". Dialogue is simply the way ordinary people say ordinary things. So, how can dramatisation be used in the "corporate context"?

The most obvious place is in training programmes. There is no better way to illustrate the wrong and the right ways of doing things, than by a dramatised example. This is particularly true where you're training people to deal with other people – "inter-personal skills", they call it. But another way in which dramatisation can be useful is in product or process demonstration. Instead of describing what something does, show some actors using it in a realistic plot.

In corporate work, there is usually a need for some kind of

documentary style explanation to accompany dramatisations. This is fine, but don't clutter one up with the other. Let your actors do their bit without the narrator breathing down their necks every thirty seconds. Use the narrator to link, and let the characters do the teaching or demonstrating. In some contexts, you don't need a straight narration at all; the occasional caption is enough. In fact, you can even make a feature of the relationship between the narrator and dramatised characters, creating a slightly surreal effect. (The treatment we have included as a sample, and the full script of the same programme that follows later in this chapter, use this technique.)

One problem: amateur actors, as we touched on earlier. If you can't afford trained actors (for anything other than very minor parts) don't do a dramatisation. It doesn't matter how many times your financial director has done "*A Streetcar Named Desire*" with his local amateur Dramatic society, he won't impress your viewers by trying to play an agitated customer. Amateur acting looks tacky; tacky content in your programme will make your company or organisation look tacky, too.

VIDEO: COMEDY

Watch comedy; don't let the tail wag the dog. In the late 1970s and the early 1980s ago when Video Arts — the well-known production company specialising in humorous corporate training programmes — was in its heyday in Britain, everyone wanted training and other corporate programmes to be shot at Fawlty Towers or the Ministry of Funny Walks ... both classic examples of a special type of humour attributed to John Cleese, one of the original Monty Python creators.

The Cleese-esque humour is still brilliant, but it got done to death, and badly at that, by "me-too" production companies and in-house units everywhere. People were so entranced by it that they would even try to force it into subject matters that were totally unsuitable for humorous portrayal. The result was that not only did the genre become tired, but it made a lot of companies look very silly. Other types of humour were exploited to death, as well — especially sitcoms. Many professional writers like us were called upon to rip off a number of popular sitcoms, in a corporate context, with very mixed results.

Writing for this type of work is a specialised job, best left to experts. There are comedy writing courses available in many major cities, plus a number of books, if you're interested in this type of scriptwriting. But whatever you do, don't try to tackle humour unless you're certain you can do it well. Comedy writing runs a close second to children's stories in the league table of the most difficult writing styles, and no one should take it lightly. And a corporate programme that uses bad comedy is the fastest way we know to make your company's image look very funny indeed.

Humorous programmes, if you do use this approach, work best when you tailor the content to the purpose. In-jokes, within an organisation, will bring the house down – and make a point. Trying to bend a well-known entertainer's style of humour around a specific brief and set of objectives takes practice, but it works, too.

Comedy is often a case not of writing lots of funny one-liners, but of placing ordinary actions in extraordinary circumstances. A man sneezing in the bathroom isn't funny; but the same man sneezing over the kitchen table just as his wife dumps a huge bowl of sifted flour on it, is. If you want to tackle humour, do remember not to labour it ... use it sparingly, and don't let it dictate your programme content.

WRITING STYLE

There are only two worthwhile points to remember about writing style, both of which we've covered a number of times in this book. *One*, is write as people speak; not as you were taught at school. *Two*, is keep it simple ... no long words, no long sentences, no meaningless clichés and jargon.

Easy, isn't it? Wrong. These two points, together, are difficult to learn. When professional writers look back at scripts they wrote even five years earlier, they often cringe. They are not as good as the scripts they are producing now. And in five years' time, they will be better still. As we point out earlier, simple, "spoken" speech sounds as easy to write as it does to say. But as is often the case in life, the simplest things are sometimes the hardest to achieve.

The best way to practise writing for the spoken word is to be observant. You don't need a RADA degree in speech and drama to write dialogue or narration; just a pair of ears and a pair of eyes. Listen to the ways in which people talk, watch how they behave. This is especially true when it comes to creating characters and *dialogue*.

Make your characters real. Even in the thick of business life, business people are thinking and reacting to other issues. Sports, current events, food, each other. Bring some personality to them; nobody is just a truck driver or just a middle manager. Have their motives in mind. People tend to say things because they want something or need something, or have some hidden agenda that lies behind their spoken words. Always be reasonably sure what the subtext is, underlying the spoken words. And don't be linear. Conversation tends to be circuitous. One person has a pet topic, another has another concern altogether. One person says something and the next person says something that sounds unrelated, but has a perfectly clear relation *for that person*.

When you're writing dialogue, don't write it – so to speak. Talk it through to yourself ... try to project yourself into the character you're scripting. Imagine you are that person ... imagine not only what he/she would say, but how he/she is feeling at the time. In drama, you have to work yourself up to feel all the emotion of any particular plot ... sense what the murderer was feeling as he stuck the electric carving knife into his mother-in-law's jugular vein ... sense how the lovestruck girl felt when her boyfriend told her he was leaving her ... sense how the mother felt when her baby died.

In corporate work, we may not need these strong emotions quite so often. But, let's say in the case of a dramatisation of an industrial accident, there should be strong emotions. You would have to feel the pain of someone who has just tripped over a fire extinguisher and broken a leg ... feel the terrible guilt of the office manager who has forgotten to unlock the door to the fire escape. Practise good old fashioned human empathy, and you're on the way to writing good dialogue.

Narration, is almost a writing style on its own. Yes, it must be spoken speech, as with dialogue. But because it is not to be spoken in a "real-life" context, and because most professional voice artistes are very good at their jobs, you can enjoy more freedom with narration than you can with dialogue. Many of us in professional writing believe that narration is similar to poetry, where the cadence of the words has a very important role to play in supporting the message the words convey. It is important to write simply, in spoken speech, but also to balance the words and the sentences, so that there is a certain music to it all. Single words and very short sentences can be loaded with emotion by the voice artiste, and convey a great deal. They are especially useful to break up longer sections of detail or technical matter.

Very often, you'll find that you develop your writing style for a particular programme, from the visual thinking that goes into the treatment and, later, into the script. Try to balance facts with feelings, keep it uncluttered, and don't write "wall-to-wall" words. Short silences, or short passages with music and sound effects only, can say more than words.

Here are the first couple of minutes of narration for a multi-image corporate programme for a well-known computer company. As it was slidetape with no other voices, the narration had to convey all the messages, including the mood and philosophy of the company. Visually, the programme began with an exciting montage of images; the narration did not run wall-to-wall, but was punctuated with music ...

"NARRATOR: Welcome ... to the information technology partnership of the future.

Welcome ... to Company X.

Pioneers ... in partnership with a new era of progress.

The principle of partnership is not new. But the Company X style of partnership within information technology is blowing a welcome breath of invigorating air back into the industry.

Up until now, most large computer systems have been researched, developed, manufactured, marketed and supported by one organisation alone ... straining, under the weight. And many companies have found the strain of such vertical integration too heavy. A rapidly changing market, rising costs, and avid competition, have forced a number of vertically integrated organisations to lose market share, or even go out of business.

Successful business, in this evolutionary time, is created by adaptable animals ... not by lumbering dinosaurs.

Now, the new way of doing business ... the Company X way ... is to form a network of strategic partnerships, in which a company concentrates on doing what it's really good at. These companies, and their partners, are very light on their feet. They respond fast and well ... to market trends, technological advances, and customer needs. (etc ...) "

TYPES OF CORPORATE PROGRAMMES

There are a number of different uses for the audio-visual media, and here are the most important ones.

The Corporate Programme itself, is sometimes called an image/capabilities show. This is most often produced in video, although you may well see it done in multi-image format as well. It is meant to set out, in ten minutes or so, the business areas, products and essential character of the company in question. Such programmes can be sent out to customers/dealers/prospects cold, to give them an idea of your company rather as a corporate brochure does. Or they can be shown as part of a live presentation, as a warm-up to the first speaker – sometimes called a "bum settler", as this is the first part of the event, and involves getting the audience settled and in the right mood.

The Meeting Show is likely to be made in multi-image format, and is used for a number of purposes within a conference or presentation. It presents a theme or a simple message in a lively and impactful way, often punctuating a longer live presentation.

The Training Programme can be made either on video or on slidetape, although video is preferable – particularly when you're teaching people a process or sequence of actions. Video is extremely useful in demonstrating not only practical techniques but also attitudes and behaviour – handy for teaching customer care and inter-personal skills, in dramatised format. Training programmes should never be too long, and you should always remember that the audio-visual media exist to communicate broad messages and concepts ... not fine detail. The best training schemes are those which get over the broad understanding with video and, having made the audience understand that, get down to fine details on paper.

The Marketing/Sales Programme is usually about a particular product or service, perhaps with a short corporate section about the company concerned at the beginning of the programme. Some people regard these as long commercials, but be careful; a) you usually don't have nearly as much money to spend on them (see an earlier part of this chapter) and b) your target audience is likely to want to know a lot more about the product/service than a commercial would tell them. Commercials sell concepts – not the sausage, but the *sizzle* in the sausage. Sales programmes sell the sizzle, but they also tell you quite a lot about the sausage at the same time. They back up concepts with interesting, vividly presented facts.

The Short Promotional Programme is a bit more like a long commercial. These programmes are most often seen running on continuous loop playback on exhibition stands, or in-store. The main points to remember about them is that they must be short – no one passing by will stop, stand there and look at such a programme for longer than about two minutes. And make them visually self-sufficient. The sound of these programmes has to compete with a high level of ambient noise, so although you need a sound track for those who can hear it, the pictures must speak for themselves for the majority, who can't hear the sound at all.

The Recruitment Programme is often taken to be a corporate programme with a bit of information about career opportunities at the end. This is a bad mistake. Once again, put yourself in your audience's shoes; what you have to sell to customers, shareholders, dealers, suppliers, etc. is quite different from what you must sell to someone who might devote the next X years of his/her working life to your company. Identifying who you want to attract, and researching their needs and inclinations, is a very important part of making good recruitment programmes, whether they're on video or slidetape. And whatever happens, don't try to make a corporate programme do a recruiting job; it will be a waste of money in the end, because the resulting hybrid won't do either job well.

SCRIPT LAYOUT

There are three basic methods of script layout. The audio-visual format has two columns side by side; one contains all the audio material like voice-over, dialogue, documentary comments, music and sound effects cues. The other contains a description of the visuals. This can be a strict list of shots, or a general description of the images required. Slidetape and multi-image scripts are usually set out in this way, and some film and television scripts are too. The sample script that follows at the end of the chapter is laid out in side by side style.

Another way is screenplay format. This comes from the feature film business, and contains narrative, voice over and dialogue in indented sections with descriptions of visuals set out between dialogue chunks at full page width. Margins should be fairly generous, so the other members of the production team can scribble notes and comments next to relevant lines. In the full camera script version, each scene should be identified as well.

"1. INTERIOR: DOCTOR'S OFFICE   *DAY*

We open on a long shot of the doctor sitting at his consulting desk. The patient is sitting opposite him, talking in undertones. The doctor listens intently, then speaks.

DOCTOR: *Well frankly, Mrs Murphy, although I understand your concern I really can't prescribe you any more tranquillisers.*

We cut to a close reaction shot of Mrs Murphy, who looks horrified.

MRS MURPHY: *Oh, no, doctor! How can I possibly manage without them?*

We return to the original two-shot. Their conversation continues in undertones as the narrator speaks over.

NARRATOR: *Helping patients to come to terms with their dependence on benzo-diazepines takes a great deal of tact and understanding ..."*

Yet another way of laying out a script is almost the reverse of screenplay format. This is television, or television drama, format. The description of the visual side of things goes in indented sections in capital letters, with dialogue running across the page in upper and lower case. Scenes are identified in the same way.

"1. INTERIOR, DOCTOR'S OFFICE   *DAY*

WE OPEN ON A LONG SHOT OF THE DOCTOR AT HIS CONSULTING DESK. THE PATIENT IS SITTING OPPOSITE HIM, TALKING IN UNDERTONES. THE DOCTOR LISTENS INTENTLY, THEN SPEAKS.

DOCTOR: *Well frankly, Mrs Murphy, although I understand your concern I really can't prescribe you any more tranquillisers.*

*WE CUT TO A CLOSE REACTION SHOT OF MRS MURPHY,
WHO LOOKS HORRIFIED.*

MRS MURPHY: *Oh, no, doctor! How can I possibly manage without
them?!"*

The best format is a matter of preference. AV producers tend to like
the side by side format because it lays out the visuals in a more
accessible way. The screenplay and television formats flow better,
because they're sequential, and are easier for the non-producer to
understand. Although you should really pick the format that seems
easiest for you, it is a helpful courtesy to speak with whoever is going
to produce and/or direct your programme, to see what format suits him
or her best.

The script that follows, in side by side format, is the script that was
developed out of the treatment shown earlier in this chapter. This
script was a little unusual as it did not change very much from the
treatment, and the finished programme was almost exactly the same,
too. Don't be lulled into a false sense of security because of this,
though; it was the exception that proves the rule.

The other unusual point about the script is that the left hand column
which normally contains a great deal of production jargon, was written
in lay terms. This was for the benefit of the non-technical approval
committee.

VISION	*SOUND*
Opening titles	(Music)

We open with an amusing visual montage of the old-fashioned, cli-chéd view of British tourism in the past. The material could include seaside picture-postcards from the early twentieth century, archival film footage of people on the beaches at Blackpool and other resorts, complete with rolled-up trousers and knotted handkerchiefs on their heads, thirties and forties charabanc tours, shots of the West End theatres pre-war, etc.	NARRATOR: *To our parents and grandparents, the good old days of British beaches and trips out with friends and family, bring back happy memories.* *In their time, mass tourism as we know it today, was still in its infancy. To travel around Britain, and to come here from abroad, was nowhere nearly as easy … or affordable … as it is now.*
Here, we should show some old drawings or paintings of early travel, old coaching inns, religious pilgrimages, etc.	*All the same, tourism has been with us for centuries. People have been travelling away from their homes, for business or personal reasons, since well before Roman times.*
If possible, we should show some representation of the "European Grand Tour"	*Tourism for pleasure, got going in the eighteenth century … but then only for the well-to-do, who went on the Grand Tour of Europe to add to their cultural knowledge.*
We should show some Victorian archival material here.	*So it wasn't until the late eighteen hundreds, that tourism became possible for ordinary people. Standards of living were getting better; railway travel was more accessible; and many people could now afford to visit the seaside and other attractions, or travel around on business. More and more foreign visitors arrived, on the greatly improved ocean liners of the day.*
Drawings, paintings, and/or early photographs of 19th-century ocean liners.	

Montage of shots, going from early cars and aircraft, through to present-day models.

Even so, it took the invention of the motor car, and later air travel, to turn tourism from an expensive luxury into something almost everyone can afford. And these two developments, in historical terms at least, happened only yesterday.

The last shot in this sequence is a long, slow pan across a British beach. The era is indeterminate. Captions over-emphasise the brief teaching points made by the narrator.

Tourism has come a long way, in a very short time.

This industry is light years beyond the whelk-stalls and the charabancs ... the corner houses and the deck chairs ... things that represented travel even just a few generations ago.

Today, it is the third largest industry in Britain ... employing nearly 1½ million people in a huge variety of different jobs and careers.

The camera's eye comes to rest on a beachside billboard, showing two comedy figures. There are holes cut out where the figures' faces should be.

And unlike many of today's older industries, tourism is growing ... with more and more job opportunities every year.

The faces of our two characters, Mum and Son, peer straight at us. As the narrator speaks about people's ignorance of tourism today, they look perplexed, then laugh.

(IN AMUSED VOICE) Yet many people still think tourism is just about day trips to the seaside ...

NARRATOR: *(TO CHARACTERS) What does the tourist industry mean to you, then?*

Mum and Son look at each other, then smile quizzically at each other. Their faces disappear from the holes in the billboard, and a second or two later they appear in full either side of the board. They are dressed in discreet beach clothes. They lean against the board, and look at each other once again. Son scratches his head; he is deep in thought.

NARRATOR: *(TO CHARACTERS) Come on!*

Son looks straight at the camera.

SON: *Well, I hadn't really thought much. I suppose it's about people coming down here, like us. For a day out and a bit of sun, you know.*

Mum joins in the conversation.

MUM: *Yes, and all those Americans going round the Tower of London.*

SON: *And coach trips. You know, when my Nan goes to see those gardens with her club.*

Mum looks at the camera.

MUM: *Is that what you mean?*

The two characters look intrigued.

NARRATOR: *Well, yes. But that's just the tip of the iceberg.*

SON: *There's more?*

NARRATOR: *Much more. And what about job opportunities? What do you think tourism offers people like you?*

MUM: *Like us? Oh, I don't know. I reckon I'm too old to be an airline stewardess. (LAUGHING) Don't you, love?*

Mum looks over at Son, and they both giggle.

SON: *Yeah. And I couldn't be a tour guide, could I? I mean, I wasn't very good at history. Only just got my CSE. And I don't speak lots of languages.*

MUM: *No, just English.*

SON: *And Rubbish!*

Mum looks at the camera.

MUM: *(BECOMING SERIOUS) Don't suppose we'd be much use, working in tourism, would we?*

NARRATOR: *Nonsense! There's a lot more to working in tourism than being a stewardess or a guide, you know.*

Sons looks seriously at the camera.

SON: *What?*

NARRATOR: *Alright. I'm going to tell you the facts about tourism. I think you'll be surprised at the tremendous amount it involves. In fact, there is an Open College course you can take, connected with this series, that gives you a very thorough introduction to tourism.*

Show O.C. caption

Why don't you just step forward a little?

They look intrigued, but step for-ward as the narrator asks.

Great. Now if you keep your eyes on the board, we'll have a look at tour-ism in Britain today.

The camera lens zooms into the billboard. During the following sequence, we see a montage of pictures and captions, linked by modern computer-generated special effects, which reinforce the points made by the narrator. This is interspersed with short sections where the camera pulls back just enough to reveal one or two of our characters, who join in the sequence as well – and so on as the script continued.

Like I said just now, tourism is growing extremely fast. In fact, it is the biggest growth industry in the world, with nearly one and a half MILLION people working in it in Britain today, either directly or indirectly. And that number is increasing by about 50,000 jobs each year.

CHAPTER 12

WILL YOUR WORDS REALLY SELL?

Conclusion

When you've finished writing whatever it is you're writing, try to avoid the usual, post-script attitude: defensiveness. If you consider your writing as a job, as a useful task that you're performing to help your colleagues, it will help. To be defensive is to view your writing as an outpouring of self-expression, and attacks upon it as attacks upon your very soul. This makes for difficult approval sessions and may do more damage to your writing in the long run than making a few changes suggested by others.

This is not to suggest that you should abandon your own work, or not defend it. You need to start by knowing what you think of your own work. If you think it needs refinement in some places, or if you need more information in another, or if something isn't quite right yet, there is no shame in saying so. Nobody minds – not even clients – hearing your informal opinion of a piece of writing ... shortcomings and all. What people do mind is the writer trying to put one over on them. Or, worse, if they think the writing has problems but you don't, they may come to doubt your basic abilities. Once they doubt, it will be difficult to regain their confidence.

So, just as there is a method for planning and developing your writing, there are also some ways of testing what you have written. It comes down to asking yourself some nagging questions which are designed to reveal your own (possibly hidden) opinions of your own work. For example ...

Would I find this interesting, if I were reading it? When you're writing, it is quite possible to separate yourself (the writer) from yourself (the human being). This is useful, in that it allows you to become completely involved in subjects that you thought you had no interest in (let's say, the history of insurance). At the same time, this ability may allow you to immerse yourself so completely in the subject that you lose all perspective. You forget that the history of insurance has a limited interest to a limited number of people for a limited period of time.

So, ask yourself as you read, whether you, the human being – not the writer who has lived through days or minutes or weeks of research and ordering and writing – would find this of any interest or relevance. You must be extremely hard on yourself. The worst thing you can do – particularly in the visual media and advertising – is to bore people.

Is it true? No company that has a desire to stay in business wants, needs or ever should deliver selling messages that are untrue. The common offence that sales writing commits – and it does so regularly – is to tell less than the whole story. This is a function of the "good news" axiom. It is hard to fault this tendency. Not only is it fundamental to making people want to buy whatever it is you're selling, it's also fundamental to the way people operate in general. They tell the version of events that best suits their purpose, whatever that might be.

Nevertheless, ask yourself if everything you have written is true, or true as you understand it – and whether anything you have written is perhaps not untrue but might be a bit misleading. There is no profit for anybody – you, the company, the reader – in muddling up the truth.

Is it convincing? That is to say, when you read it, does it have clearly stated key messages, which are supported by credible and clearly stated supporting facts or illustrations? The writing is no good if, despite nice wordsmithing and a good flow, you're not ultimately convinced. As the writer, be careful, because you have a natural desire to want to be convinced. Show the writing to somebody else, preferably somebody who has no connection with it. See what they think.

How does it look? There is no way around the fact that the perceived quality of writing is affected by the way it looks physically. Page layout, spacing, the quality of the type, the quality of the paper, headers and footers – readers are strongly influenced by these characteristics of your writing. You make a mistake if you believe these things should not be important. There is no excuse for a rotten-looking document – not, least, an excuse that will make you look any better.

Do I really think this creative approach will work, or would I just like to think it will? This is a question to ask about scripts, in particular – but, preferably, before you've reached the script stage and are still working on a treatment. It is terribly easy to fall in love with a creative idea, and harbour a deep, internal suspicion that it *can't really work* but not admit it to yourself for a long time, because it is so lovely and clever. Give yourself the luxury of loving the idea in the abstract for as long as you can afford to, and then abandon it, for everyone's sake. If the subject is rich enough, and if you've done your preparation properly, there should be ten other ideas to replace the rejected one.

Is it positive? You may be a bit sick of this question but writers are often cynical creatures. They have a tendency to look on the dark side, and see the desperate and negative motives of others. Sometimes this attitude sneaks into the writing unnoticed – in some small aside, or turn of phrase. Keep your eyes open for it.

Is it fresh, or have I seen it before? This is a tough, but necessary, question. There is absolutely no point in producing a document that sounds like every other document, that repeats what has been said before, that has nothing new to add – however small. It should not be work for the reader to get through a piece of writing; it should be interesting, enlightening, amusing, informative – or, if nothing else – refreshingly brief. There has to be some way to make the document fresh and it's your job to find it.

Is the key message clear? When you've read it, can you honestly say that it delivers the key message directly? When someone else reads the writing and you ask them what it says, do they basically articulate the major point? For example: "It says that ZX90 CMU has much better electronics than the competition". Or, that "quality is getting it right first time".

If I removed this bit, would the whole suffer? When developing a selling argument, there is no room for the extraneous. Now and again, in a longer document – such as a brochure – or in a speech, an interesting digression is acceptable. But in an ad, a script, or a written proposal, anything that is not needed is not needed. Try taking a sentence or paragraph out and see if it is missed. Nine times out of ten, everything you write is improved when you take things out.

Is it correct? Have I checked the facts? This is a bit different from the question, "is it true?". Truth has more to do with the overall picture, But, you also want to be sure you've got your facts straight – because if they are wrong and anybody notices your credibility is shattered.

Is every thought complete? Am I mixing two ideas in one place? Does something I say raise questions that I don't answer immediately? Can a complete statement be said in a simpler way by breaking it down into smaller, complete thoughts?

Does it flow? Are there any leaps of logic or abrupt changes of direction that are shocking, confusing, unpleasant, or strange? If there are, do they hurt the document or do they add interest?

Does it levitate? Finally, a completely subjective, slightly mystical question that may or may not work for you. John Butman, upon completion of a document, always asks himself the question: "Does it levitate?" The idea in the tortured writer's mind is that, if a document is properly structured, has a brilliant flow, is well polished, true, accurate and interesting, if it was held in mid-air and dropped, it would be so strong and internally well-balanced that it would hang in mid-air suspended before gently descending to a clean desktop.

A pleasant thought.

CHAPTER 13

READ ON AND WRITE ON:

Further reading and glossary

FURTHER READING

THE A TO Z OF VIDEO AND AUDIO-VISUAL JARGON, Suzan St Maur (Routledge and Kegan Paul, 1986)

DO YOUR OWN ADVERTISING, Alastair Crompton (Century Hutchinson Better Business Guides, 1986)

THE CRAFT OF WRITING ARTICLES, Gordon Wells (Allison Busby, 1983)

THE CRAFT OF COPYWRITING, Alastair Crompton (Business Books Communica Europa, 1979)

KEEPING UP THE STYLE, Leslie Sellers (Sir Isaac Pitman Sons, 1975)

PUBLIC RELATIONS FOR YOUR BUSINESS, Frank Jefkins (Mercury Books, 1987)

RUNNING YOUR OWN MAIL ORDER BUSINESS, Malcolm Breckman (Kogan Page, 1987)

BE YOUR OWN P.R. MAN, Michael Bland (Kogan Page, 1981)

HOW TO PROMOTE YOUR OWN BUSINESS, Jim Dudley (Kogan Page, 1988)

THE SECRETS OF SUCCESSFUL LOW-BUDGET ADVERTISING, Patrick Quinn (William Heinemann, 1987)

SUCCESSFUL MARKETING FOR THE SMALL BUSINESS, Dave Patten (Kogan Page, 1985)

IMPROVING YOUR PRESENTATION SKILLS, Michael Stevens (Kogan Page, 1987)

VIDEO PRODUCTION TECHNIQUES (Kluwer Publishing)

THE WAY TO WRITE FOR TELEVISION, Eric Paice (Elm Tree Books, 1981).

GLOSSARY

A.M.
In radio transmission, this stands for Amplitude Modulation. It's a more technical way of saying medium wave band.

ABOVE-THE-LINE
In advertising, above-the-line activities are anything which involves buying space in publications, or air-time on radio, television and cinema, and the creation of advertising material to be used therein. All other activities like sales promotion, direct mail, PR, and so-on are called below-the-line. In feature films and broadcast television, above the line expenditure is the main bulk of a production, and includes all the usual expenses like hire of crew, hire of performers and location fees. Below-the-line costs are for special, one-off items, e.g., stunt performers, animals, the construction of a special prop. These terms will sometimes be used by film, videotape and television commercial production companies.

ACCOUNT
The word used to describe one client's business in an advertising agency, PR, sales promotion, or direct mail consultancy. The term is also creeping into business theatre and film/video production company terminology. An account suggests an ongoing relationship between client and supplier, rather than a one-off project basis. Hence account handler, account executive, account supervisor, account director and so on.

ACTION
The action is the actual, physical activity which takes place in a videotape programme or film. But the word is more commonly associated with what directors say on set or on location when they want the performers to perform. With videotape, where the sound and vision are in one machine, the director will tell the camera operator to get going first. With film, where sound and vision are recorded on different machines, the director will tell sound to start fractionally before the camera. Then comes the magic word: *action*!

ADSHEL
A trade name for a company in Britain which sells outdoor advertising space, particular on bus shelters – hence the name.

ADVERTORIAL
A combination of advertising and editorial which refers to editorial content "given" to advertisers by some publications in exchange for a largish purchased advertisement space. The editorial words allotted to the advertiser are normally culled from the advertiser's press release, and are often placed quite near the advertisement itself.

AIR
With artwork for ads, brochures, leaflets, slides, and graphics to be used in moving pictures, to leave "plenty of air" around an image or word means to leave plenty of clear, uncluttered space.

ANIMATIC
When a television commercial is in production, rather than show a client a raw storyboard of a production as it is drawn, the production team will shoot each section of it, in order, on videotape or film. This way clients can see the drawn images from the storyboard on a television screen, which makes it look more like the finished article. Combined with this will be either the demo of a soundtrack, or possibly the finished sound, in all the appropriate places. If it is a videotape version, it is called an animatic; if shot on film, it's sometimes referred to as a film storyboard. Another way of providing a halfway house between storyboard and finished production is to make a photomatic.

ANIMATION

Animation is a more high-falutin' word for cartoon, in the film context. People in the business don't mind referring to the Disney brand of animation as cartoons, but might get a bit upset if you were so to label a serious, "art" animated film. The word can also be used to describe clay or other models or puppets, filmed in stop motion to mimic movement. With slidetape work, animation is simply the effect of moving an image around on screen. To do this, you need quite a few projectors; three is the basic minimum. Videotape animation is not unlike that of a slide tape; however there is one major difference. Whereas the effect of moving and playing about with images on slide necessitates a lot of slide production and elbow grease, digital effects on tape can be created by hitting a few buttons.

ANSWERPRINT

The first full copy of a film, after the editing has been done. It's the intermediate stage between the cutting copy, which is the one where you play about with the scissors, and the show copy, the final product. The point of the answerprint is to reveal the film in its entirety without any editing hiccups. However, there will still be work to be done on quality, grading and colour; once these have been adjusted and commented on, the laboratory can then produce the final show copy.

ARTWORK

The original drawing, photograph or diagram, typeset words, plus any other material, from which a final piece of print is produced. These components will normally be stuck on a plain board, and the resulting artwork will then be processed for whichever printing process is to be used. Artwork is also required when slides are to be produced. This will then be photographed on a rostrum camera and converted into a 35mm slide. Similarly, artwork can be prepared and shot on a rostrum camera, to be shown as a still caption in a film or videotape programme.

ASPECT RATIO

This is the ratio of the height to the width of an image. In the case of videotape, you're talking about the ratio of the picture on screen; this is 3 to 4. 35mm slides have an aspect ratio of 2 to 3. We sometimes talk about aspect ratio when referring to the shape of multi-image screens, too.

ASSEMBLE EDIT

A videotape editing term. It's the function of re-recording all the necessary material you choose from the various different tapes you've shot, on to one blank tape, in the order you want. This will form the final programme. Insert editing, on the other hand, is replacing any segment on the final tape, with another of the same length from one of your origination tapes.

AUTOCUE

A trade name for one of the teleprompter devices in common use in business theatre, and in television/video studios. As this was one of the first such systems to be created, and has been around for a long time the name is often mistakenly used as a generic term. But Autocue *is* only a trade name, along with QTV, Portaprompt, and others.

AV
AV, standing for Audio-Visual, is probably the most abused term in the whole of the communications industry. Correctly speaking, any presentation involving the use of sound and pictures simultaneously is an audio-visual presentation. However, in common usage, AV usually means slidetape, multi-image, or any other combination of slides and a pre-recorded soundtrack. In business theatre, "AVs" mean self-contained slidetape modules, as opposed to speaker support sections. Similarly, "AV links" mean a few slides with music to allow one speaker to get down off the stage, and the next to get in place for his or her speech.

   These are the basic, technically correct definitions: *AV*: anything with co-ordinated sound and pictures, still or moving. *SLIDETAPE* or *TAPESLIDE PROGRAMME*: small format (one or two projectors) with recorded, pulsed soundtrack. *MULTI-IMAGE* (USA) or *MULTI-VISION* (UK): (three or more projectors). *PROGRAMME*, when it stands alone, and *MODULE* when either small or large format is used as part of a conference.

BAR CHART
A bar chart is a way of illustrating different amounts – of money, turnover, etc. in artwork to be used for the production of print, slide, videotape or film. Each amount is represented by a horizontal bar of solid colour, in proportion to its neighbours; a visually simple and effective way of comparing figures.

BARCO
The trade name of a type of video projector. It can be used in either front projection or back projection mode and will project videotape recordings or, if plugged into a CCTV camera, will project on to a screen what the camera picks up.

BELOW-THE-LINE
See ABOVE-THE-LINE

BETACAM
A comparatively recent addition to the range of different videotape formats. Betacam is only half-an-inch wide, like VHS, but through refined technology provides very much higher quality when used as the initiation medium. The quality is, some say, even better than that of BVU or High Band, although this is of course a matter of opinion. The advantage of Betacam is that, being smaller than High Band, its equipment is lighter and easier to use.

BETAMAX
One of the videotape cassette formats, made by the Japanese firm Sony. Along with VHS, this is a format for home use, or for showing programmes to very small audiences. The cassettes are marginally smaller than VHS.

BILLING
The combined total of all that an advertising agency's clients spend on above-the-line media in one year. Agencies' size and value are often measured on the strength of their total billing.

BODY COPY
The bulk text of written words in an advertisement, as opposed to the headlines and crossheads or sub-heads. In body copy, you expand on the headline and crossheads, and give the reader a bit more detail about the selling proposition. Body copy should always read well, but be written as we speak ...

not necessarily with correct grammar and syntax, but more as an interesting monologue in print.

BRIEF
The document, or conversation, which determines the background, audience, objectives, and other requirements of a promotional project of any kind. The brief must be put together by whoever is commissioning the project, so that everyone involved – especially the writer – is able to meet its requirements accurately. A good, full, and thorough brief is essential to the successful production of any advertising, promotional, or other business communications project.

BROADCAST QUALITY
Any videotape programme or VTR TV commercial which is of a sufficiently high technical standard to be transmitted on television. This normally means that the videotape programme has been made on either one-inch or two-inch tape.

BUILD-UP
A sequence of graphics coming up on screen in a slidetape or business theatre presentation. This can be a series of words or phrases, as in bullet points; it can be figures; and it can also be parts of a chart building up to a whole, as in the case of bar charts or column charts. The term is sometimes abbreviated to *B/U*.

BULLET POINTS
Part of the artwork, graphics and caption world. When you've got several points to list on a piece of artwork, you can arrange the phrases in bullet points. This means each phrase is preceded by an asterisk, dash, or other graphic symbol, and the list of bullet points is neatly arranged within the artwork area.

BUSINESS-TO-BUSINESS
Business-to-business describes any form of communication which is from one business to another. This is as opposed to a communication from a business to its employees, sales force or consumer-level customers. Business-to-business communications, whether they're advertising, corporate video, or whatever, arise when you're selling to other businesses, and your product or service is aimed at the business market and business user only.

BVU
A ¾-inch wide videotape format, also known as *High Band*. This is quite widely used for taping non-broadcast VT programmes, as the quality is quite reasonable and the cost of it is low when compared to 1-inch or 2-inch. However it is not of sufficiently good quality to make television commercials.

CAMERA LEFT, RIGHT
The direction as if you were looking through the lens of the film, videotape or stills camera. As opposed to *stage left* or *right*, which is the other way round.

CAMERA SCRIPT
The full script for a film, programme or television commercial containing the dialogue and/or narration, plus detailed camera instructions for each shot. Also called *shooting script* or *dope sheet*.

CAMPAIGN
In advertising, a complete promotional/selling project. An advertising campaign can consist of material for a number of different media like press,

television, direct mail, but what makes it a campaign is that all the material is working towards the same goal – to launch a new product, relaunch an old product, or whatever.

CIRCULATION
The number of copies of a publication sold or otherwise distributed in the first instance. This is as opposed to *readership*, which is the number of people who actually read the publication. Usually, although only one person or company may buy or receive a copy of a publication, more than one individual will read it, so readership figures are often higher than circulation figures. Readership figures, not surprisingly, are normally more difficult to assess.

COLUMN CHART
Basically falls within the area of artwork and graphics, although column charts can be computer generated. Very like a bar chart, except the bars run vertically. Used to illustrate different quantities in artwork for print or for the screen, often with each column in a different colour.

COMMENTARY.
Although this word is often used in film, videotape and commercials as a synonym for a narration, this is not correct. A commentary should be an *un*-scripted voice over, with someone "commentating" on a specific event.

COMPUTER-GENERATED
This refers largely to graphics and special effects in slidetape and videotape. With slides, you can use a computer with a special graphics package to design artwork or captions. Then through a special method that image is photo-graphed on 35mm stills film, and processed in the normal way. Digital effects, the fancy tricks you do with videotape, are similarly computer generated.

CONFERENCE ORGANISER
Someone who organises the administration of a conference. This person is more usually encountered when the conference is a self-financing, hopefully profit-making venture in its own right, as opposed to the in-company variety. Conference organisers handle things like invitations and catering, but nor-mally turn to a conference producer to handle equipment, software and suitably qualified employees for the all-singing-and-dancing bit. In business theatre, suitably qualified employees at the conference production company will usually handle the organisation as well as the production.

CONFERENCE PRODUCER
A conference producer takes care of everything that actually concerns the sight and sound within a conference. In a smaller production company, the producer will sometimes act as conference organiser as well. But more often than not, the producer has his or her hands full with arranging slidetape, multi-image modules, any film or videotape to be shown, plus hiring, setting up and running all the hardware needed for sound and pictures. The producer will also organise actors, dancers, musicians, and every other component part of the presentation. Often the producer will act as director as well, running all on-stage performances, coaching speakers, and so on.

CONTINUITY
The simplest way to define *continuity* is that it is the "logic" of a film, videotape or television commercial production. Strictly speaking, it means the painstak-ing record of every detail of every scene shot, so that when it is edited you

don't have props appearing to have moved, or people transporting themselves thousands of miles in a split second. Needless to say, of course, most productions are shot in anything but the right order – hence the need for careful continuity. The reasons for shooting in the wrong order are wide and varied, but usually boil down to cost and logic. Continuity makes sure the production ends up in the right order, and that the whole thing flows in a logical fashion.

COPY
The words of a press advertisement, brochure, leaflet, or whatever, or the verbal section of a television or radio commercial (although this is more usually known as part of the script). A copywriter writes the words of print ads, but will normally write both the words and suggestions for visual input in the case of a television commercial. In modern advertising agencies, copywriters work in teams with an art director, and often there is no clear demarcation between their two areas of responsibility; art directors often come up with great headlines, and copywriters often come up with stunning visual ideas. Watch the jargon, though; a copywriter writes copy, but does not copywrite.

COPY PLATFORM
A few words, or a few lines, which sum up the gist of what the copy of an advertisement should get across. Something of an old-fashioned term, but still useful, especially for the non-specialist copywriter who needs to sort out his or her thoughts after conducting research, and crystallise those thoughts into a main selling message for the product or service concerned.

CORPORATE
A word used to describe the image, both external and sometimes internal, of a company. *Corporate identity* is the visual representation of this; the company's colours, logo, typestyle and so on, displayed right across its stationery, reception area, advertising and promotional material, right down to its delivery vans. *Corporate video* is a general umbrella term which describes the production of non-broadcast videotape programmes about companies. Strictly speaking, though, a corporate VTR programme is one which, in a promotional way, describes a company and what it does, as opposed to a training or motivational programme.

CRAB
Remember how a crab moves? Sideways. To instruct a film or videotape camera to *crab left of right* means that it should move, without turning, to whichever side is indicated.

CROSSHEAD
In advertising copy, a crosshead is a kind of secondary headline which breaks up sections of body copy in an ad, brochure or leaflet. Most experienced copywriters agree that crossheads are very important, because read in sequence (starting with the headline that grabs the reader's attention, and working through to the end) the crossheads get over the gist of the selling message and encourage the reader to go back and read all the body copy through. Studies have shown that most readers do scan the headline and crossheads first, especially in longer brochure copy, so good flow and continuity in these short phrases is essential.

CUE
A cue is a signal, verbal, written or gesticulated, that indicates a time or place when something in a film, slidetape, videotape, business theatre, television or radio commercial production, should happen. Used as a verb, *to cue* means to provide that signal.

CUT
A film/videotape term with a number of meanings. First, as an editing term, it means a simple, no-tricks transition from one shot to the next. In scripts, you'll sometimes see the instruction "cut to ..." This has the same meaning, i.e. to cut from one scene to the next. Second, this is the word a director will use when he or she wants the action to stop in a hurry. On hearing that word, camera, sound and performers all stop what they're doing. And third, the verb *to cut* means to edit a film.

CUTAWAY
A useful device that creates a refreshing break from the main action in a film, videotape programme or television commercial, and allows performers to move from one location to another. For example, in a production which consists mainly of a talking head describing a product or service, you might use a few cutaway shots of the product or other information for short periods on screen, accompanied just by the presenter's voice over. Or, if your presenter is talking to camera in New York, you can't just cut to another scene of him doing the same thing in London. That provides one big continuity problem, unless he's Superman. So between those two shots, you insert a cutaway shot – one of a 'plane in the air is probably a bit corny, but that's the idea.

CUT-OUT
A figure, product or other item which has been photographed against a neutral background, cut out, and stuck on an artwork board against another background for reproduction in an ad, brochure or leaflet.

DEMONSTRATION
One of the great advantages of audio-visual media; the opportunity to *show* your audience or viewers what you're telling them about. Long theoretical explanations about a product, service or technique belong in text books and brochures. Demonstration, with the vision complemented by the sound, is by far the best way to educate and motivate. Good demonstration means showing the audience or viewer as much as possible of the topic concerned. Long lectures from a speaker or presenter, with little or no other visual material, defeats the object of the exercise. Audiences and viewers have eyes as well as ears. And anyone who produces programmes, films and commercials should rate both ears and eyes as equally important recipients of a client's mesage.

DIALOGUE
Scripted, spoken speech which is performed as live action by actors or other performers. This is as opposed to commentary which is unscripted, and ad-libbed – either to camera or out of vision – and narration which is usually scripted and spoken out of vision.

DIGITAL EFFECTS
An umbrella term for all the fancy, computer generated effects you can achieve with a well-equipped videotape editing suite. These are sometimes referred to as DVE, which stands for *Digital Video Effects*.

DIRECT MAIL
Advertising through the post. Advertising material in the shape of a sales letter, plus any other sales material like leaflets and samples, sent directly to the consumer's home or office. He or she is usually expected to respond directly to the seller, as opposed to buying the product or service from a third party like a shop.

DIRECT MARKETING
The umbrella term for any marketing/selling activity which involves direct communication between seller and consumer, with the consumer expected to respond directly to the seller, so cutting out any middle agent such as a retail shop. This can include both direct mail and direct response advertising, mail order, and also telephone sales.

DIRECT RESPONSE
Direct response advertising is not dissimilar to direct mail, in as much as the consumer is expected to purchase the advertised product or service directly from the advertiser rather than from a shop. However, the sales material in this case is in the form of an advertisement placed in a publication. The normal procedure is that the consumer fills in a coupon stating either that he/she wants more information, or that he/she encloses a cheque or other payment and is ordering the goods advertised. Often, consumers may also telephone credit card orders.

DIRECTOR
In the case of videotape and film, the director is the person who directs the creative aspects of both the performers and the camera crew. He or she also officiates at the edit stage, working hand-in-hand with the VT or film editor, and will make final decisions on casting, too. In business theatre, the director will usually just be concerned with directing on stage performances; the producer runs the crew. In fact, in all but the largest of shows, the producer performs both functions. In advertising and allied disciplines, people called directors are not necessarily board directors, but are usually involved in overseeing their own area of responsibility. Account directors are in charge of the administration of an advertising, PR or business communications account (client); creative directors run the creative side of advertising or business communication agencies; art directors visualise and design the art output of their own accounts.

DISSOLVE
A technique in slidetape, videotape and film whereby one picture fades down slowly as the next picture fades up. With slide, you need two projectors to do it; with videotape, a properly equipped edit suite. With film, the dissolve is done in the laboratory, not the cutting room. A dissolve can also be called a mix.

DOCUMENTARY
A straightforward, factual representation of a film, audiotape or videotape story or message; a script that comes over in the un-fussy way of a news broadcast or television documentary.

DOORSTEPPING
In radio or television, doorstepping is when an interviewer (plus crew) attempt to get an instant interview with an unsuspecting person by turning up on his

or her doorstep. A much-favoured technique with consumer-programme champions, hard news reporters, and journalists following politicians on the campaign trail.

DRAMATISATION

The enacting of a fictitious story, using actors or models, on film, videotape or audiotape. A typical dramatisation might occur in a safety training film where actors portray what can happen in an office or factory if fire breaks out. Or, in sales training, where actors demonstrate the "right" and "wrong" selling techniques to a customer. In a television commercial, it could be a scene showing a family out on a picnic, spreading their bread with the brand of butter to be advertised; in a radio commercial for an antiseptic solution, it could be sound effects and dialogue of a child crying, followed by its mother comforting it and dressing its wound with the product.

DRY HIRE

A film and videotape expression used to show that equipment hired comes just as it stands; the hire does not include crew or operators for it, and the hirer must operate it him or herself. Opposite of wet hire.

DUBBING

Basically, dubbing means to assemble all prerecorded sound material for a videotape programme, film or television commercial, and re-record it into one harmonious mix. Sometimes, too, actors will "dub" their own voice on to a soundtrack for a film; very often the sound quality recorded on location is poor – so to do it over again in a studio gives far better results. Professional singers will dub their voices over an actor's on film where the actors appear to be singing, in lip sync, and foreign languages can be dubbed on to a film originated in another language.

DUPE

A duplicate copy of just about anything from a still photograph, to an entire film. Hence the verb to *dupe*; in the communications business, it does not necessarily mean "to deceive"!

EDITING SUITE

The rooms in which videotape editing is done. With all the electronic and computerised equipment used nowadays, even small editing suites look like the main control room in *Startrek*. But don't be baffled by science. Most engineers will be glad to explain what everything does; and what you can expect to see is this.

First, a selection of television screens on the wall in front of you – these are called monitors. Naturally, the numbers and placings will vary from suite to suite. But in the main, you'll see some small black and white screens, on which you can look through and call up each of your original tapes. Then, there'll be two larger, colour screens. One, usually on the left, will be the preview or rehearse monitor – on which you preview the edit in question. Then, the other large colour screen will show you what you have on your master tape. Other machinery will include the main control panel, plus perhaps such machinery as caption generators, and other special effects devices. The machines that actually play all the tapes will be in another room – certainly in the case of one inch editing suites and above. The editor will talk to the people in the other rooms over a microphone link.

EDITORIAL
In publications, all matter which is *not* advertising. This basically means articles and non-advertising photographs.

EFFECTS
Anything which is not part of the mainstream, live-action subject matter of videotaping, filming and audiotaping. Special effects on film include such space battle scenes as you'll have seen in *Starwars*. Videotape effects, often called digital effects, are used to move pictures around and create fancy scenes such as you might see in a rock music video. Theatrical special effects can include dry ice fog, smoke machines, and the like. Slide-tape effects will include elaborate graphics sequences, complicated build-ups, and so on. And sound effects are any prerecorded sound you add on to the main subject – like a ringing doorbell, or street noises.

EMBARGO
This is a word that originally came from the shipping world, meaning an order to stop ships from moving in or out of harbours. In journalism (and therefore writing for public relations purposes) to place an embargo on an article or press release is a request on your part that the story be held back until a given date. The release would be labelled "embargoed until 9.00 am January 16th", or whatever. Publications are not legally obliged to observe embargoes (in the UK at least) but most will respect them.

ENCODING
The act of placing electronic pulses in the master sound tape of a slidetape programme. These pulses direct the projectors, through suitable intermediary equipment.

ELEVATE
A film/videotape camera instruction. It means to raise the camera vertically; opposite of *depress*.

ESTABLISHING SHOT
An expression used in film, videotape or television commercial scripts. Establishing shots are mood setters, really; Usually short, general background shots to show a certain amount of information about the action which follows – for example, the outside of a building, inside which the next scene takes place; or a panoramic view of a city where the story is set.

F.M.
Stands for Frequency Modulation; a broadcast term, and another way of saying the transmission method used for UHF (Ultra High Frequency.)

FACILITIES HOUSE
A company which offers all the facilities required to make a programme, film or television commercial, except for the functions of producing, directing and writing. Normally, smaller production companies don't have all their own facilities like costumes, cameras, editing suite, slidemaking equipment, and so on. So when such a production company has been hired by a client, it will in turn hire a facilities house to provide all the back-up and production services required.

FILM STORYBOARD
A way of demonstrating how a finished production – usually a commercial – will look, without going to all the expense and trouble of making it first.

Elements from the drawn storyboard are rostrum filmed in sequence, and sometimes a demo soundtrack is produced to go with it. This can then be shown to the client for approval, before going on to the final production. Film storyboards have now been largely replaced by animatics, which are the videotape equivalents. Animatics cost less because you don't have any processing costs, and editing is minimised.

FINISHED ART
Finished artwork; artwork which is all stuck down and ready to go under the camera that produces the film that produces the printing plate. A finished artist, unfortunately named, is someone who prepares this camera-ready artwork.

FLOP
To turn an image, generated on transparency for slide or print work, over on the horizontal plane. Sometimes handy to create special "mirror image" effects. Also done accidentally, when it's hard to tell – unless there are any words on the picture, of course....

FLY ON THE WALL
A camera approach, usually in documentary film or videotape productions. The camera becomes an eavesdropper, in effect; recording a natural, unrehearsed conversation or meeting with no one speaking directly to camera, and no narration to describe what's going on. It allows the viewer to feel that he or she is actually present during that meeting, albeit without a speaking part, through the eye of the camera lens.

FMCG
Stands for *fast moving consumer goods*. These represent just about anything with a low unit cost that gets stocked up on store or supermarket shelves and purchased in high volume. FMCG's can be anything from chocolate bars to boxes of paper tissues to frozen foods to kitchen scourers. This is a term you will hear a lot of in the advertising business, as FMCG manufacturers tend to spend a lot of money on advertising campaigns.

FREELANCE
Freelance, means to be self-employed, working on your own. Many people in the communications industry are freelance – especially people like copywriters, art directors, scriptwriters, market researchers, and film directors. A few producers are freelance, but most work as employees or principals of production companies. Some clients, advertising agencies, consultancies and production companies get a bit nervous about there being a number of freelance people on a project. They feel that for security and continuity reasons everyone should be a member of the company's staff. But what they forget is that – quite apart from the obvious financial good sense of hiring freelance people only when you need them – you can pick the best in the business for a given job. And if anyone is worried about loyalty and security, they can forget that, too. A freelance person would only manage to leak confidential information, or be disloyal to his or her clients, once. The communications business is still small, even in the United States – and word gets around so fast that the disloyal freelance would never work again. The other truth is that if you're making a good living as a freelance, you're bound to be good at your job – so, from a client's point of view, hiring a busy, successful freelancer is a reasonable guarantee of quality.

G.V.
A videotape, film or television commercial script term, which stands for *general view*. A G.V. might be used as an establishing shot, or to show a general outlook on screen while the narration goes over some background points.

GENERATION
The stages of copying of a recording, programme or film, beyond the master. A VHS copy of a videotape programme, copied froma U-matic version which has been taken from a one-inch master, would be third "generation". If you copied some more VHS tapes from your original VHS. they would be fourth "generation". And the quality would be bad – the more generations, the worse it gets.

HALF TONE
Refers to an illustration in print. In order to reproduce a photograph in any printing process, so that the right amount of ink goes in the right place to reproduce the image, a screen is put over the original. On the final printing plate, the photograph is then represented by the number of dots created by the screen. The number of dots per square millimetre varies according to the printing process involved, and to the type of publication. The finer and more numerous the dots, the better the quality of reproduction.

HARDWARE
A term relating primarily to film, videotape and business theatre, but applicable to all disciplines within the communications industry. All the hard equipment used in production and projection – e.g., cameras, editing equipment, projectors. As opposed to *software*, which is the tapes, slides and so on. Borrowed from computer terminology.

INTERACTIVE
Any videotape/videodisk programme and playback system which offers a choice of options to the viewer. Used largely for training, interactive techniques are based on a monitor screen, a micro-computer, and either a videotape or videodisk playback system. Typically a programme will set up a proposition, then set some questions for the viewer. Depending on his or her answer, the micro-computer will instruct the tape or disk machine to search for the appropriate next part of the programme, which will then be played back – and so on to the end of the training session.

INTERIOR
A film, videotape or television commercial script term. Any shot or scene which is done indoors. Usually abbreviated to *INT*.

INTERVIEW
A very useful way for viewers or listeners to hear information "from the horse's mouth". Interviews can be scripted, but these tend to sound stilted. Far better is for the interviewer to ask carefully thought out questions, and go through them with the interviewee beforehand so he or she has a chance to figure out what best to say. Location interviews can be tricky if there is a lot of ambient noise, but they are very realistic – especially if you can show the interviewee actually in his or her place of work. Studio interviews are easier to control, but can frighten the less experienced interviewee.

JINGLE
A piece of music, either vocal or instrumental only, composed and recorded especially for a television, radio or cinema commercial.

JUMP CUT

In a film, videotape programme or television commercial, a cut from one scene to another, where there is a hiccup in continuity – e.g., a shot of someone in New York, immediately followed by a shot of the same person in Paris. Avoided by inserting a cutaway in the middle; perhaps a shot of an aircraft in mid flight.

LANDSCAPE FORMAT

A picture or ad shape which is wider than it is high. In original 35mm photography, this means holding the camera the right way up, horizontally rather than turning it round 90 degrees to the vertical, or "portrait", format. Slidetape photography is always done in landscape format, as that is the way in which the slides are always projected.

LAUNCH

An advertising, PR, or promotional campaign, or business theatre event, or all together, where a new product or service is introduced to the public or audience for the first time.

LAYOUT

A preliminary design of an advertisement, or pages of a brochure or leaflet, to show all interested parties how the finished product will look. A rough layout will be pencilled and pretty basic; a finished layout will be properly drawn, using good hand-lettering for headlines and crossheads. It is from the layout that finished artwork is then produced.

LINEAR

An expression used to describe a videotape programme where the viewer's only participation is to watch it – i.e., a straightforward playback programme. Often used to differentiate between ordinary and inter-active programmes; a linear programme is non-inter-active.

LIST

A mailing list of names and addresses of potentially interested parties to whom a direct mailshot is sent. Lists are valuable commodities to companies involved in direct marketing. They are compiled by the company concerned out of anything from business directories to electoral rolls, or purchased from large organisations like mail order companies or credit card companies.

LITH

Lith – short for lithographic – is line film which produces a negative result in slidetape productions. If your original artwork consist of black letters on white paper, the final slide photographed on lith will show clear (transparent) letters on a black background. On screen, this will project as white letters on a black background. If another projector is simultaneously projecting a plain coloured slide at the same screen area, on screen you will see the coloured background with the white lettering of the lith "burning out" of the colour. If you place a piece of coloured "gel" (gelatine, originally, but plastic these days) in the slide mounting along with the lith film, you will see coloured letters on screen, against a black background.

LIP SYNC

When you simultaneously hear and see someone speak on screen. The sound will usually be recorded at the same time as taping or filming. In the case of film though, the performer may well dub his or her words on afresh – location sound recording quality is seldom as good as the studio variety.

LIVE ACTION
Film or videotape action that consists of production with real human activity, as opposed to animation (cartoon) graphics and special effects.

LOGO
A design or symbol which represents a company's name or corporate image. Sometimes it will just be the company's name, in a specified typeface – in other cases, it will be a symbol, plus the name.

LOW BAND
One of the videotape formats; ¾-inch wide. Very seldom used as the master taping format as the quality is not quite up to it. However, the quality is better than the domestic formats – of VHS and Betamax, and low band is often used for business use playback. Sometimes called *low band U-matic.*

MAILSHOT
A single unit of direct mail; one envelope-full of direct mail material. A mailshot can consist of a single letter, or it can include a number of pieces like a letter, a leaflet, a reply-paid card, even a sample or other promotional piece.

MAGAZINE
Container – normally circular – for 35 mm slides, to be placed on top of the projector in a slide-tape programme or speaker presentation; sometimes called a carousel, which is in fact a trade name for a type of circular magazine. Also, a container for film either in a camera or projector. Sometimes shortened to *mag.*

MASTER SHOT
The main framework of a particular film or videotape sequence. For example, in an interview; the master shot would be of the interview itself. Afterwards, cutaways illustrating various points the speaker makes would be added at editing stage. In a dramatic sequence, the master shot would be all performers doing their bits together. Close-up, reverse angles and so-on would be shot afterwards (yes, actors have to do it all again, unless there's enough money in the budget to pay for more than one camera to be used at the same time) and edited in later.

MECHANICALS
These are all the artwork components for an advertisement, brochure or whatever, ready for the print plate-making process.

MERCHANDISING
This is the activity of making the product look at its best at the point of sale. It involves the design and use of promotional material and displays.

MIX
A mix, in film or video vision terms, is a slightly faster version of a dissolve – a gentle transition from one picture to the next by fading the last one down as you bring the next one up. In sound, the mix is when all the individual tracks are done, and you blend them together on one master tape. This will normally involve a great deal of tweaking of levels and sound quality – especially if the recording is of a piece of music. In advertising, you'll sometimes hear the term *marketing mix.* This generally refers to all the different marketing activities (advertising, PR, sales promotion, etc) planned, or in progress, for the promotion of one particular product.

MODULE
A "free-standing" slidetape or multi-image programme with prerecorded soundtrack. In business theatre, you refer to modules in this way to differentiate between them and the speaker support slides, which have no sound and are manually cued. Modules are driven by the electronic pulses put on one track of the audio tape. You'll also hear modules referred to as AV's – but this is technically wrong. See AV.

MONITOR
Any "television" set which is not used to pick up broadcast television signals. Some monitors, like those in a videotape editing suite cannot physically pick up broadcast – they're designed purely for tape playback. Similarly, the monitors used in teleprompter devices can only do the one job – transmit the script as picked up by the closed circuit camera (CCTV). However, if you have a normal television set in your home or office, and it's plugged in to a video cassette recorder, that set is functioning as a monitor – although it's capable of doing both jobs.

MONO
Sound that has been recorded through one single input track, sound which is played back through one single output source, or both. Stereo, or even quadrophonic, sound can be played back over mono equipment, although some quality is lost. Also used as an abbreviation of *monochrome*, meaning a black and white picture, piece of film or videotape, or television/video monitor.

MOVE LEFT/RIGHT
A film or videotape camera instruction. Means the same as *to crab left* or *right* moving sideways without swivelling.

MULTI-IMAGE
See MULTIVISION

MULTI-SCREEN
In business theatre, people often get this term mixed up with *multi-image*, or *multi-projector*, and use it freely in these contexts. However, multi-screen means just that – more than one screen area. Each screen area you use will have the aspect ratio appropriate for slides, but some may overlap. A popular example of this is two screen areas side by side, giving a very wide overall look. Slides can be projected over both areas for a "panavision effect" during modules, with another bank of projectors pointing at the centre of the two adjacent screens creating the effect of a single screen area, for single speaker support slides. This is known as "two into one", or "two over one".

MULTIPLEXER
This is an ingenious system which is used to transfer multi-image slidetape programmes to videotape. With a clever arrangement of mirrors or prisms, placing projectors around the four sides of a square and using a special videotape camera, you get a very good, sharp image. Of course, the slidetape programme has to have been made in a single screen format to start with, and all its slides should have been made television safe.

MULTIVISION
The British word for any slidetape programme that involves the use of three or more projectors. Now largely replaced by the American word, *multi-image*.

NARRATION
A narration is a scripted commentary in film, videotape and slidetape productions (commentary is strictly speaking supposed to be ad-libbed – as in sports commentating). Narrations provide voices which are heard but not seen, usually, but some techniques do involve a narrator performing to camera for part of the time at least. Some people say voice over when they mean narration, but in fact the voice over is a sound term rather than a script term.

NODDIES
A way of making a film or videotape interview shot with one camera look as though it has been done with two. After the main interview has been finished, with the camera on the interviewee all that time, you'll then shoot a few angles of the interviewer "listening to" the interviewee – who's probably off to the canteen by then. The interviewer smiles, then looks intent, and nods – hence the nickname. These shots are then edited into the interview later on, cut in here and there while the interviewee's voice is heard OOV. Sometimes, if the interviewer has not performed too well during the interview, the director will shoot his or her questions again as well.

NTSC
Stands for *National Television Systems Committee*. This is the television standard used all over North America, and in Japan. It operates on the basis of 525 lines, as opposed to the European standards of PAL and SECAM which are based on 625 lines.

OFF-LINE EDIT
See ON-LINE EDIT

ON-CAMERA
In theory, any performance which takes place in front of the film or videotape camera lens. In practice, usually used to refer to an interviewer or presenter who appears on screen while doing his or her bit. Used to differentiate between this way, and either off-camera interviews, or voice-over presentations.

ON-LINE EDIT
When editing videotape, the process of rerecording the selected sections of origination tape straight on to the top quality master. This is done after the off-line (preliminary) edit, where the same process has been done but with the selected sections rerecorded on to VHS, or lowband, both of which are cheaper and easier to work with.

ONE-INCH
A larger videotape format. Technically it is considered to be of broadcast standard and some television programmes are shot and mastered on one-inch although two-inch is generally considered best. For business communications and some television commercials, though, one-inch is fine.

OOV
Out of vision – usually referring to a performer on film or videotape who can be heard but not seen, if only for a line or two.

OUTLINE
A brief, general overview of how a proposed film, videotape or slidetape production will look and sound. The outline is usually the first stage of

production and will present the bare bones of the ideas for discussion between client and production company. From there, once the outline is agreed, you proceed to a treatment and after that a full script.

OUT-TAKES
A general term used for the bits of videotape, film or audio tape which are not used in the final master, for whatever reason. Very often out-takes include scenes which have gone wrong, with effects not working, performers getting their lines wrong and cursing in a highly undignified manner, etc. Needless to say the funnier out-takes are frequently pirated out of studios all over the world, and provide hours of hilarious entertainment. In fact, some out-takes find their way on to broadcast television screens as comedy shows or items in their own right.

OVER THE SHOULDER SHOT
Sometimes abbreviated to O/S. When the film, videotape or stills camera is behind the performer, shooting over his or her shoulder and with that particular bit of anatomy in shot. A popular technique for the introductory shot in an interview, with the camera behind the interviewer's shoulder pointing at the interviewee.

OVERHEAD PROJECTOR
The *bête-noire* of the business theatre producer – and the pet of many high-ranking conference speakers. An overhead projector consists of a machine that projects, via a system of mirrors, an image which is being drawn or shown on a lighted lectern. The projection device is such that it projects the image over the speaker's head, and on to the screen or wall behind – hence the name. Speakers like OHPs because they can draw their own particular hieroglyphics and have them instantly projected, as well as being able to show pre-drawn or written slides.

The OHP slide is several inches square, allowing plenty of space for drawing or writing on clear celluloid. The problem producers have with OHPs is that the quality of the projected image is very poor – with bad definition and pale, – washy colour. Speaker presentations look a hundred times more professional if slides are thought out beforehand, professionally created and shot on MM35, and projected by a professional programmer – while the speaker just gets on with the speech. OHP presentations are frequently stilted and patchy, with long silences while the speaker draws a chart or hunts around in a briefcase for a missing word slide. To make matters worse, an OHP presentation mixed in with other presentations using MM35 slides looks like a poor country cousin. All the same, the overhead projector has its devotees.

PACK SHOT
Any photograph, still or moving, of the client's product.

PAL
Stands for *Phase Alternate Line*. This is the television standard used in the UK and most of Western Europe except for France. It's based on a 625 line structure.

PAL M
A variation on the television/video PAL TV standard, but this time of only 525 lines rather than 625 (see above). PAL M is used in Brazil.

PAN LEFT/RIGHT
A camera instruction. Means that the camera should swivel left or right on its mounting, with the tripod or dolly staying put.

PASTE-UP
A paste-up is artwork for an ad, brochure, slide, or even for a videotape programme or film, if appropriate. (Graphics for videotape are also generated electronically.) A paste-up consists of a white art board (or clear plastic "cell", if the paste-up is to be photographed for slide or film) on which the various artwork components like drawings, photographs and typeset copy are pasted up in the right place. Hence *paste-up artist*.

PHOTOMATIC
A way of making a demo of a video programme, film or television commercial. Unlike an animatic, which is a taped or filmed version of the drawn storyboard, a photomatic uses still photographs of models, packs, etc. Usually the pictures are synchronised to a demo sound track for a more realistic feel, then videotaped.

POS
Stands for *point of sale*; the place – usually a retail or wholesale outlet of some kind – where a product is actually sold, and money changes hands.

POST-PRODUCTION
The period between the end of motion picture taping or filming, and the actual finished product. Mainly consists of editing, dubbing sound, finalising the master and getting either tape copies or film prints made.

POV
Stands for *point of view*; a script term, e.g. "cut to new angle; from interviewee's POV".

PRE-PRODUCTION
The period before you actually tape or film a programme, film or commercial. This is the time when you write and finalise the script and storyboard, cast any actors, hire the crew, arrange any locations that are needed, plus all the ancillary items like crew accommodation, costumes and props.

PRESS RELEASE
A promotional piece of prose written in an editorial style, sent out to publications by a company wishing to promote itself or its products and services. Although no one is fooled as to the selling nature of a press release, provided that it has some genuine news value for the publication concerned all or parts of it may well be used by the publication as editorial matter.

PRODUCER
First of all, let's take videotape and film. Here, the producer is the chief organiser of a production, with little creative in-put. That is left largely to the director and scriptwriter. In slidetape production, the producer also acts as the director and is usually the person who dreams up the whole show, although the producer will not necessarily write the script. In sound, the producer will direct the recording session as well as organise it, and will have a great deal of say in how the performers behave and how the mix is done. In business theatre, there is the conference producer – see separate entry.

PRODUCTION
A general videotape/film term, meaning a project, programme, film or recording. With sound and business theatre, a project is "in production" when it is

actually being made. The only areas in which the terminology is more specific are in videotape and film; a project is "in pre-production before" photography takes place, "in production" when it is actually being taped or filmed, and "in post-production" when it is being edited and finished.

PRODUCTION COMPANY
A company which works directly for a client in the making of a videotape programme or film, and handles all the creative initiation – scripts, story-boards, etc., – plus the financing and administration of a project. In the case of television and radio commercials, however, the production company will not normally write and visualise the script; this will either be done by the client directly, or more usually by the client's advertising agency. Bigger production companies will also have their own facilities (see *facilities house*), so all or most of the production can be made in-house. Smaller production companies, of the one-man and a dog variety, have to hire in everything from scriptwriter to cameraman. The advantage of this, though, is that the small company can pick the most suitable people from the selection of freelance talent available. Big production companies, although they use freelancers as well, tend to use their own staff as much as they can – whether they are suitable or not.

PROGRAMME (Verb)
The act of assembling all the slides for a slidetape programme or business theatre show, loading them into magazines, feeding instructions into the machine or computer, plus recording pulses on the audiotape.

PROJECTOR
Modern slide projectors are a far cry from the old magic lanterns. These days they are small, neat boxes with a powerful light and lens. The rotary magazine of slides sits elegantly on top, and the whole assembly could be fitted into a shopping bag. Film projectors are bigger of course, especially when you get into 16 and 35mm sizes. And videotape projectors are becoming more popular. Some come in whole units with their own screen. But in business theatre the current favourite – at the time of writing – can either front- or back project on to the normal screens used for slides. The on-screen quality is not as good as film or MM35 slides, though.

PULL BACK
A motion picture camera direction. It means to pull back the whole camera and mounting assembly, on its dolly, backwards while shooting. This gives the impression that the image is gradually disappearing towards the horizon.

PULL FOCUS
To pull focus is to change the focus of a film or videotape camera from the foreground to the background as the subject or performer moves. Taping or filming does not stop while this is being done so it requires the steady hand of a trained focus puller.

PULSE
The electronic signals on the audiotape of a slidetape presentation. These "pulses" drive the projectors.

Q & A
A structured interview with Questions and Answers so arranged that the interviewee, who is likely to be an expert of some kind, can get over a message. A more interesting way of putting information over, than merely sticking the expert in front of the camera to talk in a monologue.

Q. T. V.
A brandname for a type of teleprompter, similar in operation to Autocue systems.

READERSHIP
See CIRCULATION

R.O.P.
A media term; it stands for *run of paper*. This means that an advertiser books a space in a publication, but has no say in where in the publication the ad will appear. It goes wherever there is space available. This will obviously cost the advertiser less than if he or she were to specify a position.

RECORDING TO PICTURE
Putting a narration on to a videotape or film production is best done with the voice over artist keeping one eye on the visual side of the actual production. He or she will sit in a sound-proof area, equipped with a screen or VT monitor, and record the narration while viewing the film or tape.

REVEAL
A reveal is when a new product or service is shown on screen or stage for the first time, usually after a preamble of some kind. On screen, it's likely that suitably exciting music and special effects will be used to create a bit of drama. On stage, some clients go to extraordinary lengths to create theatrical thrills when revealing new product. Winching a new car model down from the ceiling and moving an audience's seating around, raising a wall and revealing an airline's new livery on a real commercial jet, are just real examples.

ROADSHOW
A travelling conference or business presentation – not unlike the rock music business's tour of one-night stands. Many clients find it is cheaper to take the conference to their regions, rather than have hundreds or thousands of delegates shipped into one central location. Roadshows are particularly useful for internal sales conferences when a client company's sales force is widely dispersed; similarly, in the case of dealer conferences. For external selling, a roadshow is a good way of getting customers together in a way that is convenient for them; i.e., you are not asking them to travel very far in order to see and hear your sales message.

RUSHES
The first prints of a day's film shooting, processed quickly so they can be looked at the same evening or next morning. Also called dailies. The term *rushes* is sometimes used to refer to videotape as well, although that can be watched straight away as VT doesn't have to be processed first.

SALES PROMOTION
Promotional activities designed to give sales an added boost towards the end of the marketing process. Normally, sales promotional activities will be at their most visible at or near the point of sale, or the moment of purchase in the case of mail order. Sales promotion activities include a wide variety of things, like competitions (win a holiday for two with your next purchase of Brand X), gift token schemes (collect so many tokens when you buy Brand Y petrol and save for these wonderful gifts), money-off coupons, giveaways, and so on. Generally speaking, sales promotional activities are designed to clinch a sale; media advertising creates the initial interest, and sales promotion gives the final boost to make sure the consumer actually goes ahead and buys.

SCENARIO

Some say, another word for shooting script in videotape or film; the document which contains not only all the words for a production, but the camera instruction and any other directions which may be necessary. Others say it is used to describe the action of a production. There is some argument as to which is the correct definition so, when in doubt, check with an ordinary dictionary. *The Concise Oxford Dictionary* says "...written version of play, details of scenes, etc., in film production". Hey, presto.

SCENE

One continuous section of dramatic action on film or tape, where the performance or activity taking place remains in the same place and at the same time. One scene can contain several different shots, and can go on for anything from a few seconds to half-an-hour or so. But the important thing to remember about a scene is that, however long it is, it is just one occurrence in one place at one time. This definition can be roughly attributed to the live theatrical version as well. The non-fiction, non-drama equivalent of "scene" is "sequence". However, to a certain extent, the two terms are interchangeable.

SECAM

Stands for *sequence avec memoire*. This is the television standard used in several countries, but most notably in France and the USSR. Like the PAL standard used in the UK, SECAM is based on a picture of 625 lines.

SEQUENCE

As "phrase" is to "sentence" so *sequence* is to a videotape, film or slidetape production. A sequence is a relatively self-contained chunk of a whole production lasting anything from a few seconds to several minutes. In videotape or film production, a sequence can be one long shot, or can consist of several shots all pertaining to the same subject matter. In slidetape production, a sequence will consist of several slides – for example, a graphics sequence to show a company's logo, or several shots, taken from different angles, of a machine.

SHOOT

Slang for the verb *to photograph*. If you *shoot* stills, videotape or film, you are actually taking the pictures. It is useful in that it is the one word you can use that applies equally to videotape and film; otherwise you *record* or *tape* videotape and *film* film. You'll also hear the word used as a noun; e.g. *location shoot, film shoot, stills shoot*.

SHOOTING SCRIPT

The detailed version of a videotape or film script which not only gives the narration or a dialogue, but all the camera directions as well. Also called *camera script* or *dopesheet*.

SHOT

Slang for a still photograph, sequence of film or videotape, usually of something in particular. In other words, you would refer to a *shot* of your product (still); an *aerial shot* of something, taken from a plane or helicopter. The word "shot" is also used as an abbreviation of "mailshot"; *see under appropriate heading*.

SHOT LENGTHS

These are the strange initials you'll see in film and videotape scripts. Basically they tell the director how far the camera should be away from the subject at any given time. Here are the most widely used shot lengths, described in relation to the camera's distance from a human figure, to give you an idea of their meanings:

BCU: Big Close Up – the face, excluding hair, ears, etc.

CU: Close Up – head and neck with top of shoulders.

MCU: Medium Close Up – head, shoulders and upper trunk

MS: Medium Shot – three-quarters of figure.

LS: Long Shot – full length of figure, head to foot.

VLS: Very Long Shot – full length of figure covering about half height of frame.

ELS: Extra Long Shot – figure in distance.

SLIDE
A single frame of processed MM35 stills transparency film mounted in a plastic and glass mount. This is the most widely used variety of slide. Other types include overhead projector slides, which are fully described under *overhead projector*, and "2¼ square" with an image size of 2¼ inches by 2¼ inches (54mm x 54mm). Lastly, there is the super slide, which has the sames size mount as MM35 (2 inches square overall) but a larger image area; 40mm square rather than 36mm by 24 mm. The trouble with these last two formats is that not many projectors can do justice to them, and they are more expensive to produce.

SLIDE TAPE
The term you use to desribe any slide programme driven by electronic pulses on an audio tape, with synchronised sound. Some people perversely call it tape slide – which is equally correct. What is not correct is *AV* – athough that misnomer is so widespread that even the professionals slip into it now and again.

SOLUS
A media term, referring to an advertising space. Booking a solus space means that your ad is the only one on the page of the publication; the rest of the space will be taken up by editorial matter only. A solus space will be more expensive than ROP.

SPEAKER
A non-professional performer at a business theatre event. In other words, anyone who gives a speech or presentation apart from any professional actor or presenters you hire.

SPEAKER SUPPORT
Although this in theory could be any aids used by a speaker at a business theatre event, even to the large brandy he or she consumes beforehand, in normal practice we take it to mean speaker support slides. These are slides which do not have any accompanying sound track, and which are normally cued by a programmer. The programmer takes his or her cues from a copy of the speaker's script, putting up the appropriate slide at the right time. Speaker support slides can consist of almost any subject matter, from elaborate photographs to word slides, graphs and charts.

STAGE DIRECTIONS
Stage directions, used in conventional theatre but equally applicable to business theatre, can be confusing as they are the precise opposite of some

camera directions – e.g. *stage left*, would be *camera right*, and so-on. Here are the basics.

Stage Left: the right hand side of the stage, looking at it from the audience.
Stage Right: the left hand side of the stage, looking at it from the audience.
Upstage: the part of the stage at the back, furthest away from the audience.
Downstage: the part of the stage near the footlights, nearest the audience,

STORYBOARD
A storyboard gives clients and producers an idea, on paper, of what the eventual videotape or film production will look like. Usually a storyboard is done on normal sheets of paper, with a row of little boxes – to represent frames or sequences – down one side. In the boxes, an artist will draw an approximation of what would be appearing on screen at that particular point. On the opposite side of the paper, you'll often see the relevant words from the proposed script to match the picture.

STRAPLINE
An advertising term. A strapline is a phrase or sentence of copy, which summarises the main selling or corporate message. If used with a company's name and/or logo, it will encapsulate corporate image; *"Brand X Property: a better way to build a home"*. It can also refer to an individual product; *"Brand X Boiled Sweets: the sweets that really satisfy"*. Also referred to as *"tag lines"*, *"base lines"* or sometimes (in the good old days) as *"slogans"*.

TAKE
One continuous, unbroken section of film/videotape shooting or sound recording. If a take is less than satisfactory, it will be done again and again until all concerned are happy about it. Takes are normally numbered by the production staff, and the most acceptable one is noted for later editing purposes.

TALKBACK
The system in a recording studio, radio or television station, that allows studio staff to talk to each other without it being recorded or picked up by the transmission. Basically, it's a kind of intercom arrangement.

TALKING HEAD
Any person who appears in a production, usually shot from the waist or shoulders up, talking straight to camera. A typical example of this is the well-known style of the television newsreader. Talking heads are very popular in corporate and training programmes and films; but too much of this approach, without cutaway visuals to break it up, tends to be tedious.

TELECINE
A machine – or a process – which generates television pictures, and/or videotapes them, from film.

TELECONFERENCE
A comparatively new, and interesting, way of bringing speakers together from all over the world for a conference. This is done over a private television broadcast, via DBS (direct broadcast by satellite), if necessary. Each group of people is shot live on camera, and the images are then transmitted to monitor screens in the presence of all groups involved. The principle works much as does a networked live television broadcast. Naturally it is expensive. But if the alternative is for a company to pay out a small fortune in hundreds of first class

return air fares from four corners of the world, plus executive-style accommodation in a central venue, teleconferencing can suddenly begin to look viable.

TELEPROMPTER
Affectionately known, in the business theatre/television trade, as the *idiot box*. The speaker's script is typed onto a continuous roll of paper. Its contents are transmitted via a closed circuit TV camera to a specially coated glass screen. Although the speaker can see the words on the screen, those looking at the screen from the other direction (or a camera in a television or video studio) just see clear glass. An operator listens to the speaker reading the script, and controls the speed at which the roll travels past the CCTV camera lens.

TRACK IN / OUT
A camera direction. This involves moving the camera either towards or away from the subject, along a specially built track.

TV SAFE
If any piece of artwork is to be transferred to videotape, the main picture area must conform to the aspect ratio of the television screen. This is particularly relevant when the medium to be transferred to videotape is a 35mm slide, which has a different aspect ratio.

TYPESETTING
Typesetting is part of the artwork process, using machinery that produces the necessary letters and figures either mechanically or photo-electronically, and prints them out on to shiny white paper. The paper is then cut into strips and the strips pasted down on the artwork, with the words and numbers in their correct places.

U-MATIC
A videotape format, created by Sony. In the UK there are two qualities of U-matic; low band and high band. U-matic comes in video cassette form.

UHF
Stands for *ultra high frequency*. In television, it refers to transmission on 625 lines, as you do with *PAL* and *SECAM*.

USP
Stands for *unique selling proposition, unique sales proposition,* or *unique selling point*. All mean that vital quality in a product or service which makes it different from and better than its competitors; not a quality every product has, but one for which copywriters search high and low. A product with a USP is much easier to position in the market, and to advertise.

VCR
Stands for *video cassette recorder*; normally, the type of machine people use in their homes.

VHS
Stands for *video home system,* and was developed by Japan's JVC organisation. This is one of the two small cassette formats suitable for use in the home, and for small audience business, corporate or educational playback. The other small format is *Betamax*.

VIDEO EIGHT
A home video format, now offered by several different manufacturers. Although it is sometimes confused with MM 8 film, there is no connection

apart from the fact that in this instance the videotape inside the cassette is 8mm wide. The cassettes used are about the same size as the audio compact cassette. Video 8 cameras, sometimes known as Camcorders – depending on the manufacturer – contain video recorders built in. This means that when you want to play back your videotape you simply connect the camera unit to your television set; there is no need for a separate video playback machine.

VIDEO FILM
A physical impossibility, if you think about it. You can have a videotape programme, or a film; all other terms are technically wrong. However, some are less unacceptable than others, particularly in the case of the word "video" which only means "vision" but can be used to describe anything from a VHS cassette to a rock music promotion on broadcast television! The only time when use of *video film* is almost logical is in the context of a feature film available for home viewing on videotape. These are the "video films" you can rent from a local shop or club; major movies which have done the round of cinemas first, and have then been transferred to videotape for domestic sale or hire.

VIDEO WALL
This is a device whereby a number of video monitors are stacked up to form a giant milti-screen viewing "wall". Videotape programmes or sequences can be made to show one normal-sized image repeated on each of the screens, or one large image – with the relevant portion on each screen – covering the entire wall. Because you benefit from the brightness and sharpness of each individual normal-sized monitor, video walls create a much sharper, brighter effect than you would normally get with videotape conventionally projected from a single source on the same screen area. Video walls are often used for selling purposes at permanent or temporary exhibition sites, and run specially designed programmes.

VIDEODISK
The same as a sound disc, but producing a picture as well. At the time of writing, videodisk can only be used for playback – you can't record directly on to it. And also at the time of writing, there are two main types of videodisk in existance; a mechanically produced variety, which spins 25 times fatser than an LP record, and the optical laser light produced variety which spins 50 times faster than an LP record.

VISUALISER
A visualiser is someone who interprets written copy or script ideas in terms of drawn images. He or she may also add quite a lot of ideas, to flesh out and develop the visual side of the project. In advertising and design, these people are also referred to as art directors, although in the main an art director is a more senior variety of visualiser.

VOICE OVER
Basically, a voice in a film or videotape programme which is heard, but not seen. This invisible person speaks a narration to picture in the case of slide and videotape programmes, and films. With radio, these people provide a narration to link other parts of a programme or commercial, although of course any voice on a soundtrack with no picture will technically be "over". The term *voice over*, or "V/O", is informally used to describe both the person and the job; but,

technically, it should only be used for the job. V/Os are normally hired from specialist agencies.

VTR
Stands for Video Tape Recording, or for Video Tape Recorder.

WALLPAPER
Any pictures or sound in a motion picture or audio production which act as "fillers", or general background material.

WET HIRE
An expression used to show that camera or other equipment hired comes with all necessary personnel to operate it. Opposite of *dry hire*.

WIPE
An optical (film) or electronic (videotape) device used for quick changes from one picture to the next. A line appears at one edge or corner of the screen and moves across it, obliterating the old picture and pulling the new one in with it. This line can either be hard and sharp, or soft-edged; and it can move horizontally, vertically or diagonally.

ZOOM
Any type of lens, whether for still or motion pictures, that has a length of focus which is variable – in the case of motion pictures, variable even when shooting is going on.

ZOOM IN/OUT
A camera direction. This means to activate a zoom lens to either close in on the subject or to pull away from it.

Notes

Notes

Notes

Notes

Notes